NEW PHILANTHROPY AND SOCIAL JUSTICE

Debating the conceptual and policy discourse

Edited by
Behrooz Morvaridi

First published in Great Britain in 2015 by

Policy Press
University of Bristol
1-9 Old Park Hill
Bristol
BS2 8BB
UK
t: +44 (0)117 954 5940
pp-info@bristol.ac.uk
www.policypress.co.uk

North America office:
Policy Press
c/o The University of Chicago Press
1427 East 60th Street
Chicago, IL 60637, USA
t: +1 773 702 7700
f: +1 773-702-9756
sales@press.uchicago.edu
www.press.uchicago.edu

British Library Cataloguing in Publication Data
A catalogue record for this book is available from the British Library

Library of Congress Cataloging-in-Publication Data
A catalog record for this book has been requested

ISBN 978-1-4473-1697-8 hardcover

Cover design by Qube, Bristol
Printed and bound in Great Britain by CPI Group (UK) Ltd,
Croydon, CR0 4YY
Policy Press uses environmentally responsible print partners

Contents

Notes on contributors

Kate Bradley is senior lecturer in social history and social policy at the University of Kent's School of Social Policy, Sociology and Social Research. Kate is interested in the interactions between working-class communities, charities, the state and private sector bodies in social welfare issues in the twentieth century, and has explored this through research on the settlement house movement, the juvenile courts, and legal advice provision. Kate is interested in the creation of discourses around 'social justice' in the 1960s and 1970s. She worked with Balihar Sanghera on 'Perceptions of social justice by philanthropic foundations and grant-makers in the UK', which was funded by the Economic and Social Research Council.

Sally Brooks is lecturer in international development at the University of York; and has more than 20 years' experience in development, as a researcher, teacher and practitioner. Her research focuses on decision making in international 'science for development' organisations, programmes and networks, particularly in food security and smallholder agriculture; and the extent to which these respond to lived realities and local knowledge in diverse contexts. She is author of *Rice Biofortification: Lessons for Global Science and Development* (Earthscan: 2010).

Ayşe Buğra is professor of political economy at the Ataturk Institute of Modern Turkish History at Bogazici University, Istanbul. She has conducted research and published in the fields of history and methodology of economics, business history and comparative social policy. She is the co-founder and the current director of the Bogazici University Research Centre Social Policy Forum where she initiated and conducted several studies on inequality, poverty and different foundations of social solidarity. Ayşe Buğra is the translator of Karl Polanyi's *The Great Transformation* into Turkish, and author of *New Capitalism in Turkey: The Relationship between Politics, Religion and Business*, co-authored with Osman Savaşkan, (Edward Elgar Publishing: 2014).

Sam Cameron is Professor of Economics at the University of Bradford. He is co-editor of *Journal of Cultural Economics*. He is the author of the books *Music in the Marketplace: A Social Economics Approach* (2015), *Economics of Hate, Economics of Sin, Econometrics, Playing the Love Market: Dating, Romance and the Real World* (with Alan Collins). He has also edited the book *A Handbook of Leisure Economics* and contributed numerous book and encyclopedia entries and articles in academic journals. Outlets for these works has covered economics but also the fields of psychology, marketing, law, sociology, politics and creativity research. His current research is mainly on the subjective valuation of creative output with specific reference to the establishment of a body of work and also the social positioning of fakes and frauds.

Hugh Cunningham is Emeritus Professor of Social History at the University of Kent. His recent work on philanthropy was broadcast in a series of programmes on BBC Radio 4 entitled 'How New is the New Philanthropy?' (2011). He co-edited with Joanna Innes *Charity, Philanthropy and Reform* (1998). His books on the history of childhood include *The Invention of Childhood* which accompanied a Radio 4 series in 2006.

Michael Edwards is a distinguished senior fellow at Demos, New York, and the author of *Small Change: Why Business Won't Save the World* (2010). From 1999 to 2008 he was the director of the Ford Foundation's Governance and Civil Society Programme. He has worked in senior management positions for Oxfam (as Regional Director for Southern Africa); Voluntary Service Overseas (as Head of Development Education); Save the Children (as Director of Research, Evaluation and Advocacy), the World Bank (as a Senior Civil Society Specialist) and Ford Foundation (as director of its Governance and Civil Society Program). He also co-founded the Seasons Fund for Social Transformation, which makes grants to organisations that link their work for social justice with spiritual principles and contemplative practices. His writings examine the global role of civil society and its institutions, the purpose and impact of philanthropy and the not-for-profit sector, the role of business in solving social problems and the links between personal and social transformation. He is currently a distinguished senior fellow at Demos in New York. In 2011, he received the Gandhi, King, Ikeda Award.

Rachel Hayman is head of research at the International NGO Training and Research Centre (INTRAC), Oxford. She was previously based in the School of Social and Political Science at the University of Edinburgh. Her research broadly covers the politics of international development and civil society. Rachel has published in journals and books on aid effectiveness, governance and Rwanda. Current research projects at INTRAC include: how the evidence-based policy-making agenda is affecting NGOs; the changing aid architecture and civil society partnerships; collaborative research in international development between NGOs and academics, and relationships between civil society organisations and private funders.

George Holmes is a lecturer in Critical Environmental Social Science at the School of Earth and Environment, University of Leeds, with an interest in the politics of protected areas, particularly their relationship with local communities, and private protected areas. From 2011-2013, he worked on a two-year Leverhulme-funded fellowship, looking at private protected areas in Patagonia. At the bottom end of South America there are a significant number of privately owned nature reserves, in contrast to the majority of protected areas globally, which are run by governments. Some of these are owned by rich philanthropists, others by families, businesses and NGOs. His project looked at why this strange phenomenon has happed here, and what it means for biodiversity. George is a member of the World Commission for Protected Areas, a fellow of the Royal Geographical Society and a member of the Association of American Geographers. He also participates in the Poverty and Conservation Learning Group, a forum of scholars and practitioners looking at linkages between poverty alleviation and biodiversity conservation, which is coordinated by the International Institute for Environment and Development.

John Mohan is professor of social policy at the University of Southampton, and also deputy director of the Third Sector Research Centre (www.tsrc.ac.uk) and director of Spoke 2 of the work programme of the Centre for Charitable Giving and Philanthropy (www.cgap.org.uk). His current research is focused on the contemporary British voluntary sector, including projects on the distribution of resources and the pattern of engagement in voluntary activity. Previous work has included work on the development of the hospital contributory scheme movement in the 20th century (with Martin Gorsky, *Mutualism and Health Care*, Manchester University Press, 2006) and various publications on the social and political geography of the UK.

Behrooz Morvaridi teaches development theory and policy at the Faculty of Social Sciences, University of Bradford. Morvaridi's theoretical and empirical research experience displays an interdisciplinary approach and covers a range of specialist areas within political economy of developing, including poverty and inequality, rural development, food security, forced migration, the politics of social protection, migration, displacement and resettlement. He has conducted fieldwork research in Turkey, Cyprus, Iran, Oman, Tunisia, India, Zimbabwe, Senegal with funding from a number of different agencies. His book, *Social Justice and Development* (2008, Macmillan) extends the theory of social justice from a local to global level. The focus of recent work is new philanthropy and social justice and understanding the relationship between the agency associated with philanthropy and business approaches and interests. He completed a research project on the political economy of social protection (2014). This looked at social protection, social safety nets and targeting mechanisms in Islamic countries. The research was funded by the Ministry of Development in Turkey on behalf of Organisation of Islamic Countries. The research involved field work in Turkey, Tunisia, Oman and Senegal.

Behrooz Morvaridi has acted as an advisor to UNDP, DFID, EU (Social Affair), Export Credit Agency of UK, Ministry of Development in Turkey.

Filipo Osella is professor of anthropology and South Asian studies at the University of Sussex. He has conducted research in Kerala, south India, since 1989, and published two joint monographs (with Caroline Osella): one on issues of stratification, identity and social mobility among an 'ex-untouchable' community (*Social Mobility in Kerala*, 2000, Pluto Press), and another on masculinities (*Men and Masculinity in South India*, 2007, Anthem Press). His recent research examines contemporary transformations among south Indian Muslims, with fieldwork in Kozhikode (Calicut) and a number of Gulf countries. He has co-edited a special issue of *Modern Asian Studies* on 'Islamic reform movements in South Asia' (with C. Osella), a special issue of *South Asia: Journal of South Asian Studies* on 'The politics of food in South Asia' (with C. Osella) and a special issue of *Journal of the Royal Anthropological Institute* on 'Islam, politics and modernity' (with B. Soares). He has recently concluded a joint ESRC/DfID-funded research project (with R. Stirrat and T. Widger) on charity, philanthropy and development in Colombo, Sri Lanka.

Tom Parr is a PhD candidate in politics and international studies at the University of Warwick. His main interests are in political theory and, in particular, in the moral principles and social institutions that ought to guide society's arrangement and distribution of work. His current research is on the right to freedom of occupational choice and its limits. His research is jointly funded by a Warwick Postgraduate Research Scholarship and the Economic and Social Research Council (ESRC).

Balihar Sanghera is the director of graduate studies (taught) and senior lecturer in sociology at the University of Kent's School of Social Policy, Sociology and Social Research. His main interests are political economy and ethics. He examines how moral sentiments, judgments and concerns shape and are shaped by economic and social structures and institutions. In particular his research explores how class, inequalities and poverty affect everyday morality and politics. His recent research grant from the British Academy was on moral reflexivity, the ethics of ordinary life and charitable giving in the UK. Balijar's current research projects on 'Perceptions of social justice by philanthropic foundations and grant-makers in the UK' is funded by the Economic and Social Research Council (ESRC). This investigation into philanthropy involved 34 semi-structured interviews with executive directors or senior project managers of social change and community-based foundations and grant makers.

Acknowledgments

Many people have helped with this book, and I would like to thank some individuals in particular. I would like to thank Charles Husband for his support in organising the symposium from which the papers in this book were drawn. Both Charles and Andrew Sayers provided scrupulous comments on the book that were extremely helpful. Maya Vachkova provided essential help in assisting with the editing of different chapters and in ensuring that the sources for each chapter were correct. My thanks also go to Maria Ambrozy, Anastasia Belynskaia, Ulli Immler, Marijke Synhave and Sumaila Asuru for their help with the symposium. In addition to all of those mentioned above, I want to thank all of the contributors to this book who provided me with a special opportunity to work with each of them on a very important and stimulating discourse. And last I would like to thank the staff and editors of Policy Press for running the show smoothly.

Introduction

Behrooz Morvaridi

This book is concerned with the current conceptual and policy debate on the new philanthropy and social justice that has been prompted by increases in the flow of giving for poverty reduction. The theoretical underpinning of mainstream philanthropy entails the idea that involving non-state actors such as philanthropists and civil society organisations in social policy issues can lead to more effective outcomes through a 'sharing of responsibilities'. The objective of the book is to consider the potential of philanthropy for social transformation. It takes a critical view of the prevailing conceptualisation in which philanthropy is considered to be an integral part of the neoliberal strategy to disperse state responsibilities in line with declining social expenditure.

Globalisation is having a profound impact on how philanthropy interfaces with social protection and poverty reduction. A new form of philanthropy has emerged on the back of neoliberal economic globalisation which has encouraged wealth concentration in the hands of a few 'super-rich' individuals and families emanating from both the global south and the global north. Over the last two decades individual capitalists and private corporations have become increasingly involved in philanthropy, often through the establishment of foundations targeted at helping to reduce social problems such as poverty, disease and food security. These new structures of philanthropy are considered unique in imbuing business principles into the non-profit sector to support social transformation, as reflected in descriptors such as 'venture philanthropy' (Letts et al, 1997), 'entrepreneurial philanthropy' (Harvey et al, 2011), 'strategic philanthropy' (Sandfort, 2008), 'philanthrocapitalism' (Bishop & Green, 2008), and 'capitalist philanthropy' (Morvaridi, 2012). Bill Gates and Warren Buffet are perhaps the most well-known new philanthropists, between them having donated more than US$62 billion to poverty reduction objectives. Azim Premji, an Indian software billionaire, has devoted US$2 billion to an endowment fund for education. Other philanthropic individuals, whose wealth comes from entrepreneurial activity, include the Hariri family (Lebanon); the Tata family (India); Carlos Slim Helú (Mexico); Miloud Chaabi (Morocco); Patrice Motsepe (South Africa); the Sabanci family (Turkey); Peter

Kellner (Czech Republic); Lee Kun-hee (South Korea), eBay founder Pierre Omidyar (USA) and Richard Branson (UK), to name just a few.[1]

The political underpinning for this kind of giving is the belief that what works for the market should also work for citizen action. This idea hinges on the view that social justice and the distribution or transfer of resources to address poverty or provide social protection do not necessarily have to be between the state and civil society, but can be achieved by linking philanthropy to the poor, whether directly to individuals or through partnerships. Private aid and philanthropic charities are often considered an integral part of a neoliberal strategy to reduce state responsibility for the provision of many services considered essential to securing social rights. The devolution of welfare responsibilities to non-state actors is a means to minimising state social expenditure. Such a construction ostensibly depicts philanthropic non-state actors as agents of social justice that, in contributing to poverty reduction, play a role in social transformation. Despite an increasing dependency on philanthropy to deliver social protection, the political consequences of this form of non-state provision have not been analysed. The chapters in this book debate the current conceptual and policy discourse on philanthropy and social justice drawing on case studies from different geographical and cultural contexts. Common themes emerge across the different trajectories of philanthropy reflecting that the philanthropy and social justice debate extends far beyond the boundaries of the nation state.

While philanthropic activities may be considered worthy in themselves, this book questions the political and ideological reasons why rich individuals, charities and large companies are engaged in poverty reduction through philanthropy. It considers the political framework for giving and the idea that what works for the market (innovation, technology and modern management methods) also work for citizen action. New philanthropy is both politically and ideologically committed to market-based social investment through partnerships that aim to make the market work, or work better, for capital. An overlooked but very pertinent question that we should be asking is whether giving is truly altruistic, for the good of society? Or is its intent to sustain the ideology of market-led capitalist development? Whose interests are ultimately being served and are

---

[1]   For the first time in history the number of billionaires has reached roughly 1210, who between them have a total net wealth of US$4.5 trillion. Billionaires at the top of the list have become increasingly involved in philanthropy, setting up foundations targeted at helping to reduce social problems.

there any conflicting interests? The chapters in this book look at these questions from different perspectives. In response to these questions some authors (Parr, Mohan) argue for the value of philanthropic activity and charitable donations, focusing on their transformative potential. Others (Cunningham, Edwards) question the basic legitimacy of new philanthropists where they are effectively operating as delegated agents of the state, but do not provide systematic social protection and are not accountable for their actions.

Philanthropy – an act of moral duty or self-interest?

Liberalism of one sort or another argues that philanthropy is driven by altruism and the desire to help improve the experiences of others. While philanthropy is quite an open concept, it is generally understood to reflect support for a cause from which the individual (or organisation) concerned is not likely to benefit personally. Much of the debate about philanthropy centres on motivation and objective in the context of whether philanthropic activities have a moral value, in the Kantian sense. In Chapter 1, Cunningham provides a historical analysis of the development of philanthropy, which acts as a backdrop to other chapters in this book. In a compelling narrative that re-examines germane polemics about philanthropy in the context of different eras, Cunningham shows that there is a whole range of motivations behind giving: from 'a love of humankind and a desire to promote human wellbeing' associated with the social justice agenda of early charities such as poor relief to political and ideological motivations. Cunningham argues that philanthropy is inseparably connected to the history of capitalism. In the 19th century, political economists did not hide their enmity to charity and philanthropy, maintaining vehemently that philanthropists' interference with the free market through generous donations hampered capital accumulation and industrial development.

Even contemporary political economists such as Friedman – one of the 'neoliberal ideologues' and architects of free market ideals – argue that the social responsibility of the capitalist is to make a profit and maximise economic welfare, and that any deviation from this is therefore morally problematic. In a similar vein, but with different political and ideological objectives, Marx believed that capital and social responsibility do not resonate, because the main motivation of capital is profit maximisation. Radical political economists were prone to view any charitable wealth transfers as an affront to the poor's agency. Gramsci (1971) vehemently believed that philanthropy was an instrument of hegemony by which the capitalist class maintained its control of the market, workers and peasants, and one that served to avert attention away from the malevolence of the rich and the concentration of wealth in the hands of the few. As in wider society, hegemony is realised within the field of civil society. In other words, philanthropic donations support the domination of politics by the powerful and this is effectively reinforced through consensus rather than force.

For Bourdieu (2001, p15), the 'gratuitous gift does not exist'. For all intents and purposes, the act of giving assumes either some form of reciprocal response or it is motivated by the status that it can generate. Philanthropic activities are consciously driven by specific identified goals and strategies, shaped by personal character and qualities in the social field and through its external relations with other fields, such as business, politics, religion, as well as a grounding in the class system. In Bourdieu's theoretical framework, philanthropists embody not only economic capital – that is, individual capitalists who are dominant actors in the economics field (such as Ford in the car industry, Rockefeller in the oil industry, and most recently Gates in computer technology) – but also symbolic capital. The relationship is synergistic: philanthropists both use and gain symbolic capital through philanthropic activity. In other words, they convert economic capital into symbolic capital and symbolic capital functions to reproduce economic capital. The two fields of activities they are engaged in – capitalist activities for profit and philanthropy not for profit – are far from being separate and distinct but are related symbiotically one to another (Harvey et al, 2011). What distinguishes symbolic capital from other types of capital is that it acts as a source of power to the field of participants through values, recognition, prestige and reputation. Their status, or symbolic capital, is often enhanced by the media and public relations agency that they employ, to the point that there are examples where the media presents philanthropists as having a form of celebrity status, thus generating free publicity about them. A good example is the media attention paid to Bill Gates and Warren Buffet when they announced their decisions to donate a large proportion of their wealth to charitable causes. Bill Gates's philanthropic activities in health, such as the anti-malaria field, have gained him a global reputation for doing good for the wellbeing of humanity, further reinforcing his individual status and the status of associated corporate organisations. As a result, Bill Gates has been able to establish a network that involves other rich capitalists in philanthropic work through the 'Giving Pledge' initiative, through which 40 US billionaires pledged in 2010 to donate half their wealth to philanthropic foundations (either during their lifetime or posthumously), with the number rising since to more than 450. If new philanthropists base decisions about giving on an analysis of the benefits both to others and themselves in terms of power and influence, and political and economic control of outcomes, does this mean that giving only serves to ease the capitalist's conscience?

In the early 21st century, new philanthropy could not have come into being had there not been accumulation of capital in the hands of a few individuals. In fact, the new philanthropy is the price that now needs to be paid to justify neoliberalism, argues Cunningham. According to Bishop and Green (2008), who coined the word 'philanthrocapitalism', what we are witnessing are new 'global movements' initiated by individual capitalists who want to do 'good' and help the poor, in order to make the world a better place in which to live. However in Chapter 2, with meticulous scrutiny, Edwards is critical of this position. He considers how the new philanthropist's practice of helping others hinges on notions of self-transformation and status in the social corporate responsibility stakes. In this context, when the action of giving is not an act of 'duty' it lacks moral worth and value. This aligns with Polanyi's (2002) argument that what characterises 'market society' (capitalism) is its social disembeddedness, in that morality and values tend to be excluded from consideration under a market economy: the aim is to produce what is profitable, not what is socially desirable. Edwards sets out how new philanthropists, some of whom earned much of their wealth in the Silicon Valley and dot.com boom, have developed an approach to solving the problems of extreme poverty based on the principles that made them successful in business. Branded the 'Silicon Valley Consensus', innovation, technology and modern management methods are seen as the framework for solving the poor's problems and global poverty.

The consensus asserts that private aid delivered through a network of public–private and philanthropic–civil society partnerships is more effective than government-led assistance at tackling the problem of poverty. Some capitalist philanthropists (Bill Gates and Pierre Omidyar, for example) are directly involved in running their foundations and shaping how they fund projects within a market-based, knowledge-driven and results-oriented system. They aim to 'make profits and do good' at the same time. Bill Gates is open about the marketisation of philanthropy: 'to have a sustained and strategic impact, philanthropy must be conducted like business – with discipline, strategy and a strong focus on outcomes' (Wall Street Journal, 2011). More importantly 'this approach has nothing to do with the old aid model of donors and recipients. This is about business and … investment' (Hultman, 2011). Edwards dismantles the notion of 'newness' in philanthropy, claiming that it is either always or never new. Irrespective of whether the backdrop is the Industrial Revolution or the Silicon Valley Consensus, innovation and progress result in the perpetual displacement of old ways of conceptualising and implementing philanthropy. Edwards concludes that philanthropy in the 21st century is losing its 'transformative potential' and being replaced by a 'new philanthropy' that is elitist to its core. He argues that if philanthropists really sought to deliver positive change and social reform, they would support a radical restructure of philanthropy from above and the system of funding to one based on democratic and grassroots activity.

There is therefore a paradoxical tension between their engagement in philanthropic activities that help to ease conditions of poverty and their business activity. Philanthropic projects and programmes coexist in a highly competitive environment. The resultant donor-centricity can have numerous adverse implications, such as undermining the much-needed agency of the groups and organisations they fund. In Chapter 3, Cameron argues that, in line with rational choice theory, selflessness is far from the true motive behind philanthropy. Economic theory is premised on the assumption that greediness and selfishness are inextricable from human nature. Their adverse effects may only be mollified through external regulation, be it by the family or the enveloping social framework. At the individual level, giving up resources (money or labour) could be driven by empathy for a group of worse-off individuals, but this is considered to be merely a rational decision to restore one's inner peace if and when it is disturbed by the misery of others. Underlying motivations are considered to reflect the self-maximising assumption in orthodox economic theory that philanthropy is inherently selfish.

By contrast, Singer (2009) and Pogge (2002) have both argued that there is a moral or religious purpose to philanthropy and that individuals of reasonable income and wealth are morally obliged to give a proportion of their income to charities that aim to combat global poverty, with their conscience acting as the 'ultimate unit of moral concern' (Pogge, 2002, p169). Attributing a moral value to philanthropic activities in the Kantian sense makes them not simply acts of kindness or compassion, but acts of duty based upon the universal belief that suffering is bad. This duty becomes operative only if the cost of preventing the harm is not greater than the moral cost to the 'rescuer' of mediating harmful effects and through the disassembly of the structural causes of injustice. Both Singer (2009) and Pogge (2002) believe that it is possible to resolve world poverty and remedy the suffering of the poor through transfers of resources, aid and money from the philanthropists of the global north to the global south using instruments of redistribution, such as a Global Resource Dividend (GRD), which would use the tax system to divert a proportion of individuals' income in rich countries towards poverty alleviation activities (Pogge, 2002). Parr's chapter considers giving as a moral obligation within Singer and Pogge's conceptual framework. He explores why the scope of philanthropic endeavours extends beyond the passive surrender of wealth and posits that philanthropy is a duty which cannot be discharged through discrete donor transactions but one that involves challenge to social, economic and political injustice. In a way, Parr advocates the abolition of the elitist criteria from philanthropy; in its place, philanthropy can be practised as a career and in this way the pursuit of social justice is elevated to the status of a duty to make charitable donations. Parr does not deny the philanthropic value of charitable donations, but suggests that it constitutes a mode of social justice delivery even if philanthropists are self-interested. He argues that there is value in philanthropy careers that mitigate the harmful effect of injustice but only where the benefits of philanthropy outweigh the costs. Individuals that both 'make charitable donations *and* work, say, in international development do more to mitigate (the harmful effects of) injustice than those who merely make charitable donations'.

Holmes (Chapter 5) and Brooks (Chapter 6) offer particular insights into new philanthropic activities in two diverse local contexts. They both conclude that new philanthropy is dominated by elites and handed down through increasingly control-oriented practices from donors to recipients. In a case study of southern Chile, Holmes scrutinises new methods of environmental preservation and the commodification of biodiversity, which have been initiated by philanthrocapitalists. Chile is well-known for its deeply entrenched neoliberal policies and poor social justice delivery. Large-scale privatisation has engendered severe inequalities, such as unequal access to fundamental public goods like water and education. Based on interviews with over 40 entrepreneurs and managers of Privately Owned Protected Areas (PPAs), Holmes provides a detailed examination of the aspirations of contemporary philanthrocapitalists towards natural preservation in Chilean Patagonia. He shows that, while the intent is to sustain biodiversity, landgrabs and the privatisation of natural resources have led to significant profits from high-class eco-tourism, land brokerage and carbon credit sales for some individuals at the expense of local communities.

Can philanthropy and capitalism, underpinned by globalisation, coexist symbiotically? The main motivation for this type of market-based philanthropy is ideological, with activities driven by the intent to commodify and marketise public goods. Brooks examines similar issues in reviewing the projects and programmes that the Bill and Melinda Gates Foundation supports and the actors with whom they partner. Since 2006, the Bill and Melinda Gates Foundation (Gates Foundation) has dedicated US$1.7 billion to assisting small family farmers in Sub-Saharan Africa. This has involved partnerships with a number of private sector partners, whereby the Foundation invests in research and development activities and in-field delivery. In 2010, the Foundation invested US$23 million in the purchase of 500,000 shares in the multinational company Monsanto, one of the world largest producers of GM seeds. In addition, the Gates and Buffett Foundations have together given US$47 million in grants towards Monsanto's five-year project to develop water-efficient maize varieties that the small-scale farmers can afford. The Gates Foundation has also partnered with Cargill, an international producer and marketer of food, together with agricultural, financial and industrial products and services on a venture to improve the incomes of cocoa farmers in West Africa. These kinds of partnerships may be considered essential by philanthropists to support the commodification and marketisation of small-holding farmers and peasants. Brooks examines the Golden Rice and drought-tolerant maize project in Sub-Saharan Africa, setting out how the strategy is to restructure agriculture through public–private partnerships with a particular focus on technology and innovation. Besides introducing supposedly life-saving technology, the Golden Rice and drought maze project also introduce genetically modified foods to an unassuming public. Promotion of highly contentious GM crops would be considered sabotage to social justice at a global level. However, through the promise of life-saving technology, philanthrocapitalists and their partners have managed to successfully bend legislation in many countries in the global south. New regulations open local economies in Sub-Saharan Africa to a profitable GM market, which, for the time being at least, is firmly regulated in the global north. These kinds of activities consolidate corporate global agribusiness chains' hold on agriculture in Sub-Saharan Africa under the auspices of establishing food security, outside of a regulatory framework. Brooks raises the issue of the legitimacy of new philanthropists, given that they are effectively operating as delegated agents of the state but outside of any accountability framework. Given that the agency of small farmers is not being harnessed in this process, it is not clear how social transformation is going to take place that is sustainable.

The Green Revolution in the 1960s and 1970s was a product of a carefully negotiated partnership between philanthropists and states, and was designed to capitalise farming and expand the agribusiness market in an era of state-led development. Under neoliberalism the notion of philanthropy is fundamentally different, in that it is embedded in a concept of governance through partnerships that involve private sector interests and devolve power to non-state actors. The aim is to reduce the need for government intervention to eradicate food insecurity based on the assumption that partnerships between non-state actors – such as private corporations, philanthropists and civil society organizations – can lead to more effective outcomes, through a 'sharing of responsibilities' (World Bank, 2008). The ideological motivation is to reduce the need for government intervention in food security by shifting aspects of governance to private sector interests.

Philanthropy and social protection

Neoliberalism scholars argue that social justice and the redistribution of resources to address poverty do not have to be achieved through a direct relationship between the state and civil society. Instead, linking philanthropy to the poor – whether directly to individuals or through partnerships, regardless of the location in which they live – is considered to be a new conceptualisation of state and civil society. This 'self-development' approach, according to neoliberal economists, involves three steps: 1) raising money from individuals or philanthropists, 2) activities that deal directly with beneficiaries and not through governments, and 3) transferring funds to the poor (Kapur, 2004; Milanovic, 2005; The suggestion is that private aid is more likely to go to the people who really need it if it bypasses government bureaucracy, thereby generating 'more benefit for beneficiaries. The perceived benefits of such individual giving are that it does not require a costly government bureaucracy on the giving side and on the receiving side there is less opportunity for money to be siphoned off into the pockets of corrupt government officials' (Kapur, 2004, p7). Thus philanthropy appears to be good for equity and for poverty, while imposing few budgetary costs. In this conception it would seem that philanthropy in its different forms confers a moral obligation upon the organisation or individual involved to contribute towards the objectives of social justice and development for the wellbeing of individuals, communities and wider society in ways that, according to the World Bank (2008), are 'good for business' and 'good for development'.

The political dimensions of these partnerships are often ideologically articulated within the parameters of the neoliberal market economy. Buğra (Chapter 7) and Osella, Stirrat and Widger (Chapter 8) present cases from Turkey and Sri Lanka respectively that show the different shapes that partnership between philanthropists and the state can take. Services that provide social safety nets and social security provision are a prime example of such partnerships. In both countries, the delivery of services is no longer solely the responsibility of the state, but is effectively devolved through partnerships between state agencies and non-state actors, such as faith-based organisations, the private sector and philanthropists. There is a long and strong tradition of philanthropic activity in both countries, which in its most traditional form is shaped by religious donations (Zakat, Vakif, Sadaka, Zekat al-fitr and Kurbani in Islam, and daane in Buddhism). These forms of giving have a moral value, in that they are not simply acts of kindness or compassion but constitute a duty that aims to bring donors closer to God and paradise, with individual giving considered to reflect the sincerity of the donor's belief.

Since the 1990s, there has been a steady growth of faith-based organisations (FBOs) globally that are involved in service delivery and community development, in part a response to the vacuum in delivery of social services left by the shrinking of the state. FBOs have reciprocal benefits in mobilising support for states that use them to satisfy welfare needs. Buğra focuses on the political dimensions of modern philanthropy in Turkey and the relationships between a conservative neoliberal state and benign political Islam in the context of social protection and service delivery. She argues that the neoliberal state has reinvigorated opportunities for faith-based civil society activity in the public sphere, as part of a wider cultural-political repositioning. The 'mildly' Islamist Justice and Development (AKP) regime has transformed welfare institutions by adorning them with a religious halo. By emphasising family-oriented corporatism as the crucial unit for social cohesion and using FBOs to plug the welfare system gap (such as care for the elderly and street children), the AKP appeals to the norms and institutions of traditional and Islamic solidarity. Buğra shows that, where local government is controlled by the AKP, FBO characters have been successful in mobilising charitable donations and channelling them to the destitute. The outreach potential is why FBOs are coopted into implementing the government's social and development policy as a new form of welfare governance. FBOs actively engage people who provide ideological support to the state and influence public opinion to favour and therefore legitimise political projects. This new government management structure is based on diverse partnerships between FBOs, state departments and/or local municipalities and businesses, building links with groups like the Independent Industrialist and Businessmen

Association (MÜSIAD), which was founded in 1990 and organises Islamic entrepreneurs into a collective group that can network with other actors (Adas, 2006). MÜSIAD functions as an interest group for lobbying the government on behalf of the business community, but its members are also a powerful force in shaping the state's social and economic policies through the political influence gained through financial and practical support for charitable activities.

The use of a common set of values pertaining to solidarity, culture, family and religious philanthropy as a basis for new partnerships provides a framework for linking local traditions with the politics of philanthropy and everyday social protection. This type of 'indigenous charity' is distinct to the global south, according to Osella, Stirrat and Widger. Giving is embedded in culture and religion, such that the poor tend to give as much as the rich through donations towards specific projects. Such decisions are moral and reflect how giving is embedded to varying degrees in everyday life. Individuals can also make genuinely 'disinterested judgements about moral worth and can adopt an impartial and critically reflexive instance towards others' (Sayer, 2005, p24). They provide evidence to show how philanthropic activities are allied to community objectives such that civil society and the state together set the development agenda. Colombo is a tapestry of religions and ethnicities that coexist, including Hinduism, Buddhism, Christianity and Islam. There is, however, an ongoing controversy over whether donations should be categorised as social protection tools, given the perceivably targeted nature of religious donations that will benefit a restricted group. Open almsgiving invites social support and facilitates entry into new social networks, but this becomes particularly complex in the case of donations from large corporations that have political underpinnings and are based on an analysis of the benefits of giving both to others and for themselves in terms of power and control of outcomes. The chapter concludes that philanthropic ventures in Colombo are fragmented and unaccountable, but are increasingly being shaped by the neoliberal discourse of international development agencies (such as empowerment, sustainability and participation). While philanthropy in Sri Lanka provides some social safety nets for the economically deprived, it fails to provide a long-term solution to inequality and injustice. Moreover, this approach to social fairness reinforces existing patterns of power relations.

Hayman pursues this argument on the relationship between new philanthropy and 'indigenous' charity, suggesting that new philanthropy encourages neglect for structural causes of social injustice and in so doing hampers development. In an African context, she examines the negative impacts on grassroots, bottom-up development of new philanthropists' influence on local development policies. Due to distrust of local capacity, new philanthropists often ignore local actors and assign foreign NGOs to be programme implementers based on their preferred or existing partnerships. Hayman argues that distinguishing 'indigenous' charity and local NGOs from new philanthropic activity perpetuates new philantopists' fixation with technical solutions. Technical solutions stem from the marketisation of philanthropy by champions, who are usually successful businessmen armed with a particular set of expertise. This in turn encourages a result-oriented evaluative culture whereby projects' successes are measured against standardised indices. Given that projects and programmes coexist in a donor-driven, highly competitive environment, we find that donor dominance undermines the much-needed agency and empowerment of the local groups and organisations they fund. Paradoxically, Hayman points out, in NGO taxonomy a holistic approach to development is one that is based on inclusion, participation, respect for local culture and capacity building. African civil society organisations tend to advocate increased support for institutional change and social justice, rather than technical fixes, as a basis for tackling inequality. External funders tend to display reluctance for political engagement, whereas by contrast, African philanthropic foundations tend to be driven by more robust social policy objectives. Hayman argues that a possible escape from 'the technical fix' predicament, would be to encourage philanthropists to engage in open dialogue with civil society and to embrace the political nature of social change and development.

Sanghera and Bradley (in Chapter 10) and Mohan (in Chapter 11) delve into the operations of philanthropists in a different cultural context. They use a conceptual framework based on Rawls's social justice theory to analyse philanthropy in the UK, framed around how social and political institutions distribute fundamental rights and duties so that benefits and responsibilities are fairly distributed and shared. This presupposes that capitalist society can be changed to offer a shared institutional order, which maintains genuinely equal treatment of individuals. Following this argument, the authors argue that philanthropy can be transformative – in contrast to the critical perspectives of Cunningham and Edwards (chapters 1 and 2 respectively) – if they first pursue the 'liberty principle' (that is, the protection of equal rights for each individual) and second and more importantly the 'different principle' (that is, socioeconomics of opportunity that benefit all citizens, in particular the marginal and most deprived in society). Social justice in this conceptual framework is concerned with fair distribution across society that supports civil and political rights on an equal basis and thus also delivers personal security. It may require access to resources, which are essential not only for the livelihoods of citizens but also to ensure equal opportunity. Hence we would expect people to have access to education and jobs, for example, without prejudice on any basis. Sanghera and Bradley argue that charities, foundations and organisations that are actively involved in challenging inequality and poverty in capitalist society are effectively ascribed to 'social justice philanthropy'. Basing their arguments on a study of ten philanthropic organisations in the UK, they attempt to show that not all philanthropic organisations can be considered to be in the category of social justice philanthropy.

Despite the fact that many charities and foundations have a commitment to liberalism and social justice principles, Sanghera and Bradley conclude that many philanthropists steer clear of clamorous notions about 'social justice' in their official statements and do not incorporate an overt social justice agenda into their programmes for a number of reasons. 'Social justice' implies bearing the responsibility to 'practice what you preach'. Foundations need to be able to pass the same test of fairness as the ones they would impose on other social structures. Moreover, 'social justice' is reminiscent of left-wing egalitarianism, which is not well received in contemporary British society. Unsurprisingly, agents of philanthropy avoid the bright badge of 'social justice' because it would fit neither their suits nor those of their donors.

Mohan also raises concern about social justice issues relating to regional inequality in the distribution of charitable organisations and charitable resources in England. The needs of people in some of the poorest, most deprived areas are often not matched by resources, and we find 'charity deserts' where philanthropic activity is scarce. Their findings show that motivations for philanthropic giving are complex and not always driven by a social justice agenda. Mohan estimates that the national average of charities per 1000 people is 2.56. However, the ratio changes dramatically according to the locus. Rich local areas have a ratio much higher than economically deprived areas (the ratio of the City of London is 30 times above the average). The ratio approach has a flaw: not all charities work within the locality in which they are registered, and many extend their work nationwide or worldwide. The average ratio of local charities is calculated as 1.6 charities per 1000 persons. The most disadvantaged local authorities, however, tend to suffer the lowest ratios. The median expenditure of charities also indicates a misbalance in favour of rich areas, with charities in prosperous areas saturated with funding compared to poorer ones. He concludes that there is a strong link between charity concentration and economic prosperity and implies that notions about the 'Big Society' stretch further existing gaps between communities rather than bringing them closer together.

References

Adas, BE, 2006, The Making of entrepreneurial Islam and the Islamic spirit of capitalism, *Cultural Research*, 10 2 pp11-136

Bishop, M and Green, M, 2008 *Philanthro-capitalism: how the rich can save the world*, London: Bloomsbury Press

Gramsci, A, 1971, *Selection from the prison notebook*, New York: International Publishers

Harvey, C, Maclean, M, Gordon, J and Shaw, E, 2011, Andrew Carnegie and the foundations of contemporary entrepreneurial philanthropy, *Business History*, 53, 3, 424-48

Hultman, T, 2011, Best chance to end polio: Bill Gates promotes vaccines and food programs to attack poverty, *All Africa*, 9 February, available from: http://allafrica.com/stories/201102091101. html?viewall=1

Kapur, D, 2004, Remittances: the new development mantra?, G24 discussion paper no. 29, *UN Conference on Trade and Development*, Geneva: United Nations

Letts, C, Ryan, W and Grossman, A, 1997, Virtuous capital: what foundations can learn from venture capitalists, *Harvard Business Review*, 75, 2, 36-44

Milanovic, B, 2005, *World apart: global and international inequality 1950–2000*, Princeton: Princeton University Press

Morvaridi, B, 2008, *Social justice and development*, London: Palgrave

Morvaridi, B, 2012, Capitalist philanthropy and hegemonic partnerships, *Third World Quarterly*, 33, 7, 1191-210

Pogge, T, 2002, *World poverty and human rights*, Cambridge: Polity Press

Polanyi, K, 2002, *The great transformation: the political and economic origins of our time*, Boston, MA: Beacon Press

Sandfort, J, 2008, Using lessons from public affairs to inform strategic philanthropy, *Non-Profit and Voluntary Sector Quarterly*, 37, 3, 537-52

Sayer, A, 2005 *The moral significance of class*, Cambridge: Cambridge University Press

Singer, P, 2009, *The life you can save*, New York: Random House

Wall Street Journal, 2011, Should philanthropies operate like businesses?, *Wall Street Journal*, 5 December

World Bank, 2008, *Agriculture for development: World Development Report 2008*, Washington, DC: World Bank

Part One
New philanthropy and social transformation

ONE

Philanthropy and its critics: a history

Hugh Cunningham

Introduction

In 1795, the English Unitarian George Dyer set out his vision of the relationship between philanthropy and justice (Dyer, 1795, pp35-6):

> There would be less occasion to erect so many temples to Charity, if we erected more to Justice. To remove the defects and excesses of governments; to give a just direction to the laws; and to preserve the course of industry from being obstructed, would be attended with more advantages to the poor, than the erecting of a thousand hospitals; and, on this ground, every philanthropist should be a reformer.

Dyer (1795) believed that 'in proportion as a country abounds in poor, the state of society is bad' (p47). He was a supporter of the newly-formed Philanthropic Society's plans to reform convicts' children and 'add citizens to society'. In the late 18th century, philanthropy as a word indicating a love of humankind and a desire to promote human wellbeing was radiating out from its French base, and Dyer's statement reflects this moment of hope. Old charity with its temples and its hospitals was neither adequate nor necessary. Instead philanthropists should focus on removing 'the defects and excesses of governments'. In short, philanthropy was a political project: to be a reformer was to engage in politics. For people like Dyer the point of philanthropy was to deliver social justice.

This late-18th-century moment stands out in the history of charity and philanthropy. Before and after it social justice was rarely absent, but it was equally rarely an overriding concern. In part this was because charity and philanthropy faced criticisms which had the effect of deflecting their activities onto what seemed safer terrain than the promotion of social justice. This was particularly the case in the 19th century, when philanthropy was criticised for interfering with the workings of a free market. In setting out some of the criticisms made of philanthropy (or charity, as it is properly called before the late 18th century) I aim to show how and why a concern for social justice became marginalised.

Charity and poor relief

From the late 15th century charity was intimately bound up with poor relief and there were only a limited number of possible policies that could be utilised. At one extreme lay indiscriminate giving to the poor as you encountered them on the street, at the other the incarceration of beggars. In between was domiciliary help for the poor, based on assessments of need determined by visitors from a higher class. Whichever policy was favoured, charity was frequently criticised as inefficient and liable to demoralise the poor whom it was meant to be helping. Critics urged a more rigorous charity, an end to indiscriminate giving, an attack on begging, careful examination of claimants and, with shades of today, a measurement of outcomes. In the wake of this criticism things changed, but with the passage of time old habits returned, and it was time for another round of criticism.

The late fifteenth and early sixteenth centuries provide a starting point to examine this pattern. Previous to this in the West, in the early Christian centuries and in the Middle Ages, there was a degree of reciprocity in gifting. The rich gave, and in return the poor – sometimes thought of as close to Christ – prayed for the souls of the rich. It was particularly common in the later Middle Ages for the wealthy to try to reduce their time and sufferings in purgatory by paying for chantries, where prayers would be offered. But in the late fifteenth and early sixteenth centuries in Europe, attitudes to the poor became harsher; rather than being considered close to Christ they became thought of as idle, licentious and dangerous. Most historians ascribe this new attitude to a changing economic climate which then, and subsequently up to the late 19th century, condemned about one-third of the population to poverty. Charity became inextricably bound up with poor relief and reciprocity in the gift relationship came to an end. Further, if charity was helping in the relief of poverty it was also criticised for exacerbating the bad behaviour of the poor.

The new attitude was most evident in the northern European countries that turned Protestant. In Germany, Luther was scathing in his attack on Catholic mendicant orders. He, and others like him in the 1520s, drew up schemes of poor relief based on funding from a common chest, the engagement of town authorities, and delivery in the recipient's home rather than an institution (Grell, 1997). Move forward two hundred years to Hamburg, and we find the poor relief system criticised and, consciously or not, the advocacy of policies such as opposition to begging, very similar to what had been proposed and implemented in the 16th century. Mary Lindemann (2002) emphasises the new economic conditions that underlay the Hamburg initiatives. Hamburg was a port town with an unsettled population, its residents subject to the vagaries of global trade. Alongside the Protestant input to the reform proposals there was concern to maintain the economic order. The Hamburg reforms (Lindemann, 2002) became well-known and were copied elsewhere, but they formed only part of wider criticism in the 18th century of charitable practices.

One criticism focused on donors. In England, the Dutchman Bernard Mandeville turned his acid pen against them. Charity, he argued, sprang from donor selfishness; what he called 'the reward of virtuous action' - that is 'a certain pleasure [a man] procures to himself by contemplating on his own worth' (Williams, 1996, p84). Too often, Mandeville went on, this pleasure was celebrated communally in annual dinners, where donors feasted and congratulated themselves and 'the objects' of the charity were paraded round on display. Benevolence as a part of human nature was much celebrated in the 18th century, but did it, as Mandeville suggested, spring from self-love?

As to the recipients of benevolence, the 'objects', Mandeville was one of a long line of critics, reaching its height in the mid 19th century, who argued that the unregulated exercise of benevolence would do more harm than good: in a nutshell, it encouraged dependency and idleness and sapped the springs of industry. Thomas Secker, who became Archbishop of Canterbury in 1758, argued that 'Love to our Fellow-Creatures is one of our natural inclinations. ... If we succeed, we have exquisite Joy: if we fail, it is no inconsiderable Comfort, that we meant well' (Andrew, 1992, p584). Nonsense, said Mandeville, you have to weigh the consequences of your benevolence. Even David Hume – a proponent of benevolence – acknowledged that if you looked at the encouragement 'to idleness and debauchery' arising from giving alms to a common beggar, you had to view 'that species of charity rather as a weakness than a virtue' (Hume, 1975, p10).

This kind of thinking was widespread throughout Europe. In Modena in Italy in the early 18th century, Ludovico Ricci worried that all forms of charity were potentially vicious, since they might undermine self-sufficiency and encourage improvidence (Davis, 2005, p12). France was the epicentre of the critique. In Montpellier, indiscriminate giving was thought to have far exceeded donations to the city's charitable institutions – leading Bishop Colbert in 1735 to urge his flock to stop it altogether, to 'regulate your alms'. This criticism of charity, fuelled by anti-clericalism, became a leading theme of Enlightenment thinkers. In the words of Turgot in 1757, too much and ill-directed relief 'made the condition of the idle preferable to that of the man who works'. In place of traditional charity the Enlightenment advocated *bienfaisance*, a term popularised by Voltaire, suggesting a universal human propensity to give in the face of suffering – but one that needed to be ordered and well-directed. This led in the Revolution to the establishment of *bureaux de bienfaisance* (Jones, 1982, pp2-3, p77).

The Enlightenment critique of charity gave birth to the *Société Philanthropique de Paris* in 1780, an elitist reforming institution (Duprat, 1993). It was the first clear sign of the emergence of a new and enduring vocabulary of 'philanthropy' and 'philanthropists', disengagement from the Church a key aspect of their approach. The Parisian model spread and Philanthropic Societies were soon founded in other French towns, in London, and in Brussels. They put much of their energy into the prevention of youth crime and the reform of prisons. The first person to be described as a 'philanthropist' in England was John Howard, famous for visiting prisons all over Europe.

The new thinking associated with the Enlightenment was gendered. To some people the 'man of feeling', never ashamed to shed a tear when occasion demanded, was indeed an ideal. Isaac Wood, for example – who established the Shrewsbury House of Industry for children in 1783 – recorded how the scene of children working, 'never fails to interest the intelligent spectator. I have seen the tear of benevolent sensibility trembling in the eye of a HOWARD [John Howard the prison reformer], and several other exalted characters, as I have accompanied them through the working rooms; where they frequently stopped to indulge their generous emotions' (Cunningham, 1991, p26). But if such a passage was moving to some readers, to others it exposed itself to ridicule and attack. The trembling 'tear of benevolent sensibility', the indulgence of the 'generous emotions', smacked of self-regard. Worse still, they suggested that most heinous of late-18th-century crimes: effeminacy. It was 'unmanly' to behave in such a way. Softening hearts, trembling tears, the indulgence of the emotions: these were women's province.

Philanthropy and political economy

By the late 18th century, the chorus of criticism of the consequences of indiscriminate giving was deafening. This reflected the growing dominance of political economy, as it fast became the ideology of capitalism. The course of philanthropy was in many ways determined by that dominance, the two at first in partnership, later at odds. What was at stake was set out by a preacher at Addenbrooke's Hospital in Cambridge in 1797: 'Indiscriminate donations ... are not found infrequently to defeat the purposes of industry, and in a commercial kingdom may do as much harm as the most unfeeling parsimony' (Andrew, 1992, p588). Britain was undoubtedly 'a commercial kingdom', and the time for indiscriminate giving was over. Nothing did more harm, it was said in 1815, than 'the misplaced benevolence of the charitable and humane'; their 'injudicious benevolence' that so encouraged vagrancy and begging (Coats, 1973, 'Mendicity', pp121, 139). That comes from the *Tory Quarterly Review*. Even more stridently, an anonymous writer in the utilitarian *Westminster Review* in 1824 argued that '[B]enevolence is useless or mischievous without knowledge', and the knowledge that was required was knowledge of political economy:

> To convince the public, twenty or thirty years ago, of the goodness of a charity, it was sufficient to shew that the objects relieved were in a state of real distress. ... But now, that the circumstances are more generally known, on which the condition of the labouring classes depends, all former reasonings on the subject of charity ... are invalidated. ... The condition of the labouring classes with regard to the necessaries and comforts of life, is evidently determined by the rate of wages. (Coats, 1973, 'Charitable Institutions', p 99)

This writer got to the heart of the political economy case against charity: the rate of wages should be determined by the market and the market only; charity's meddling interfered with that. Political economy caused much anguish amongst those distressed by the condition of the poor but wary of doing anything that might break its laws. Unitarians, for example, on both sides of the Atlantic – as David Turley has shown (Turley, 1998, pp235–40) – tussled with this dilemma.

The problem didn't go away. In 1865, Joseph Rowntree was withering in his assessment of giving: 'Charity as ordinarily practised, the charity of endowment, the charity of emotion, the charity which takes the place of justice, creates much of the misery it relieves, but does not relieve all the misery it creates' (Vernon, 1958, p64). Indiscriminate almsgiving, asserted another writer in 1869, was 'a public nuisance, if not a grave moral offence ' (Coats, 1973, 'Charity', p684).

In the 1820s, claims were made that 'philanthropy' was the means by which political economy could set bounds to unlimited charity (Coats, 1973, 'Charitable Institutions', p113). Teaching the poor 'the knowledge of the laws which regulate wages ... depends in a great measure upon the exertions of enlightened philanthropists' (Coats, 1973, 'Charitable Institutions', p113). Thirty years later, in an article tellingly entitled *Charity, noxious and beneficent*, the message was still being drummed home. It said:

> The profession of philanthropy, like every other, can be safely and serviceably practised only by those who have mastered its principles and graduated in its soundest schools. It is as dangerous to practise charity, as to practise physic without a diploma. He who would benefit mankind must first qualify himself for the task. (Coats, 1973, 'Charity, noxious and beneficent', p81)

What that meant was 'ascertaining and enforcing those principles of social science by which alone misery can be permanently removed or prevented, and distress, effectually and without mischief, relieved' (Coats, 1973, 'Charity, noxious and beneficent', p81). Once the principles of social science (i.e. political economy) were firmly established, 'our kindly impulses and deep consciousness of the debt we owe to others, will cast off the lazy shape of charity, and rise into the attitude and assume the garb of true philanthropy'(Coats, 1973, 'Charity, noxious and beneficent', p88).

Philanthropy, however, never entirely separated itself from 'the lazy shape of charity'. In an 1869 article, *The philanthropy of the age and its relation to social evils* (anonymous author), there was much criticism of 'a misguided and sanguine philanthropy', and reference to an essay read before the Social Science Association *On misdirected philanthropy as an economical question* (Coats, 1973). The misdirection arose from ignoring the lessons of political economy, and philanthropy and charity were in danger of doing precisely that. In 1872, Walter Bagehot questioned:

> whether the benevolence of mankind does most good or harm. Great good, no doubt, philanthropy does, but then it

also does great evil. It augments so much vice, it multiplies so much suffering, it brings to life such great populations to suffer and to be vicious, that it is open to argument whether it be or be not an evil to the world. (Bagehot, 1947, p124)

The reason for the evil, said Bagehot, arguing a social Darwinist case, was that philanthropists had 'inherited from their barbarous forefathers a wild passion for instant action'. If philanthropy was to do good, it must be the product of careful forethought and preparation, of adherence to the laws of political economy, not of a desire by otherwise excellent people to 'relieve their own feelings' in face of an 'evil' (Bagehot, 1947).

Politicians absorbed the anxieties of political economists. Gladstone in 1875 feared that if W.E. Forster became Liberal party leader he might lean towards over-government and, 'in … the propagandism of a vague philanthropy, he might go constantly astray' – astray, that is, from the principles of political economy. In 1877, G. J. Goschen, another Liberal, feared that political economy had been dethroned 'and Philanthropy has been allowed to take its place. Political economy was the bugbear of the working classes, and philanthropy, he was sorry to say, was their idol' (Harrison, 1982, p246). From the Conservative side, Salisbury complained about Gladstone's 'vague philanthropic phraseology'(Harrison, 1982, p246). Philanthropy had lost any claim to be better than the charity or benevolence from which it had tried to emancipate itself. It was no longer working in accordance with the so-called laws of political economy. As Brian Harrison concluded, 'Philanthropy had become a pejorative term for some Mid-Victorians, a synonym almost for soft-headedness' (Harrison, 1982, p246).

Reading warnings about the dangers of giving could reduce well-intentioned people to a state of paralysing uncertainty. In the mid-1840s Mary Carpenter wrote for advice on the matter and her mentor, James Martineau, a Unitarian with much experience of poverty in Liverpool, replied, 'I can discover no satisfactory guiding principle to determine the conflict between Christian *compassion* and Christian *economy*, so that I never give, and never withhold without compunction. I fear it is quite impossible to disentangle the mischief of charity from its good' (Manton, 1976, p73). Of John Ruskin, it was said that 'he never dares to give any thing in the streets without looking on all sides to see whether there is a political economist coming' (Roberts, 1991, pp229-30). But it was not only political economists he had to worry about; it was also Christians. When Brooke Lambert, a vicar in London's East End, preached before the University of Oxford in 1868, he lamented the money that had poured indiscriminately into the area from the

West End. 'The marvel of Christ's life', he said, 'is His repression of His powers of beneficence' (Lambert, 1869, p11). It was, if nothing else, a new take on the Gospel. Christians, like Christ, should repress their 'powers of beneficence'.

This call for repression represented a minority voice at a time when many trumpeted the generosity of philanthropists – amounts given in London alone greater than the budgets of smaller European states. But against this there was a persistent line of criticism that claimed that assertions by philanthropists of their generosity failed to recognise that, in fact, the poor gave more to the poor than did the rich (Prochaska, 1990, pp362-6). Exactly what the poor gave could never be accurately counted, but a clergyman in south London in 1908 commented on the:

> unostentatious, wholly unselfish charity of the poor amongst themselves, which is startling in its extent. The poor breathe an atmosphere of charity. They cannot understand life without it. And it is largely this kindness of the poor to the poor which stands between our present civilization and revolution. (Conybeare, 1908, p6)

There was a further problem with charity and philanthropy. Many people, echoing Mandeville, pondered the motives of donors. According to Lord Hobhouse, 'love of power, ostentation, and vanity' were the principal motives driving them, along with superstition (the belief that you would benefit in the afterlife) and spite (disappointing expectant heirs) (Finlayson, 1994, p50). Benjamin Jowett asked Florence Nightingale rather pointedly: 'Do you ever observe how persons take refuge from family unhappiness in philanthropy?' (Prochaska, 2006, p 88). In Liverpool *Porcupine* in 1861 reported its belief that:

> The most fashionable amusement of the present age is philanthropy. ... No small number of these benevolent persons are philanthropic because it is the fashion to be so; because it brings them into passing contact with this Bishop or that Earl, or even with Mr Cropper or Mr Rathbone, or any other of our leading local philanthropists. (Simey, 1992, pp56-7)

Such social observations were meat and drink for novelists. It comes as something of a shock, however, to see how critical they were of charity and philanthropy. They didn't simply poke fun at fundraising bazaars. Take Dickens: he was actively engaged in a range of philanthropic or charitable projects, but he didn't disguise his feelings about the approach and attitude of some philanthropists, especially concerned about their focus on 'telescopic philanthropy'. In *Bleak House*, Jo sweeps the doorstep of the Society for the Propagation of the Gospel in Foreign Parts; Mrs Jellyby is preoccupied with her project for Borrioboola-Gha on the left bank of the Niger – to the neglect of her own family; and the fearsome Mrs Pardiggle focuses her attention on the Tockahoopo Indians. In part this was an attack on Christianity gone wrong, but it also had in its sights the neglect of problems at home in favour of those being faced by missionaries on the front line of what Alison Twells (2008) has called 'global missionary philanthropy'. George Eliot in *Middlemarch* was more wide-ranging in her criticism of philanthropy. She too picked up on the neglect of home problems in favour of those overseas. 'We all know the wag's definition of a philanthropist', she has a journalist write, 'a man whose charity increases directly as the square of the distance'. But it was in her extended portrait of two types of philanthropist, the secular Mr Brooke and the evangelical 'philanthropic banker', Mr Bulstrode, that she came close to questioning philanthropy as a whole. Brooke, for whom philanthropy is mainly about 'punishments and that kind of thing', is vague and ineffective; his deficiencies mercilessly exposed by the public and the newspapers when he makes the mistake of standing for Parliament. Bulstrode, under the guise of philanthropy, seeks to exercise power while keeping the lid on his own misdemeanours. Dorothea dutifully surrounds herself with 'her particular little heap of books on political economy' as a guide to action, but quickly puts them aside to follow the dictates of her heart. She alone comes through with a clean bill of health.

Philanthropy and the state

By the late 19th century, philanthropy was facing a new challenge from those who argued that it was simply incapable of coping with the problems of an urban and industrial society. In *Toiling Liverpool* (1886), Hugh Farrie doubted 'whether charity is doing any good at all to society' (Simey, 1992, p107). From York, Joseph Rowntree concluded in 1904 that 'much of our present philanthropic effort is directed to remedying the more superficial manifestations of weakness or evil' (Vernon, 1958, p154). George Cadbury in Birmingham agreed. Rowntree's son, B. S. Rowntree, described how the impact of charity was no more than marginal. General Booth, of the Salvation Army, was dismissive of the miscellaneous and heterogeneous efforts which are clubbed together under the generic head of Charity. Faced with the 'great and appalling mass of human misery', remedies, claimed Booth, were 'beyond the imagination of most of those who spend their lives in philanthropic work' (Finlayson, 1994, p38). The radical Countess of Warwick agreed: with hungry children, the unemployed and the aged all in need of help, 'of what possible use is it', she asked, 'to plaster this state of things with philanthropy?' Even the Charity Organisation Society admitted in 1886 that there were 'permanent causes of distress which it is impossible for philanthropy alone to cope with or even in any sufficient degree to palliate by schemes of direct relief' (Finlayson, 1994, pp138-40, pp159-60, p171). These commentators all had a vision of social justice and all felt that philanthropy on its own was unable to deliver it.

From a different angle altogether, the Social Democratic Federation regularly denounced charity and philanthropy for their patronising attitude, as well as the inadequacy of what they offered. In *A word to philanthropists* in 1894, Sunderland's socialist paper claimed that the attitude of philanthropists to those they set out to help was to 'treat them as things to be amused, educated, restricted, lectured, advised; to have everything except fair play'. We were working out our own salvation, claimed the writer, and there was no need for the 'canting sympathy and foolish patronage' of philanthropists (Waters, 1990, pp71-2). The state alone, it was asserted, could tackle the problems that beset a late-19th- and early-20th-century city: unemployment; homelessness; poverty, especially in childhood and old age; environmental degradation and ill health. In Rotherham in 1906 the Cinderella Club, set up to feed schoolchildren, was uneasy about engaging in philanthropy. The club said, 'Our main work as socialists is to abolish the need for charity by establishing a system of justice for the workers, and making it the duty of the State to care for the sick and the needy' (Waters, 1990, p88). Through the Liberal welfare reforms before the First World War, the state made its move. It was not that charity and philanthropy had lost their raison d'être, far from it. Rather they lost any claim to be leading partners in the mixed economy of welfare, and they could not establish 'a system of justice'.

By the interwar period charity and philanthropy were detested even more. In the late 1970s, Richard Crossman recalled how 1930s philanthropy had been seen as 'an odious expression of social oligarchy and churchy bourgeois attitudes' (Harrison, 1982, p247), and he said that, like others, he had 'detested voluntary hospitals maintained by flag days' (Finlayson, 1994, p272). In 1946, Nye Bevan claimed it was 'repugnant in a civilized community for hospitals to have to rely upon private charity.... I have always felt a shudder of repulsion when I see nurses and sisters who ought to be at their work ... going about the streets collecting money for the hospitals' (Finlayson, 1994, p272).

The attack on philanthropy from the Right by political economists, and from the Left by Fabians and socialists, was resisted. The Charity Organisation Society embodied this resistance. In 1913 its leader, C. S. Loch, deplored 'state philanthropy' with the state as 'caterer in chief for its citizens' (Finlayson, 1994, p195). And yet the narrowing of the sphere in which philanthropy operated, shifting the emphasis away from direct involvement in poor relief, opened up new opportunities.

New directions

So what could would-be philanthropists safely do? One approach was to attempt to solve social problems by building institutions for those in need. By taking the poor out of the environment in which they lived there seemed less danger, than by direct poor relief, of infringing the laws of political economy. Moreover, and this had been of fundamental concern since the late middle ages, this could contribute to good order. Michel Foucault dated the 'great confinement' of the different categories of those who threatened disorder from the mid-17th century to the end of the 18th, but confinement itself had 16th-century precedents, as he acknowledges, and did not end with the 18th century (Foucault, 2006, pp44-77). The practice of it in the 19th century in the United States has been brilliantly explored by David Rothman. How was it, he asked, that this reform movement – which began in the 1820s – 'would eventually turn into a snake pit'? (Rothman, 1971, pp14-15). Criminals, the insane, the old, the ill, and children were all placed in institutions. Sometimes, as with early mental hospitals or asylums, the progenitors set out with admirable motives, only to find that the institution took on a life of its own. The investment in buildings, often named after donors, induced conservatism in thought and administration. Criticisms of institutionalisation, particularly harmful for children, were commonplace in the later 19th century – but did little to slow down the rate of institution building. Only in the second half of the 20th century was there a concerted and largely successful campaign to close these institutions.

The boldest social experiment undertaken largely by charity involved the removal of British children thought likely to be troublesome: to Canada and later Australia. Barnardo defended the practice and called it 'philanthropic abduction' (Wagner, 1979, p208). Around 80,000 children were taken to Canada in the late 19th and early 20th centuries, most of them under 14 years old. There followed, almost inevitably, scandals of mistreatment. Criticism was vociferous, but the practice continued until the 1960s. Incredibly, some children were wrongly told that their parents were dead, and only in the late 20th century was there acknowledgement of the damage that had been done.

As founding institutions or sending children abroad attracted criticism a safer option for philanthropists was to engage in what was seen as the civilising mission to provide a cultural infrastructure in the towns and cities where they lived and worked. Parks, libraries, museums, art galleries, concert halls and gymnasiums became the norm in urban communities – some the result of municipal initiative, many the outcome of a donation by the rich. An advantage for the donor was that they often carried his, or more rarely her, name. Philanthropists also turned their attention to housing problems, engaging in an early form of social enterprise known as 5% philanthropy. This entailed building worker apartment blocks – with an anticipated 5% investment return for the philanthropists.

By the end of the 19th century this philanthropic engagement in urban infrastructure seems to have run out of steam. The urban bourgeoisie, previously staunchly loyal to their towns, began to fragment as people moved to London, built country houses, and widened their interests across the country and in the Empire.

In the 20th century it was in the United States that new opportunities for philanthropy were most enthusiastically adopted. The philanthropic foundations that came into being in the early 20th century were, as the Rockefellers put it, 'wholesale, not retail', and emancipated from the tiresome business of dealing with the needs of individual human beings (Sealander, 2003). With a global perspective, and with the profound belief that science held the key to the realisation of their goals, philanthropists directed their money towards universities and research institutes (Sealander, 2003). Philanthropy and poor relief, long indissolubly linked, could now go their separate ways – poor relief a problem for the state and local do-gooders.

The same disassociation of philanthropy and the problems of poverty was happening in Britain. The foundations that were established, like their American counterparts, focused on medicine and medical research as the main way they could contribute to the welfare of humanity. Many of them became funding bodies for other people's research. One unforeseen outcome of these developments was a lasting divide between the world of philanthropy and that of the social services and the voluntary sector. The former was the world of big money, the latter of professionalisation – especially of women – and an increasing reliance on the state for funding.

Conclusion

Historians, learning from anthropology, have in recent years studied charity and philanthropy primarily as forms of gift relationship. Motives for giving in such studies are shown to be complex and wide-ranging, Power, patronage, social status and fear of disorder are part of the complex alongside compassion, religious motivation and a concern for social justice (Van Leeuwen, 1994; Kidd, 1996). Poor relief was at the heart of charitable activity for many centuries. No one who studies it could pretend that such activity arose dominantly from a concern for social justice. If nothing else, the criticisms that such a concern prompted steered donors in other directions.

The history of philanthropy from the late 18th century is intimately bound up with the history of capitalism. The key factor in its development lay in its relationship to political economy. Prevented from doing anything that might interfere with the free workings of a market economy, philanthropists sought different and safer spheres of action – keeping clear of poor relief. This is not to say that they did not strive to do good; rather that social justice rarely featured high on their agenda. Philanthropy was also linked to capitalism in a different sense. By the late 19th century it had become associated with the giving of large sums of money. Up to then, anyone who demonstrated a love of humankind might be considered a philanthropist, and there were mutual aid societies which had philanthropy in their titles. But capitalism changed all that, making possible the emergence of a plutocracy. The early-20th-century American foundations, like the early-21st-century 'New Philanthropy', could not have come into being had there not been vast fortunes coming into the hands of a few individuals. It is possible to argue that the welfare states of Europe in the second half of the 20th century were the price capitalism paid for political survival, after the world depression of the 1930s. Philanthropy, some argue, is the price that now needs to be paid to justify neoliberalism. The "New Philanthropists", Charles Handy has argued, have provided 'a social justification for the free enterprise system' (Handy, 2007, p10). And Bishop and Green have warned: 'with populist anti-rich policies on the rise it is in the enlightened self-interest of the wealthy to be philanthropic' (2008, p11). They argue for a social contract between the rich and everyone else. If the rich paid taxes, earned money honestly and gave generously and effectively about one-third of their fortunes, everyone else would stop sniping at them (Bishop & Green, 2008, p11, p261). History suggests that won't happen. Philanthropy has always been criticised and the criticisms have and will continue to shape the directions it takes.

References

Andrew, D T, 1992, On reading charity sermons: eighteenth-century Anglican solicitation and exhortation, *Journal of Ecclesiastical History*, 43, 581-91

Bagehot, W, 1974, *Collected works*, vol 7, London: The Economist

Bishop, M and Green, M, 2008, *Philanthrocapitalism: How the rich can save the world and why we should let them*, London: A and C Black

Coats, A W (ed) 1973, *Poverty in the Victorian age volume III: charity 1815-1870*, Farnborough: Gregg International Publishers

Conybeare, W, 1908, *Charity of poor to poor: Facts collected in South London at the suggestion of the Bishop of Southwark*, London: SPCK

Cunningham, H, 1991, *The children of the poor: representations of childhood since the seventeenth century*, Oxford: Blackwell

Davis, J A, 2005, Health care and poor relief in southern Europe in the 18th and 19th centuries', in Grell, O P, Cunningham, A and Roeck, B (eds) 2005, *Health care and poor relief in 18th and 19th Southern Europe*, Aldershot: Ashgate, pp10-33

Duprat, C, 1993, *Le temps des philanthropes*, Paris: Éditions du C. T. H. S.

Dyer, G, 1795, *A dissertation on the theory and practice of benevolence*, London: Kearsley

Finlayson, G, 1994, *Citizen, state and social welfare in Britain 1830-1990*, Oxford: Clarendon Press

Foucault, M, 2006, *History of madness*, Abingdon: Routledge

Grell, O P, 1997, The protestant imperative of Christian care and neighbourly love, in Grell, O P and Cunningham, A (eds) 1997, *Health care and poor relief in Protestant Europe 1500-1700*, London: Routledge, pp43-65

Handy, C, 2007, *The new philanthropists: the new generosity*, London: William Heinemann

Harrison, B, 1982, *Peaceable kingdom: stability and change in modern Britain*, Oxford: Clarendon Press

Hume, D, 1975, *Enquiries concerning human understanding and concerning the principles of morals*, Oxford: Clarendon Press

Jones, C, 1982, *Charity and bienfaisance: The treatment of the poor in the Montpellier region 1740-1815*, Cambridge: Cambridge University Press

Kidd, A J, 1996, Philanthropy and the 'social history paradigm', *Social History*, 21, 2, pp180-92

Lambert, B, 1869, *East End pauperism*, London: James Parker and Co

Lindemann, M, 2002, Urban charity and the relief of the sick poor in Northern Germany, 1750-1850', in Grell, O P, Cunningham, A and Jütte, R (eds) 2002, *Health care and poor relief in 18th and 19th century Northern Europe*, Aldershot: Ashgate, pp136-54

Manton, J, 1976, *Mary Carpenter and the children of the streets*, London: Heinemann

Prochaska, F K, 1990, Philanthropy, in Thompson, F M L (ed) *The Cambridge social history of Britain 1750-1950,* vol 3, pp357-93

Prochaska, F K, 2006, *Christianity and social service in modern Britain: The disinherited spirit,* Oxford: Oxford University Press

Roberts, M J D, 1991, Reshaping the gift relationship: the London Mendicity Society and the suppression of begging in England 1818-1869, *International Review of Social History*, 36, 2, pp201-31

Rothman, D J, 1971, *The discovery of the asylum: social order and disorder in the new republic*, Boston: Little, Brown and Company

Sealander, J, 2003, 'Curing evils at their source: the arrival of scientific giving', in Friedman, L J and McGarvie, M D (eds) 2003, *Charity, philanthropy and civility in American history*, Cambridge: Cambridge University Press, pp217-39

Simey, M, 1992, *Charity rediscovered: a study of philanthropic effort in nineteenth-century Liverpool*, Liverpool: Liverpool University Press

Turley, D, 1998, The Anglo-American Unitarian connection and urban poverty, in Cunningham, H and Innes, J (eds) 1998, *Charity, philanthropy and reform from the 1690s to 1850*, Basingstoke: Macmillan

Twells, A, 2008, *The civilising mission and the English middle class 1792-1850: the 'heathen' at home and overseas*, Basingstoke: Palgrave Macmillan

Van Leeuwen, M H D, 1994, Logic of charity: poor relief in pre-industrial Europe, *Journal of Interdisciplinary History*, 24, 4, pp589-613

Vernon, A, 1958, *A Quaker business man: The Life of Joseph Rowntree 1836-1925*, London: George Allen and Unwin

Wagner, G, 1979, *Barnardo*, London: Eyre and Spottiswoode

Waters, C, 1990, *British socialists and the politics of popular culture, 1884-1914*, Manchester: Manchester University Press

Williams, C D, 1996, 'The Luxury of Doing Good': benevolence, sensibility and the Royal Humane Society', in Porter, R and Roberts, M M (eds) 1996, *Pleasure in the eighteenth century*, Basingstoke: Macmillan, pp77-107

TWO

From love to money: can philanthropy ever foster social transformation?

Michael Edwards

Introduction

The central argument of this chapter is that philanthropy is losing whatever transformative potential it possessed as it moves further away from its original meaning as 'love of humankind', along the historical trajectory sketched out by Hugh Cunningham in Chapter 1. In its place, the 'new philanthropy' is defined in terms of money that is concentrated among elites and handed down through increasingly control-oriented practices from 'donors' to 'recipients'. When this happens, at least in the highly unequal societies that characterise contemporary capitalism, philanthropy becomes a divisive force by separating those who need it but don't have it from those who have it but don't need it and so decide to give some of it away – but only on their own terms. These trends raise a wide array of questions about transparency, accountability and impact in philanthropy and the changing balance between public and private action for the common good.

   Three questions are considered in the argument that follows. First, what is happening in the world of philanthropy and why? The answers to that question are located in the rise of what has been called the 'Silicon Valley Consensus' – related to the use of technology and markets for solving social problems – which provides the context for the arrival of 'new philanthropy'. Second, why does this matter? What are the strengths and weaknesses of the 'new philanthropists', especially in terms of the 'distributional effects' of their giving (that is, who wins and who loses in the short and longer terms?), and their impact on democracy – with regard to issues of public participation in, and public accountability for, social policy choices? And third, what can be done to address these effects through regulation, institutional reform, or influencing the new philanthropists; and/or by building up alternative forms of philanthropy that are more satisfactory – if the goal is to transform society rather than to reform or ameliorate the costs of capitalism in its present form? By way of conclusion, I call for questions of giving and sharing to be reunited with their moral, political and spiritual underpinnings – which are rooted in the search for a world defined by love and social justice, rather than by money and the power it represents.

A changing context: the marketisation of philanthropy

Let me begin with some quotations that help to sum up what is going on (Edwards, 2010). Julie Meyer, Chief Executive of Ariadne Capital Investment in the United Kingdom, says:

> The sphere of social action has radically changed due to the emergence of mega-social entrepreneurship, new technologies and business-minded foundations ... in fact the business of doing good should be just that – a business ... it should not be left to government, volunteers and non-profits.

"The profit motive", says Larry Ellison, the founder of software giant Oracle "could be the best tool we've ever found for solving the world's problems". Implying that other approaches are outdated or ineffective, two other enthusiasts assert:

> In the past philanthropy was rarely about impact. But now for the first time, donors have sought to make a difference. [T]hey are ready to make use of the sophisticated management instruments they have developed in their business life to achieve greater performance in this new arena. [T]hey give purposefully, think strategically, and rely on measurements and regular monitoring. (Bronfman and Solomon, 2009, p15)

This approach is quite explicit about the use of market mechanisms, technology and 'big data' to guide decisions, like rates-of-return on investment, enforced competition to weed out the weak, close supervision over the organisations you support, and standardised outputs as indicators of success – an entrepreneurial results-oriented framework that emphasises leverage, personal engagement and impatience (Edwards, 2010).

The superiority of this framework is advocated, consolidated and legitimised through an endless stream of books, reports and articles that describe new philanthropy as smarter and more strategic in delivering value-for-money for donors, and, by implication, for society at large (Brest and Harvey, 2008; Pallotta, 2010; Morino, 2011; Tierney and Fleishman, 2011). A powerful 'echo chamber' has been created to promote this message by a small but well-connected network of philanthropists, writers, business leaders, journals and consultants who all think the same way. These approaches are relentlessly donor-centric, emphasising the assets and ideas that funders bring to the table, instead of building the agency of those who are doing the work on the ground. As a result, it is increasingly common for foundations in the US to close their doors to unsolicited applications and simply select the groups they want to implement the programmes the foundation has designed.

These ideas are actually less innovative than they often claim to be, since the booms and busts of technology-driven growth have always thrown up vast fortunes for a small number of individuals at certain points in time – some of which has been reinvested in good causes for a mix of altruistic reasons and self-interest, in ways that were heavily conditioned by their business interests and experience and their desire for results through so-called scientific approaches to social change (Zunz, 2012). In that sense there has never been philanthropy that was not new. Hence, spikes in giving have always accompanied inflection points in the trajectory of capitalism, including financial recessions and the rapid growth of inequality – which threaten the stability of the system. Philanthropy is part of the historical response to these trends, acting as a safety valve or a barrier against more fundamental change or an essential element in recovery and reconstruction, depending on the viewpoint of the commentator (Callahan, 2010; Freeland, 2012; Dalzell, 2013).

Perhaps what is different this time around is that there is more confidence in the transformative potential of markets and technology to address the problems of capitalism by themselves, a view that has been termed the Silicon Valley Consensus. Rather than relying on external pressure and regulation to tame, pressurise and reform capitalism through government and civil society – as has been practiced in the past – the current zeitgeist emphasises the power of factors that are internal to the market. It is this consensus that underpins the rise of market- and technology-based approaches to philanthropy as a natural component of a much wider and more deliberate trend to introduce the logic of capitalism into increasing areas of our lives at the 'softer end' of the neoliberal revolution initiated in the UK and the US in the

1980s. In this context, why *not* advocate for the market as the preferred mechanism for allocating resources to social goods like health care, education and poverty-reduction – with philanthropy in lockstep with these arrangements?

In Silicon Valley culture everything is solvable, so all problems can be fixed through markets, technology and the drive of the entrepreneur – without recourse to the messy realities of collective action, democracy and struggle and avoiding the unforeseen effects of any human intervention. 'Sunny, smooth and clean, with Silicon Valley at the helm, our life will become one long California highway', was the way Evgeny Morozov put it in an article in the *New York Times* (Morozov, 2013). In place of the essential friction that human agency and difference impose on decision making, the Silicon Valley Consensus offers us a frictionless engagement with the challenges of social change. And who could resist a seductive vision of gain with no pain, progress without politics, and philanthropy that is rendered as elegant as an algorithm or the latest piece of software code?

Against the background of these much bigger forces, one might say that it was only a matter of time before philanthropy also fell in love with technocracy and the market. And while the importance of the new philanthropy should not be overestimated in quantitative terms (it is still a small proportion of the resources available for social change), there is no doubt that big ideas plus big money can generate a powerful wave in society. So let me move to question number two and examine the impact of this wave on questions of democracy and distribution.

Distributional effects of the new philanthropy

Clearly, there are situations where markets and technology can really help, and in those areas the distinctive features of the new philanthropy could be of real assistance – for example, in getting new vaccines to those who need them more cost-effectively, or more efficient cooking stoves to communities in Africa, or raising commercial revenue streams for NGOs if that is something they want to do. I see no problem in using some of the tools of business where they make sense but, as a general philosophy, using business thinking to attack deep-rooted problems of inequality or discrimination is akin to using a typewriter to plough a field or a tractor to write a book. It is simply the wrong choice of instrument for the task in hand; the characteristics of some problems make markets inappropriate, ineffective or inadequate for generating solutions.

The function of markets is to facilitate exchange, not to negotiate solutions democratically. Markets work according to supply and demand, not solidarity or fairness or the satisfaction of human rights. They utilise competition, not the cooperation and collaboration that build successful social movements and strong alliances for change. They measure success against a clear bottom line, which is easy to evaluate but absent from pretty much every situation in which non-profits work. And to succeed in the marketplace you need to exert a high degree of control over supply chains and other variables, which is the opposite of empowering others for independent action. Importing markets into the very domain in which people seek to challenge their distributional failures is deeply ill conceived.

So when the logic of the market is applied to social questions, problems of distribution soon arise – as when philanthropy migrates to some groups or strategies or causes at the expense of others that may actually be more valuable. That can happen through mission drift, when NGOs gravitate to areas with more revenue-generating potential and away from activities, like advocacy and community organising, which though crucial to long-term social impact are more expensive and controversial to undertake. Or by diverting support away from organisations that aim to change society in fundamental ways to those that are satisfied with reforms and improvements around the edges. Examples include the promotion of social enterprise and microfinance; high-technology agriculture – as carried out by the Alliance for a New Green Revolution in Africa, which is enthusiastically supported by the Gates and Rockefeller Foundations; and the focus on the delivery of retroviral drugs for HIV instead of building up health systems that can meet the broader needs of the population over time.

Such diversion effects are already occurring in the United States, where only 12% of philanthropy goes to causes defined in terms of social justice (Edwards, 2010). Any group that speaks the language of social innovation or impact investing will have ready access to multiple lines of funding – despite the novelty of these ideas and the absence of hard evidence that they produce significant systems change. In the meantime, those who want to organise communities or deepen democracy face severe restrictions, despite the proven historical importance of their work. And while there are no data that can prove or disprove these assertions (since no-one is collecting them in this form), there is plenty of anecdotal evidence to suggest that funders increasingly favour the larger and more established advocacy and service-providing groups. In 2009, for example, environmental NGOs with budgets of US$5 million or more received over half of all foundation grants in the US, despite the fact that they represented only 2% of non-profits working on environmental issues (Hansen, 2011).

At a deeper level the new philanthropy could influence social norms in directions that may be harmful to long-term social change, by reorienting attention to the possibilities of individual achievement instead of collective action, or by eroding trust, cooperation, self-sacrifice and solidarity as groups are forced to compete with each other for resources in order to capture easily-measurable financial returns and results. By ignoring social movements, politics and government – which seem to be too messy or conflicted for most new philanthropists to fund – some of the most important capacities for long-term social change may be denuded over time, since redistributive governments and independent civil societies have been the prime movers in securing rights and equality in both industrialised and developing countries over the last hundred years. Indeed, government and civil society form the very ground from which citizens can challenge and reconstruct all human institutions, and when that ground is eroded we risk losing the ability to create a different vision of the future as communities of equal persons, and not as recipients, contractors, clients or consumers. That is why this debate is so important, beyond the details of who gives what to whom, and it provides the link to the second set of effects we must consider around the impact of the new philanthropy on democracy and decision making.

Characteristically, social questions have no easy or undisputed answers because different people have different views about the priority of combating climate change when compared with job creation, for example, or the efficacy of private versus public solutions to these problems. Philanthropy and democracy have always been uneasy bedfellows, because philanthropy – at least in its concentrated form – gives some people more influence than others in answering these questions. When the new philanthropists say that problems can be fixed, they must select which problem they want to work on and how it should be solved. 'It's my money and I'll do what I want with it' is so often the refrain. Except life is never so simple, especially when the tax advantages of philanthropy impose an obligation on the giver to satisfy a public benefit requirement and to be accountable for doing so in some way, shape or form. As philanthropy becomes more important and more directive in key areas of public policy, these accountability questions are going to grow – yet we have no answers to them at present.

Hence, while it is worthy that Bill Gates and other billionaire philanthropists want to strengthen health and education, that does not give them the right to decide which drugs should be subsidised in developing countries or how schools should be reformed in the US – yet that is exactly what is happening. A network of business–oriented philanthropists is engaged in a systematic effort to reform public schools along free market lines by introducing vouchers, charters, and corporate salaries, weakening the power of the teachers' unions, and relying on standardised test scores to close schools and fire teachers who don't measure up (Ravitch, 2010).

Goodness knows schools in America need improving, but when one digs a little more deeply one finds that for-profit charter schools do not perform any better than not-for-profit public schools; that standardised tests are an unreliable measure of educational achievement; that even great teachers struggle in schools that have lots of pupils from poor socioeconomic backgrounds; and that rising inequalities in salaries contribute to low morale. It turns out that Bill Gates is just as fallible as the rest of us. His resources could have a bigger impact or they could simply finance mistakes on a much larger scale – similar to the mistakes that the Gates Foundation made in previous experiments with small schools, which were supposed to be a 'magic bullet' for public education ten years ago but also had a disappointing record.

More insidiously, the new philanthropists are beginning to merge their grant-making strategies with advocacy and lobbying and even the promotion of candidates for political office – creating a much bigger threat to democracy by entrenching permanent elite control over important areas of public policy. Take the US$4 million that Bill Gates gave through an NGO called Learn New York to Michael Bloomberg's campaign to abolish term limits for mayors in New York City. Unsurprisingly, once re-elected Bloomberg reinforced official support for the school reforms that Gates continues to fund (Edwards, 2010). Or take Mark Zuckerberg of Facebook fame, who donated US$100 million to the same kind of school reforms in Newark, New Jersey and who later hosted a major fundraising event for State Governor Chris Christie. Part of Christie's election platform was the continuation of these reforms (Cohen, 2013). Even more blatant is the case of the Broad Foundation, which inserted a clause in the contract governing its donations to school reform in New Jersey that specified that Governor Christie must continue in office in order to secure ongoing support, and that the state must recruit a schools' superintendent who is pre-approved by the Foundation (Cohen, 2012).

The key point here has less to do with the details of school reform and more to do with the general question of what happens when definitions of the public good are appropriated by private interests under the seductive cloak of philanthropy, in a much more aggressive way than has been experienced with foundations in the past. If this is happening to public education today, then why not health care and social security tomorrow? So what can be done?

An agenda for action

Money lies at the heart of inequality in market-based societies because it is used as an instrument to concentrate wealth, centralise power and subvert democratic choices, as well as to fight against these things by funding work for social change. That is why the debate over the future of philanthropy is so important. Who owns and controls philanthropy, and how other forms of influence become attached to it, are questions that lie at the heart of any transformational agenda. Recognising and acting on this fact is vital, rather than pretending that money is somehow neutral or separated from the broader processes in which it is accumulated, expended and exchanged. And that means that questions of money must be integrated into the search for social transformation so that modes of funding can challenge pre-existing inequalities instead of reproducing them, as the new philanthropy tends to do. What would that mean in practice?

The obvious place to start is by reforming, regulating or otherwise pressurising new philanthropists to become more transparent and accountable for what they do. After all, they are unlikely to go away: efforts like the Giving Pledge sponsored by Bill Gates and Warren Buffet are designed to persuade the wealthy to give more of their money away, and foundations are becoming more popular as a badge of responsible wealth creation. Polls also show high levels of support for technology- and market-based philanthropy among members of the millennial generation, who will be the big givers of the future. In any case, since these approaches work well under certain circumstances, why not encourage the new philanthropists to focus on those areas where markets are useful and leave the rest to others?

Unfortunately, these goals will be very difficult to achieve, partly because the new philanthropists do not agree on a logical division of responsibility (that is part of the power of the Silicon Valley consensus), and partly because they resist any attempt to curb their ability to spend money as they please. School reform in the US is a perfect example – something that should be publicly funded and democratically debated. By contrast, foundations like Gates, Broad, and Walton have no desire to subject their efforts to broader oversight. Even simple measures, like diversifying the membership of foundation boards, have been rejected.

In a recent interview with the *Daily Telegraph*, Bill Gates described his foundation's activities as 'God's work' - which is a convenient distraction from the need to be held *humanly* accountable for its results (Tweedie, 2013). The reality is that the Gates Foundation's work is a very particular expression of the worldview and priorities of the four individuals on its board – three members of the Gates family plus Warren Buffet. The sooner they are subjected to, at least, some minimal rules about transparency and accountability, the better. The Gates Foundation is the largest funder of global public health after the US and UK governments; as such, some regulation would be appropriate.

Appropriate it may be, but it is also unlikely, since philanthropy is as easily removed as given – because it is privately held and controlled. Any attempt to strengthen accountability or alter foundation priorities will be resisted, using the threat to 'take my money elsewhere' if government interferes. And no-one wants to push scarce resources away from urgent public policy problems, especially in a context like the US where the leaders of Silicon Valley, Wall Street and the new philanthropy are part of networks that are deeply intertwined with each other and which include senior politicians – many of them in the administration of President Barack Obama.

Therefore, it is equally important to build up alternatives to the new philanthropy which have a life of their own, and which start from a different set of principles. I favour the analogy of a 'philanthropic ecosystem' instead of the 'funding monoculture' that is perpetuated by the echo chamber that was mentioned earlier. These ecosystems would contain a collection of different revenue-generating options that can be matched to the diversity of needs and conditions that social transformation requires. Those options would include market elements, but they would not be dominated or defined by them, since the definition of smart or strategic philanthropy is surely that financial needs and mechanisms are appropriately matched – not that every approach conforms to a narrow view of what is most effective across very different circumstances.

A philanthropic ecosystem would include a wide range of democratic, commercial (or market-based) and institutional elements, each of which has different characteristics that make them suited to a particular set of tasks. Crucially, *all* these elements would be encouraged, not just the ones favoured by the new philanthropists, including new kinds of foundation and democratic funding models created by individuals or groups to serve their needs and over which they exert a high degree of direct responsibility. These would include, for example, giving circles in which members decide how to allocate their resources collectively;

union and membership dues; workplace giving; house parties; and other forms of grassroots or solidarity fundraising (INCITE, 2007).

More recently, the development of social media has opened up new routes to 'peer-to-peer' funding through websites like Kiva and Global Giving, small-scale, regular online donations to groups like Wikipedia, and 'crowdfunding' techniques – in which members of the public subscribe to causes without going through a conventional intermediary like an NGO. By developing these democratic elements the influence of the new philanthropy would automatically be reduced, or, at least, balanced by alternatives which may be more suited to the support of social movements and community groups.

Going further, as markets and social activism embrace more democratic and distributed forms like commons-based production and networked campaigning, the overlaps between democratic, commercial and institutional funding will grow, and this will generate new, hybrid institutions and financing models in the process. I call these developments 'experiments in transformative financing', meaning ventures that have the *double* impact of boosting radical change in society while also transforming relationships surrounding money in ways which remove the destructive inequalities that separate donors from recipients. Instead of trying to retrofit *just* financial solutions onto an *unjust* economic system, why not start from a different premise that rejects existing patterns of ownership and control, and, by extension, philanthropy?[1]

For example, community banks, credit unions and other collective ownership arrangements show how the economic surplus can be shared and reinvested under democratic control – instead of being appropriated and hoarded by private financial institutions. Community controlled economic development initiatives can channel some of their profits into locally governed agencies and programmes. New forms of money and exchange – like alternative and non-cash currencies, and no-interest financing – are already being used to revitalise communities in, for example, Brazil, where the Green Life Bank accepts wheelbarrows of recyclable garbage in exchange for vouchers that can be spent in local stores.

Stone Circles, a non-profit in North Carolina, offers 'radical hospitality' packages at discounted rates for NGOs at its rural retreat centre, and channels the funds that accrue into its community organising programmes. Make the Road New York, a community organising

---

[1]   For further details of all the examples and experiments cited here, see Edwards, 2013.

group, works with the Brooklyn Co-Operative Credit Union to help its members obtain loans to cover their membership dues if they experience temporary economic hardship. These experiments reverse the philosophy of philanthropy that has grown up in the rich world. Instead of giving something back from the proceeds of inequality, why not give forward to create something new?

Similar experiments are possible among the institutional elements in the ecosystem, so that concentrated funding in foundations or intermediaries can be used to support transformative activities. Take the Freedom of the Press Foundation in the US, which was established to protect whistleblowers whose legal defence is prohibitively expensive – partly in response to the difficulties experienced by Wikileaks when its donations were halted by PayPal and credit card providers. Foundations could pool their money for education in democratically governed Innovation Funds that empower schools to experiment with new ideas, without the strings attached to current top-down foundation-funded programmes. NGOs and foundations could opt for radically different forms of governance and accountability that dissolve the barrier between donors and recipients. There are already examples of foundations – like the Dalit Fund in India – that have been formed by excluded groups instead of by elites acting on their behalf. Joint or downward decision-making structures are evolving to bring the users and providers of resources into more equal and co-creative relationships, like those used by the Edge Fund in the UK and by Red Umbrella in the Netherlands.

Networks like Enough and The Funding Exchange are educating a new generation of philanthropists in the need to confront their own privilege as a gateway to a much more liberating role. And quick-release, no-strings-attached funding – the opposite of the increasingly top-down and tightly-controlled ethos of the new philanthropy – is gaining ground through agencies like the Pollination Project and the Philanthropic Ventures Foundation, whose director, Bill Somerville, is on record for saying that 'we fail to realize that the chief benefits of working in a foundation – money, power and privilege – also work as the three greatest obstacles to doing a good job' (Somerville, 2008, p12).

Conclusion

As these examples show, more effective support to the transformation of society requires substantial change in the funding community itself – in how it sees, raises and uses money to pursue its objectives; in its own financial roles and relationships; and in the ways people see themselves as *participants* in processes that they share in but do not control. This implies some short-term upheavals, but the long-term benefits will be huge in terms of the size and depth of results that could be achieved. Discussions about money are never easy if they are honest, since money causes friction and friction generates discomfort. This discomfort will continue so long as money is embedded in economies and cultures of inequality, paternalism, hierarchy and control. But by acting from a different set of premises it should be possible to break down these destructive limitations and develop much more positive relationships.

Moving from the monoculture of the new philanthropy to a well-articulated ecosystem of funding options is crucial to this task, along with support for new experiments in transformative financing that can dissolve the power imbalances between donors and recipients and reconstitute philanthropy on more democratic foundations. The dominance of money in market-based societies means that philanthropy will likely never return to its purest incarnation as love of humankind, but there is no reason why philanthropy should be defined and controlled by those who accumulate more wealth and influence than others. Can philanthropy be used to transform capitalism rather than the other way around? That is the challenge for the future.

References

Brest, P and Harvey, H, 2008, *Money well spent: a strategic plan for smart philanthropy*, New York: Bloomberg Press

Bronfman, C and Solomon, J, 2009, *The art of giving: where the soul meets a business plan*, San Francisco: Jossey-Bass

Callahan, D, 2010, *Fortunes of change: the rise of the liberal rich and the remaking of America*, Hoboken, NJ: John Wiley

Cohen, R, 2012, Broad Foundation grant terms: Governor Christie must stay in office, *Non-Profit Quarterly*, 14 December, www.nonprofitquarterly.org/policysocial-context/21510-broad-foundation-grant-terms-gov-christie-must-stay-in-office.html

Cohen, R, 2013, Email trail of Zuckerberg's $100 million Newark Schools Donation Revealed, *Non-Profit Quarterly*, 10 January, www.nonprofitquarterly.org/philanthropy/21617-e-mail-trail-of-zuckerbergs-100m-newark-schools-donation-revealed.html

Dalzell, R, 2013, *The good rich and what they cost us*, New Haven: Yale University Press

Edwards, M, 2010, *Small change: why business won't save the world*, San Francisco: Berrett-Koehler

Edwards, M, 2013, *Beauty and the beast: can money ever foster social transformation?*, The Hague: Hivos

Freeland, K, 2012, *Plutocrats: the rise of the new global super-rich and the fall of everyone else*, New York: Penguin

Hansen, S, 2011, *Cultivating the grassroots: a winning approach for environment and climate funders*, Washington DC: National Committee for Responsive Philanthropy

INCITE, 2007, *The revolution will not be funded*, Boston: South End Press

Morino, M, 2011, *Leap of reason: managing to outcomes in an era of scarcity*, Washington DC: Venture Philanthropy Partners

Morozov, E, 2013, The perils of perfection, *New York Times*, 2 March www.nytimes.com/2013/03/03/opinion/sunday/the-perils-of-perfection.html?pagewanted=all&_r=0

Pallotta, D, 2010, *Uncharitable: how constraints on non-profits undermine their potential*, Boston: New England University Press

Ravitch, D, 2010, *The death and life of the great American school system*, New York: Basic Books

Somerville, B, 2008, *Grassroots philanthropy*, Berkeley: Heyday Books

Tierney, T and Fleishman, J, 2011, *Give smart: philanthropy that gets results*, New York: Public Affairs

Tweedie, N, 2013, "I have no use for money. This is God's work", *The Daily Telegraph*, 18 January, www.telegraph.co.uk/technology/bill-gates/9812672/Bill-Gates-interview-I-have-no-use-for-money.-This-is-Gods-work.html

Zunz, O, 2012, *Philanthropy in America*, Princeton: Princeton University Press

THREE

Does economic theory lead to a cynical view of philanthropy?

Samuel Cameron

Introduction

It is particularly vital that non-economists have access to a clear view of economic thinking on the general matter of philanthropy.

A casual thought about traditional mainstream economics might suggest that, as the 'dismal science', it would have little to say about ostensibly non self-directed behaviour. I will explore the extent to which this is true. In the last twenty years or so, there has been an increasing amount of economic work that acknowledges social formations – see Ostrom (2000) – and looks at psychological aspects of individual choice. This widening has become even more extended recently in the form of neuroeconomics and 'nudge economics'

Detailed interest in philanthropy is comparatively recent in economics – mainly in the last thirty years or so. The view most consistent with the traditional core of economic theory is the fundamentally selfish one in which giving to others (in whatever form) is only carried out as a source of instrumental utility to the donor. Cunningham showed in Chapter 1 the animosity of political economists to charity and philanthropy. They believed that the rate of wages should be determined by the market and market only, therefore 'charity's *meddling* interfered with that.'

For the economist, giving becomes a commodity which is traded off against other more conventional commodities. Some economists attempt to give this a more rigorous foundation by rooting the degree of philanthropy in sociobiology. But this is still a fundamentally selfish approach, even though textbook accounts such as Frank (2008, p212) call the person who is donating 'non-egoistic'. Particularly worrying is the tendency that some economists have to bandy about the word 'natural' in an ill-considered way. For example, the short paper by Scharf (2012), an economist who seems strongly supportive of prosocial behaviour, describes the work of Benabou and Tirole (2006) as assuming that individuals are '*naturally* greedy'. Ideas that individuals are naturally weak in prosociality might lead to the proposal that some intervention is needed by government, independent charities and corporations. Thus social justice cannot be attained by individual initiative alone in the framework of a market economy. New philanthropy can be seen as a challenge to the 'natural greediness' thesis as we see incredibly rich people not just giving but driving others to do so. The logical counter to this is that corporate philanthropy is a signifier of self-interest. The (purely economic) empirical literature on this is considered below.

Much of economic writing tends to use the term 'altruism' as the signifier of non-selfish behaviour. This was addressed by Collard (1978). Altruism continues to attract attention in the leading mainstream economic journals, most usually in relation to the analysis of intrafamilial altruism inspired by the air of paradox in Gary Becker's 'rotten kid theorem' (Becker, 1991) and more widely in empirical research on charitable donations. In economic literature, the term philanthropy tends to occur more commonly when looking at corporate behaviour. Altruism means non-selfish behaviour, while philanthropy generally signifies the practice of caring for other people. The definition of altruism is sometimes extended to animals. Caring for animals is treated as just another commodity demand in mainstream economics. Figures offered in Micklewright and Schnepf (2009) indicate that, for many people, animal aid is preferred to human aid. For economists, giving money is usually the focus, although there is some interest in volunteer labour.

My general approach in this chapter is to start at the level of the individual, then move out successively to groups of individuals, and then to consideration of corporations and charitable organisations. Finally, I will provide a critical exposition of relevant economic thinking on justice and relate this to the new philanthropy.

What has economics got to do with it?

Giving will change the distribution of resources and may also have efficiency effects in terms of production. That is, total output may fall or rise when we redistribute income.

The most obvious popular argument, in this context, is that redistributing income away from richer groups will harm lower-income groups as they are thereby deprived of 'trickle down' effects.

Traditional economic theory sees altruistic behaviour as an 'externality effect' where the behaviour, or state, of others has an impact on one's utility (wellbeing). We presume, as is standard, that individuals are 'rational' – in the sense of having consistent, well-defined and exogenous preferences. Suppose a rational individual is upset by seeing starving people on television. They will lose utility from this negative externality. The motivation is not automatically social. It is purely a 'commodity' situation. The state of the person being helped competes alongside X-Boxes, bars of chocolate and freshly-cut flowers for the choice of the individual.

This choice operates at the personal level. However, independent and private rational actions might have public consequences which are suboptimal. The traditional Edgeworth-Bowley box diagram textbook representation of a Pareto optimal social contract (Frank 2008, Chapter 18) is no longer sufficient as markets cannot take care of the interpersonal external effects arising from altruism. This will also be true in a reciprocal setup, in addition to the unilateral case given earlier. A number of economists have proposed a so-called 'public good theory of charity' (Culyer and Posnett, 1985; Cullis and Jones, 1986). This refers to the technical concept of a 'public good' in economic theory, not the specific matter of public provision.

Take the simple case of three identical people on a desert island. Two of them (M and N) have 90% of the resources between them, while the other (P) has the remaining 10%. Let us assume M and N feel sorry for P and that M acts first to give away 10 % of his resources to P. N will benefit from this giving as a 'free rider' and, hence, the amount given will decrease. This can be represented in Cournot-Nash type reaction functions familiar from duopoly models. As is common in duopoly models, without collusion or cooperation, the outcome is expected to be suboptimal for both parties. Thus we can have a prisoners' dilemma situation where two intrinsically selfish people, with some 'commodity' philanthropy, end up giving less than would most benefit them due to the problem of isolated decision making. Some people object to this as unrealistic, and there are further objections that existing empirical evidence contradicts some propositions of such an approach.

The chief opposing position to the public good model has been Kantian reciprocity (Sugden, 1998). A broader treatment of Kantian economics can be found in White (2011). This is part of a wider family of situations that describe how people get utility from giving per se. Such means- as opposed to ends-oriented behaviour still falls within the commodity-based perspective. The Kantian model does not necessarily guarantee that there will be a large volume of spontaneous individual giving. It may even lead to a zero outcome due to the 'after you' problem, where individuals wait for each other to display the behaviour that is to be emulated. These conclusions are somewhat overlooked in the emerging literature on social network (primarily digital) effects, which tends to promote an optimistic view of an incoming golden age of expanding philanthropy.

So there is no guarantee of optimal efficiency with fully rational isolated individuals. What if individuals depart from the basic economic model that assumes total free will? Some economists argue that a more complicated model is needed to deal with certain real world behaviours (Etzioni, 1987). These models variously – described as models of multiple utility, bi-utility or metapreferences – imply that there may be some kind of self-control problem. They also assume utility maximisation, known exogenous prices, and complete knowledge about preferences. The term metapreference means having 'preferences about preferences'. For completeness, we should note that in a metapreferential, lack of self-control model, we could have a reverse situation. Individuals may wish they had *not* given so much away if they feel their generosity of spirit was due to their inability to resist acquired tastes or social pressure. This implies that those who currently find themselves giving more due to bandwagon social network effects may be worse off than they would intend to be due to weakness of will.

Interestingly, there is empirical work suggesting that those trained in the discipline of economics are by far the most reluctant to give to good causes of various types (Frank, 1993). Thompson (1980) provides, perhaps, the cynical argument that is likely to be found morally objectionable to non-economists. Essentially, he puts forward a 'moral hazard' argument that those in need of aid have an incentive to distort the magnitude of their needs in order to get more. Due to imperfect information, this will alter the behaviour of givers.

Thus, we have a *layer* of causes of failure of the voluntary market (or market analogue) mechanism to achieve what is the most desirable outcome for the collective of individuals who so far only 'add up' to a *nominal* society, rather than a genuine community or society.

Before we move on to the issue of whether economic analysis reveals any 'genuine' altruism, we should say that we have, thus far, not considered *why* altruism should exist. Economists are still prone to debates about whether the version of altruism in economic accounts is 'genuine' (Ulibarri, 2000) or just selfishness masquerading as concern. The public good theory of donation is one which seems to involve elements of selfishness, despite the presence of acts to improve the wellbeing of less fortunate others.

Sociobiology/the family

It can be argued from a sociobiological perspective that there is no genuine altruism as all acts of self-sacrifice are selfish or are out-of-date customs which were previously beneficial to the apparent altruists. Sociobiology argues that all actions are determined by one's genes. Therefore, 'so-called' altruism gets weaker as propinquity (the genetic nearness of people to their relatives) decreases. Where propinquity becomes negligible, the seemingly altruistic gesture is actually a selfish act. It is done in the hope of receiving some benefit at a later date. Thus it becomes purely reciprocal and, according to economists, would only occur where it is likely to secure a higher return than the formally enforceable market alternative.

This is the logical place to address the problem of 'naturalism'. Biologists who study social behaviour see lying and cheating as 'natural' as it is manifested from birth. In *The Selfish Gene* (1976), Richard Dawkins outlines the structure of opportunism, which predisposes children to lies and deceit (Dawkins, 1976, pp148-50). This has its origins in the power asymmetry, whereby the child is dependent on adults. Parents are genetically programmed to support the children. They need to know how hungry a child is in order to optimally feed it. Reward signals are issued upon the receipt of the food, such as smiling. The offspring can engage in deception, as they may choose to give false hunger and gratification signals that are out of proportion to their true needs. This tendency will be exaggerated by the presence of rival siblings. Dawkins is at pains to claim that children do not consciously seek to cheat their parents, but that is a mere trifle on the way to his conclusion that:

> we may expect to see cheating and selfishness within families. The phrase "the child should cheat" means that genes which tend to make children cheat have an advantage in the gene pool. If there is a human moral to be drawn it is that we must teach our children altruism, for we cannot expect it to be part of their biological nature. (Dawkins, 1976, p150)

Thus, altruism in the family context is unilateral. There is no 'natural' tendency to be altruistic, other than to dependents. One might even consistently attempt to cheat one's begetters out of resources, in order to bestow them on one's own offspring. Biological altruism cannot explain assistance given to people with little gene affinity. That can only be due to genuine or atavistic self-interested cooperative behaviour.

Fluids, organs and others

The sociobiological model can produce quite precise and well-defined predictions about the likelihood of transfer of, for example, organs and fluids between specific family members. For example, you would risk your life for a family member if their gene affinity was high enough, but would otherwise likely opt to ensure your own safety. However, we observe both market and non-market means of redistributing organs, fluids and so on from the living and the dead where propinquity is low, such as with anonymous sperm and blood donation.

These can be viewed by people like Dawkins, and economists inclined to the sociobiological position, as learned behaviours which are not 'natural'.

As we have seen, the core problem for economists with philanthropy is that it involves sacrifice, in the sense of giving something up. The idea of others benefiting is not intrinsically problematic. Besides sacrificing monetary income or resource transfers such as voluntary labour, we may have a difference in kind, rather than just in degree, so far as the transfer of body materials – such as blood, eggs, sperm, and kidneys – is concerned. First, we must consider transfers while living. There is a fundamental difference between organs and fluids – mainly in terms of the risks and costs to the donor. Fluids such as semen and blood that can be replenished easily are, therefore, relatively low-cost transfers. Provided that there is a reliable extraction service, risks will be small. In the absence of cultural restrictions on such transfers, such low price barriers might suggest that giving of these materials should be widespread.

It would appear that giving organs after death has even lower costs than any of the above, as a dead person does not need their organs. As ever, this might be overridden by cultural constraints such as religious edicts. However, taking the ultra-cynical view, if there is a perfect market for organs then one could enter contingent contracts whilst alive to maximise the discounted value of the dispersal of one's constituent parts. In a world of perfect cloning, similar arrangements could apply to DNA. Literature on these matters is generally traced back to the celebrated work of Titmuss (1970) on blood donation as a 'gift' relationship. The notion of a gift, in its pure form, amounts to giving without expecting something back in return. It would seem that gifts are a phenomenon that is outside, and opposed to, the concept of a market. Notwithstanding that, economist Waldfogel (1993) has written about Christmas presents from a market analysis point of view. This reflects the cynical view expounded above that giving presents is a waste of resources due to transaction costs of not matching preferences as well as giving money does.

Titmuss believed that introducing price incentives to the previously non-priced gifting sector would produce the perverse outcome of reducing supply, as the distaste of payment eliminates more giving than could be compensated for by new organ donors. Law professor Mary Jane Radin (1996, pp96-9) discusses this in terms of the 'domimo theory', whereby the monetary ethos spreads and eventually weakens and kills off the gift motivation. Recently, some economists (Frey and Meier, 2004; Benabou and Tirole, 2006; Della Vigna, List and Malmendier, 2009; John, 2012; Scharf, 2012; Smith et al, 2012) have sought to model the Titmuss proposition, despite decades of lack of interest in this matter.

It is perhaps instructive to consider the central points of the paper by Benabou and Tirole (2006), which is the most formally developed treatment. They adopt a conventional economic setup of an individual maximising utility, subject to constraints. They introduce additional arguments to the utility function above the standard commodities. They then add some new features in terms of social interaction. The new arguments in the utility function revolve around the value of personal identity. Individuals are assumed to make rational choices trading off gains in self image. Giving to charity is perceived as good and not giving to charity as greedy. These are information goods which constitute signals of varying accuracy as we cannot always be sure how 'good' someone's actions are, for example. We may note that the Buffet-Gates pledge bandwagon has been characterised by high signalling density. Participants have not striven to keep their decisions private. The layperson might be inclined to ask 'so what, so long as recipients do actually benefit from an increased level of giving?'. Benabou and Tirole (2006) take us to the exactly opposite proposition. In fact, their abstract conveys a veritable litany of cynical economics woes.

Philanthropic endeavours result in a suboptimal outcome, and even 'perverse' responses of the Titmuss variety. The problem is caused by the signal-noise ratio in the messages generated by philanthropic endeavour. If self-sacrificial acts have no monetary return, then it must be obvious that I am, in some sense, 'good' for donating and, paradoxically, I may be seen as even *more* 'good' if I keep my actions private. *Totally* private donation gives no signals at all to others, while the much lesser sacrifice of participation in a charity run would have high signal content. As the monetary return to self-sacrifice is increased, if there is a market, then the signal becomes more obscured by the possibility of others dismissing the activity as selfish rather than selfless. In such conditions we may, for different reasons, get the Titmuss 'perverse' result, which reflects the notion that expanding incentives for prosociality decreases the supply.

In this framework the new philanthropy has high visibility, as the Gates-Buffet endeavour is far from private. However, it signals non-selfishness in that they are exhorting others like themselves to give following their example. As high levels of wealth in modern economies originate in business activity, it is time we looked at the empirical evidence on this to assess what is known about its determinants. Although it is not the primary focus of authors in this field, it is quite easy to conjure a cynical economics view from the literature.

Corporate philanthropy

If the economic view of philanthropy is indeed cynical, then we would expect this to reach its zenith in the area of corporate giving. All giving would be directed towards the gain of the company through; for example, the acquisition of a good public image in terms of corporate social responsibility, which in turn might increase sales and profits. We may note that American firms tend to brand their philanthropic activities as 'giving something back', implying that it is not a gift but is rather their reciprocation, within an implicit social contract. For example, a company may cause considerable monetary cost through dubious ethical practices in various territories but might seek to deflect attention from this by a high *doing good* profile. Or, it might be a very adroit evader and avoider of taxes, in which case the good deeds help deflect attention away from increased government control.

Corporate social responsibility is a prominent topic in the business and management literature, and has been a growing area of course development in academic institutions. It is rarely subject to formal economic analysis in terms of its policy implications. A corporation or organisation is not a person and therefore has no identity or will to determine its philanthropy. If it engages in *sacrifice* in order to help others, then it would be seen to be reducing the resources of some specific individuals. The obvious case would be shareholders, whose profits might be reduced. Or we have the case where employees are exhorted to do pro bono work. The largest American corporations show a distinct pattern of encouraging their staff to do charitable work in their own time. We should note that one ought not to confuse the high profile of some of the *individual* mega-rich with corporate philanthropy. They may have derived their wealth from running a corporation, and may have imposed their views on it, but once they leave the choice would devolve to the board or replacement dominant figure. In that case, is the behaviour of Buffet and Gates really *individual* philanthropy?

There is an obvious problem with financial markets. If shareholders are only motivated by return (that is, they do not share the corporate desire to do the specific 'good' being done) then the benevolent corporation, other things being equal, should lose out to more profit-oriented entities. In the case of pro bono work, the lower real income of the worker might be seen to be subsidising corporate philanthropy. However, in the spirit of Benabou and Tirole (2006), the worker may be selfishly using their participation to signal certain other attributes that may enhance their career prospects or even their attractiveness as a relationship partner.

Before looking at the specifics of empirical research on corporate philanthropy, I will enter into a brief case study of the McDonald's corporation, which is a highly visible embodiment of global capitalism. Its philanthropic behaviour seems to attract relatively little consideration. According to the figures generally given by *The Chronicle of Philanthropy* (see http://philanthropy.com/section/Facts-Figures/235), McDonald's does not feature in the lists of biggest corporate givers, either in absolute or percentage terms. It ranks highly as a target of those seeking to devalue the shares of non-ethical corporations (see www.karmabanque.com).

In general, large American corporate givers tend to focus on specific targets − particularly those involving children and education − and other areas are chosen very strategically to enhance the company image. Newer digital enterprises, such as Google, display a desire to break away from this traditional approach. Apple is now moving into a very proactive approach to corporate giving. Apparently, Steve Jobs declined to sign up to the Buffet-Gates pledge, and during his tenure he is reported to have said that the products of his firm did far more good to the world than any charity ever would.

In 2009, McDonald's issued its first ever CSR (Corporate Social Responsibility) statement for Malaysia (McDonald's, 2009). Not surprisingly, this gives a favourable impression. The text is extensively interspersed by copious upbeat photographic illustrations. However, many of these illustrations simply signify the compliance of McDonald's with general legal requirements of the kind that would be found in most countries. Or, they are responses to the market. Unsurprisingly, the document tells us that the corporation aims to make the world a 'better place'. It also gives the impression that expanding franchising is an act of generosity, because this will aid the economic development of the country.

McDonald's's overt demonstration of philanthropy is the Ronald McDonald House Charities (which we shall refer to as RMHCs; see www.rmhc.org). This organisation is explicitly conceived as a charity, rather than being a 'foundation' or some other more nebulous body. The RHMCs provide accommodation for children and their families who have had to travel overseas to obtain crucial medical treatment or surgery for the child's condition. In the case of McDonald's this is done by establishing a separate non-profit organisation, for which it funds the administration and management costs of the charity. It does not fund the whole operation, which requires additional specific fundraising activities, although McDonald's does provide some support for the fundraising. It should be noted that many big givers do *not* follow this model, as their transfer operates within the framework of the corporation. These differences will impact on the position a firm maintains in the philanthropy league tables.

The engagement of McDonald's in corporate philanthropy might be seen as low compared to what we might expect. Economic models attempt a greater degree of precision in making such statements. There is a considerable amount of empirical work, of an applied economics nature, on the determinants of the amount of corporate philanthropy. That is, classical statistical techniques (regression) are used to test hypotheses. Early empirical studies emphasised the role of firm size (McElroy and Siegfried, 1985; Useem, 1988; Adams and Hardwick, 1998). We might suppose that large firms are able to give more but this does not necessarily follow, as a large firm could be in a difficult financial position. It can be argued that large firms may contribute regardless of profit levels, hence implying that there is a 'pure' effect of size.

Profits have long been cited as a key independent determinant (Ullmann, 1985; McGuire et al, 1988) of giving. The argument is that profitable firms can afford to give more. Thus they are just like individual philanthropists who have more money than others. Brammer, Millington and Down (2004) claim that the influence of profits weakened during the 1990s, as firms became more sensitive to demands by stakeholders. A number of other studies offer some empirical support for the idea that investors' ethical preferences constrain the implicit selfishness of firms (for example, Graves and

Waddock, 1994; Cox et al, 2004). Wang and Coffey (1992), using a sample of 78 Fortune 500 firms from the year 1984, found positive relationships between charitable contributions and higher insider stock ownership, and more female and minority board members. The finding on female directors is replicated by Williams (2003), using a sample of 185 Fortune 500 firms for the years between 1991 and 1994.

There are many papers exploring the idea that that donation serves as a form of advertising (Fry et al, 1982; Mescon and Tilson, 1987; McWilliams and Siegel, 2000; Seifert et al, 2004; Brammer and Millington, 2005; Amato and Amato, 2007). Chai (2010) examines the relationship between firm ownership structure and corporate charitable donations, using a panel data set of 1,017 listed Korean firms. The volume of donations is related to ownership of the firm (domestic or foreign), the size of the firm and advertising intensity. Larger firms with higher advertising intensity appear to give relatively more, based on standard tests of statistical significance. The author suggests that charitable donations are, therefore, both strategic and discretionary corporate expenditures.

The empirical work on corporate philanthropy offers little explicit theoretical modelling of decision making. In particular we might expect some derivation of a production function for giving, in terms of the firms' objectives. Advertising can be analysed using the developments of the marginal conditions in the Dorfman-Steiner theorem. This model demonstrates how advertising continuously shifts the demand curve faced by the firm, but simultaneously increases the operating costs. The key point with philanthropy as a form of advertising is that it may lack the continuity and scale properties of conventional advertising. For there to be a continuous relationship between the amount of philanthropy and consumer demand, consumers would need to be monitoring donations and responding appropriately. If consumers have homogeneous preference and display a gated type of 'rational ignorance' (see below discussion on charities) there will be no scale effects. Once the individual has decided that the company is 'good' and worth endorsing they will consume its goods up to a certain level, but will not increase this in response to higher levels of philanthropy by the firm.

Philanthropic agencies

As philanthropy can be perpetuated by individuals and firms, one needs to ask why specifically charitable agencies will be formed. In addition, an economist would question why such agencies would be given non-profit status. We should pause to point out that non-profit philanthropic organisations increasingly draw on the services of for-profit provision, specifically in the area of fund-raising.

The objective of a charitable firm is to transfer resources on behalf of individuals. If individuals could do this efficiently there would be no need for the intervention of a charitable firm. Economists have devoted much less attention to the analysis of charitable firms than they have to individual donation behaviour (see Thompson (1980) for a rounded approach). Economic models of charities assume that they try to maximise something. The chosen maximand will be used to gauge the effectiveness of their performance. Tullock (1971) gives three possible maximands:

1. profits
2. size – measured by total funds raised
3. transfer of resources to the objects of the charity

A charity maximising (2) is referred to as a bureaucratic charity. Type (3) is the 'ideal' charity because it comes closest to achieving what we think of as the proper objectives of a charity.

Type (2) may expand to the point where it is enormous, in terms of revenue, but virtually no charitable payments are made. Allegedly this was the case with the Bob Hope golf charity. This happens because the managers are driven to excessive spending on promotional activities.

The problems associated with type (2) charities stem from lack of information and/or monitoring of their activities. The government could take over the role of the charity or could attempt to steer it closer to a desired outcome using punishments and/or incentives. The problem with interventionist policies is that they are not cheap, and the marginal gains of policing the charity could be less than the marginal costs of doing so.

Tullock gives an argument of the type now common in behavioural economics. He said that 'rational ignorance' prevents individual voluntary donors from closely monitoring the net outcome of their donations. Giving is not like normal commodities. The 'warm glow' feeling is ruined if the individual finds out that they have been fooled into giving to something that does not produce any transfer to the deserving. The stakeholders can demonstrate weak motives, regarding the monitoring of charitable companies.

Economics of social justice

We have seen that mainstream economic theory tends to lead to a cynical view of self-sacrificing behaviour. This is overshadowed to some extent by current empirical work on the impact of social networking, which is of an optimistic nature. One can argue that the economics of social decision making needs to incorporate some concept of justice in order to correctly structure responses to undesirable effects of the free-market economy. Such a framework could be used to assess the benefits of new philanthropy. But will this framework itself be a repository of cynicism?

Economists have struggled with finding a concept of justice that fits conveniently into the competitive markets paradigm. This has not stopped them writing about it. Technical and highly formal works in welfare economics tend to avoid the issue by delegating the administration of justice to some other entity. The theoretical mechanism of a social welfare function tends to be the primary focus of comments about justice. We are here talking solely about distributive justice rather than commutative justice. The simplest approach to social welfare functions is broadly utilitarian. That is, some method is found of adding up individual welfare to arrive at total social welfare. This approach is compatible with outcomes where there is large amounts of philanthropy or none at all. It is essentially an extension of the ideas discussed in the earlier part of this chapter.

Anything approaching a conventional idea of justice can only be found by adding restrictions to the allowable distributions of wellbeing that arise. The standard economic approach is to invoke the idea of Pareto optimality. This states that society cannot be better off if one person is made worse off by a change even though others are made better off. This is not very helpful in terms of social justice as it allows many outcomes that we would consider substantially unjust. Pareto optimality is compatible with new philanthropy as the philanthropists are assumed to be better off after their giving, as their recipients will be.

Many mainstream works on welfare economics and public sector economics give an exposition of the writings of John Rawls as an illustration of how justice can be encapsulated in social welfare functions. However they then usually go on to dismiss Rawls's approach as merely a special case of a general expected utility social welfare function (one with infinite risk aversion). The key to the Rawlsian approach is the 'veil of ignorance' whereby we do not know where we will be in the outcome of the social process and thus choose the social ordering with least bad bottom position (maximin).

The main attempt to provide an alternative to Rawls that is satisfactory to economists comes from the French economist Serge Christophe Kolm. He published a key work (in English) on this in 1969, but his work was largely ignored by English speaking economists for quite a long time. The core of his ideas is to be found at book length in a work published in 1971 (but only available in French for a long time (Kolm, 2002)). By now, Kolm's work is regarded as a major attempt to show that economists can say something useful about justice.

In essence, Kolm's work represents the attempt to chart the middle path between the two extremes of Pareto optimality (which says nothing about justice) and Rawls, which proposes what Kolm calls 'leximin dictatorship'. That is, the person who will be worse off in a social state holds everyone else to ransom by their poverty.

Progressing past this point would seem to require the ability to make judgments about distributional outcomes which are grounded in some set of principles. The first stumbling block to emerge is the problem of interpersonal utility comparisons. Kolm is bold about this issue. He asserts that it IS possible to compare the welfare of people in different situations but he is unwilling to go as far as full cardinality. Throughout he maintains a general welfarist/utilitarian position (despite some of his philosophical discussions) but with attempts to graft on judgments that cover a wider range of cases than the simple leximin argument of Rawls.

Much of his text covers technical groundwork along with restating matters covered in Arrow and Rawls. The climax of his position is to be found in Part C5 of Section III of Justice and Equality (the book is not laid out in conventional chapters). Here he comes to the following conclusions on the basis of his theoretical work (which is based on assumptions most economists are not likely to find controversial):

(i)   we need to work with a concept of 'Practical Justice' because:
(ii)   there may be no just state of social outcomes which is efficient or there may even be no just state which is possible
(iii) 'Practical Justice' is a powerful and selective criterion. Its name is drawn from Kantian usage. Practical meaning arrived at under constraints of reality. This is akin to the idea of a second-best optimum in welfare economics.

Practical justice is defined as follows. It is not egalitarian per se, as it does not seek any form of equalisation. Our first priority is to take care of the most unfortunate or unhappy. If their state rises sufficiently then we take care of the 'new' most unhappy person or group. This does not provide a decision on the desired outcomes for those higher up the distribution. Deciding on this is a problematic aspect of the approach. There may be more than one outcome that is practically just. Kolm favours the decision over which is best being based on the level of unhappiness of the worst-off group. This is not as rigid as the Rawlsian approach as the veil of ignorance is not being employed. Practical justice is compatible with new philanthropy as it implies a (Kantian) imperative to help the less fortunate. However, it does not necessarily endorse new philanthropy as being superior to alternative possible arrangements. It does not provide any ammunition against those critical of new philanthropy as being a Trojan horse for meddling activity by wealthy individuals seeking to impose their value system and interests on poorer territories.

Conclusion

This contribution has a question as its title. We might, optimistically, aim to have arrived somewhere near a definitive yes or no answer by this point. The balance of evidence seems to incline towards the *yes* solution for a number of reasons. This presumes that by 'cynical' we mean tending to the view that neither good motives nor good outcomes are likely to dominate the field of apparent philanthropic activity. The idea of selfishness would suggest that 'good' motives are weak and that we should progress to the idea that stimuli are needed to overcome this weakness. Worse still, there are economic models that extend Titmuss's observations about blood donation, and which conclude that such incentivisation produces perverse outcomes. In contrast, modern economic writings on justice and fairness are supportive of philanthropic endeavour but they do not necessarily endorse any specific form of it as superior.

References

Adams, M and Hardwick, P, 1998, An analysis of corporate donations: United Kingdom evidence, *Journal of Management Studies*, 35, 5, 641-54

Amato, L and Amato, C, 2007, The effects of firm size and industry on corporate giving, *Journal of Business Ethics*, 72, 3, 229-41

Becker, G S, 1991, *A treatise on the family*, Harvard: Harvard University Press

Benabou, R and Tirole, J, 2006, Incentives and pro-social behaviour, *American Economic Review*, 96, 5, 1652-78

Brammer, S and Millington, A, 2005, Corporate reputation and philanthropy: an empirical analysis, *Journal of Business Ethics*, 61, 1, 29-44

Brammer, S, Millington, A and Down, C, 2004, The development of corporate charitable contributions in the UK: A stakeholder analysis, *Journal of Management Studies*, 41, 8, 1411-34

Chai, D H, 2010, *Firm ownership and philanthropy,* Centre for Business Research working paper 400, Cambridge: University of Cambridge

Collard, D, 1978, *Altruism and economy: a study in non-selfish economics,* Oxford: Martin Robertson

Cox, P, Brammer, S and Millington, A, 2004, An empirical examination of institutional investor preferences for corporate social performance, *Journal of Business Ethics*, 52, 1, 27-43

Cullis, J and Jones, P, 1986, The economics of charity, *The Economic Review*, 4, 2, 12-15

Culyer, A J and Posnett, J, 1985, On caring and charity: why choose the welfare state', *Economic Affairs*, 5, 2, 40-2

Dawkins, R, 1976, *The selfish gene,* London: Oxford University Press

Della Vigna, S, List, J and Malmendier, U, 2009, *Testing for altruism and social pressure in charitable giving,* NBER Working Paper No 15629, New York, NY: NBER

Etzioni, A, 1987, Towards a Kantian socio-economics, *Review of Social Economy,* 45, 1, 37-47

Frank, R H, 2008, *Microeconomics and behaivor,* 7th edn, Singapore: McGraw-Hill

Frank, R H, 1993, Does studying economics inhibit cooperation?, *Journal of Economic Perspectives*, 7, 2, 159-71

Frey, B S and Meier, S, 2004, Social comparison and pro-social behavior: testing conditional cooperation in a field experiment, *American Economic Review*, 94, 5, 1717-22

Fry, L W, Keim, G D and Meiners, R E, 1982, Corporate contributions: altruistic or for-profit?, *Academy of Management Journal*, 25, 1, 94-106

Graves, S B and Waddock, S A, 1994, Institutional owners and corporate social performance, *Academy of Management Journal*, 37, 4, 1034-46

John, P, 2012, Pledges and publicity: an experiment in civic behaviour, *Research in Public Policy*, 14, 4-5

Kolm, S, 2002, *Justice and equity,* trans. H F See, Cambridge, MA: MIT Press

McDonald's Malaysia, 2009, *Corporate social responsibility report for Malaysia*, www.readbag.com/mcdonalds-my-abtus-csr, Accessed 7th February 2015

McElroy, K M and Siegfried, J J, 1985, The effect of firm size on corporate philanthropy, *Quarterly Review of Economics and Business*, 25, 2, 18-26

McGuire, J B, Sundgren, A and Schneeweis, T, 1988, Corporate social responsibility and firm financial performance, *Academy of Management Journal*, 31, 4, 854-72

McWilliams, A and Siegel, D, 2000, Corporate social responsibility and financial performance: correlation or misspecification?, *Strategic Management Journal*, 21, 5, 603-9

Mescon T S and Tilson, D J, 1987, Corporate philanthropy: A strategic approach to the bottom line, *California Management Review*, 29, 2, 49-61

Micklewright, J and Schnepf, S V, 2009, Who gives for overseas development?, *Journal of Social Policy*, 38, 2, 317-41

Ostrom, E, 2000, Collective action and the evolution of social norms, *Journal of Economic Perspectives*, 14, 3, 137-58

Radin, M J, 1996, *Contested commodities: the trouble with trade in sex, children, body parts and other things*, Harvard: Harvard University Press

Scharf, K, 2012, Small world economics in a big society, *Research in Public Policy*, 14, 9-10

Seifert, B, Morris, S A and Bartkus, B R, 2004, Having, giving, and getting: slack resources, corporate philanthropy, and firm financial performance', *Business and Society*, 43, 2, 135-61

Smith, S, Windmejier, F and Wright, E, 2012, *Peer effects in charitable giving: evidence from the (running) field*, CMPO Working Paper no 12/290, Bristol: University of Bristol

Sugden, R, 1998, The metric of opportunity, *Economics and Philosophy*, 14, 2, 307-37

Thompson, E A, 1980, Charity and nonprofit organizations. economics of nonproprietary organisations, *Research in Law and Economics,* Supplement 1, pp125-38

Titmuss, R M, 1970, *The gift relationship: from human blood to social policy*, New York: Random House

Tullock, G, 1971, Information without profit, repr in Lamberton, D (ed) *Economics of Information and Knowledge*, Harmonsworth: Penguin

Ulibarri, C, 2000, Rational philanthropy and cultural capital, *Journal of Cultural Economics*, 24, 2, 135-46

Ullmann, A A, 1985, Data in search of a theory: a critical examination of the relationships among social disclosure, and economic performance of US firms, *Academy of Management Review*, 10, 3, 540-57

Useem, M, 1988, Market and institutional factors in corporate contributions, *California Management Review*, 30, 2, 77-88

Waldfogel, J, 1993, The deadweight loss of Christmas, *American Economics Review,* 83, 5, 1328-36

Wang, J and Coffey, B S, 1992, Board composition and corporate philanthropy, *Journal of Business Ethics,* 11, 10, 771-8

White, M, 2011, *Kantian economic and ethics: autonomy, dignity and character,* Stanford: Stanford University Press

Williams, R J, 2003, Women on corporate boards of directors and their influence on corporate philanthropy, *Journal of Business Ethics*, 42, 1, 1

FOUR

From philanthropy to philanthropists

Tom Parr

Introduction

Philanthropy refers to practices that aim at the mitigation of (the harmful effects of) social, economic, or political injustice. These practices may be directed either 'toward assisting long-term social and economic transformations' or 'be intended to fulfill the short-term immediate needs for the recipients during a crisis generated by natural disasters, political violence, social strife, or pandemics' (Banerjee, 2013, p587).

Philanthropy is typically practiced voluntarily, in the sense that it is neither legally prohibited nor legally required. It is left to us to decide for ourselves whether or not to practice philanthropy. There is, however, emerging agreement (amongst political philosophers, at least) that we *should* be willing to practice philanthropy, at least to some degree. In other words, there is emerging agreement that there is a *duty* to practice philanthropy. Arguments in defence of this conclusion are standardly justified by reference to the demands of social justice and, in particular, the demands of social justice in a world characterised by global injustice.

It is often assumed that our philanthropic duties are best discharged through charitable giving and, in particular, by making *financial* donations to charities that are effective at mitigating (the harmful effects of) injustice.[1] This assumption has prompted theoretical inquiries into the following types of questions: why and how much money should we give? To whom and for which purposes should we give? The

---

[1]   A notable exception to this is that of *organ philanthropy*. The case of Zell Kravinsky, who donated a kidney, in addition to US$45 million, is well reported in the literature on philanthropy. See Peter Singer, 'What should a billionaire give – and what should you?' in Illingworth, Pogge and Wenar (2011)

intimate connection between philanthropy and financial donation is conveniently illustrated by the full title of a recently published book on the subject, *Giving well: the ethics of philanthropy* (Illingworth, Pogge & Wenar, 2011).

This chapter challenges the alleged intimate relationship between philanthropy and charitable giving. In particular, it is shown that we ought to resist characterising our philanthropic duties in terms of duties to engage in charitable giving. To this end, a more radical claim is established – namely, that our philanthropic duties extend to cover our choice of career as well. That is, in addition to being willing to engage in charitable giving, we ought also to be willing to pursue careers that mitigate (the harmful effects of) injustice.

This chapter begins with a brief summary of the literature on the relationship between social justice and philanthropy. Particular attention is given to arguments developed by Peter Singer (1972, 2010) and Thomas Pogge (2008), which have each been especially influential. The subsequent section consists of a defence of the claim that our philanthropic duties include not only a duty to engage in charitable giving, but also a more radical duty to pursue careers that mitigate (the harmful effects of) injustice. The thought, in a nutshell, is that by focusing on charitable giving alone, we risk letting ourselves off the moral hook too easily. Our philanthropic duties, that is, have greater scope than an exclusive focus on charitable giving might suggest. Two objections to this argument are then considered and responded to in the next two sections: the first objection challenges the plausibility of this argument by purporting to establish its *over-demandingness*, and the second objection challenges the plausibility of this argument by claiming that it rests on sociologically naïve assumptions. The respective responses to these two objections clarify further both the content and status of the position defended in this chapter. In the final section, the implications of this argument are illuminated.

Social justice and philanthropy

There are several compelling arguments that demonstrate how social justice imposes on us a duty to mitigate (the harmful effects of) injustice. Many of these arguments proceed from very modest assumptions and, as a result, are attractive to those with very different political outlooks. The ecumenical nature of these arguments is politically convenient in so far as it has facilitated a near consensus on the moral imperative to practice philanthropy, at least to some degree.

Two arguments in particular warrant being singled out for particular attention. These are the arguments developed by Singer and Pogge. Singer begins his argument in defence of a duty to practice philanthropy by asking us to consider the following:

> If I am walking past a shallow pond and see a child drowning in it, I ought to wade in and pull the child out. This will mean getting my clothes muddy, but this is insignificant, while the death of the child would presumably be a very bad thing. (1972, p231)

When analysing this case, it is natural to conclude that to refuse to attempt to rescue the child would be to act *wrongfully*. If correct, this implies the presence of a duty to attempt to rescue the child. This is the case despite the fact any attempt to rescue the child would necessarily involve bearing some costs – namely, getting one's clothes muddy. Notably, Singer asserts that the explanation for our reaction to this case is given by the following moral principle: 'if it is in our power to prevent something bad from happening, without thereby sacrificing anything of comparable moral importance, we ought, morally, to do it' (1972, p231). Let us call this the *principle of rescue*.

The principle of rescue, though apparently quite uncontroversial, has radical implications for how we conceptualise the demands that social justice makes upon us. This is because just as it is wrongful to refuse to attempt to rescue the child in the aforementioned case, so too the principle of rescue dictates that it is wrongful to refuse to attempt to rescue a child in analogous cases in which doing so would not involve bearing significant costs. For example, the principle of rescue asserts that if you had good grounds to believe that you were able to rescue a child by making a £200 donation to the Against Malaria Foundation, then it would be similarly wrongful for you to fail to do so.[2] To refuse to make the donation in this case, that is, would be exactly like refusing to attempt to rescue the drowning child from the pond.

It is sometimes suggested that the principle of rescue mistakenly directs our attention to the *symptoms* rather than the *causes* of injustice. It is concerned with who should bear the costs associated with rescuing drowning children rather than with the separate issue of how we should stop children from falling into ponds. This is problematic, so the argument goes, since the appropriate response to injustice is not

---

[2]   A helpful discussion of the cost-effectiveness of saving lives can be found in Singer (2010, pp86–7).

(only) to mitigate its harmful effects, but (also) to tackle its underlying causes. A consequence of the failure to appreciate this is that there will always remain injustice that needs correcting.

However, even if the empirical component of this objection is sound, it fails to impugn the principle of rescue. This is because the principle of rescue is indeterminate regarding the target of philanthropic action. It is likely that the principle of rescue will *in some cases* require us to make charitable donations to mitigate the harmful effects of injustice, and *in other cases* direct our philanthropic attention to progressive social movements, such as the Occupy movement, say, that tackle the causes of injustice. In any given instance, which of these two acts is required by the principle of rescue will be determined by which act is most efficient at mitigating (the harmful effects of) injustice, which in turn will be determined by the social, economic, and political facts of the situation.

While the principle of rescue has many supporters, it is not unanimously endorsed. In particular, there is a subset of libertarians who challenge the principle of rescue by denying the moral imperative to attempt to rescue the drowning child in Singer's example. They assert that, while it is no doubt praiseworthy to attempt to rescue the child, it would not be *wrongful* to refuse to do so. It is politically important to be able to offer arguments in defence of a duty to practice philanthropy that are capable of being endorsed by these libertarians. This is not because libertarianism offers a plausible alternative to the principle of rescue; rather, it is because many citizens (correctly or not) have libertarian sympathies.

A defence of the duty to practice philanthropy that is consonant with the demands of libertarianism is developed by Pogge. Pogge begins with the claim that there is a negative duty 'to ensure that others are not unduly harmed (or wronged) through one's own conduct' (2008, p136). In cases where a citizen fails to observe this requirement, he continues, she then becomes liable to compensate the victims of the wrongdoing. In simple terms: if Taylor has a negative duty not to harm Lewis, but unduly harms Lewis nonetheless, then Taylor would become liable to compensate Lewis for the harm suffered. An attractive feature of this argument is that, in grounding liability to compensate in *negative* (rather than positive) duties, it utilises a moral framework acceptable even to those libertarians who deny the duty to attempt to rescue a drowning child. That is, even libertarians acknowledge that compensation is justified when one citizen unduly harms another.

With these foundations laid, Pogge then embarks on an examination of the implications of this normative commitment. In particular,

Pogge brings to our attention an important set of facts regarding the global political economy and, more specifically, the extent to which the global political economy unduly harms the global poor. First, there are *globally shared institutions* that affect the circumstances of the global poor 'through investments, loans, trade, bribes, military aid, sex tourism, culture exports, and much else' (Pogge, 2008, p205). Often these institutions are experienced as harmful to some. Second, there is the fact that some states have appropriated an unfair share of the world's resources and, as a result, other states have been denied their fair share of the world's resources (Pogge, 2008, p207). Thirdly, there is a *common violent history*, such that current inequalities are largely the result of 'historical processes in which moral principles and legal rules were massively violated' (Pogge, 2008, p209).

These three facts reveal the extent to which contemporary global poverty is the result of (historical and ongoing) wrongdoing of the kind that renders citizens living in western parts of the world liable to pay compensation. In turn, these considerations sanction duties both to tackle the causes of ongoing global injustice *and* to issue compensation for the harmful effects of the global political economy. Let us call this the *libertarian principle*.

It is worth stressing two features of the libertarian principle. First, as noted earlier, it is more ecumenical than the principle of rescue and, as a result, is capable of securing a higher level of general support. Second, the libertarian principle is in one way more demanding than the principle of rescue. Whereas the principle of rescue renders citizens liable to bear only less than *significant costs, the libertarian principle renders citizens liable to bear costs equal in magnitude to* the level of harm for which they are responsible. It is, of course, possible that the level of harm for which a citizen is responsible will be greater than 'significant'.

Social justice and career choice

Both the principle of rescue and the libertarian principle seek to establish the conclusion that social justice imposes on citizens a duty to practice philanthropy. Typically, this duty is cashed out in terms of a duty to make charitable donations to mitigate (the harmful effects of) injustice. One worry with this, however, is that it seems fetishistic to focus exclusively on charitable donations, especially when there are other means available that are perhaps more expedient at mitigating (the harmful effects of) injustice. If there are more effective tools for mitigating (the harmful effects of) injustice, ought we not to be prepared to make use of them? Let us consider, for example, the practice of using one's career to mitigate (the harmful effects of) injustice. Just as the principle of rescue and the libertarian principle exert demands over citizens' financial decisions, perhaps similarly the principle of rescue and the libertarian principle exert demands over citizens' career choices?

As a mechanism for mitigating (the harmful effects of) injustice, the pursuit of certain types of careers is superior in at least two ways. First, assuming that one is relatively competent, it will be beneficial also to work for the cause to which one is committed in addition merely to contributing financially to that cause. Citizens who make charitable donations *and* work, say, in international development do more to mitigate (the harmful effects of) injustice than those who merely make charitable donations.[3]

Second, the pursuit of certain types of careers is also superior as a response to injustice by virtue of it being a *public* activity. Empirical evidence suggests that many citizens are *conditional contributors*, who are willing to bear burdens only if they have the assurance that others are also willing to bear equivalent burdens (Singer, 2010, pp64–5). Whether this is a morally defensible position is not relevant; what matters is that many citizens act in this way. This presence of conditional contributors is important as it alerts us to the fact that, when examining the expedience of various responses to injustice, it is important to take into account the extent to which those actions are publicly verifiable. This is because public actions are more capable of promoting assurance and, hence, more likely to lead to conditional contributors being willing to contribute.

This point is made most clearly by Andrew Walton (2012), who asks us to consider an example in which both Clive and Deborah are willing to bear certain costs in the pursuit of some valuable end. Whereas Clive has committed to bearing the necessary costs, Deborah is a conditional contributor. Deborah is only willing to bear the necessary costs if she has assurance that Clive is willing to bear his share of the costs also. Clive has the option either of making a financial donation to a just cause or of performing the more publicly verifiable act of mending broken playground rides. Walton notes that there are at least two reasons for thinking that Clive ought to mend broken playground rides, rather than make a financial donation. First, Deborah could believe that 'making a financial contribution does not constitute a genuine

---

[3] Similar affects may also be achieved indirectly: if more citizens were to desire to pursue careers in international development, this may have the effect of lowering pay in international development. This may free up funds that could then be put to better use.

contribution, perhaps because she feels that it is not in keeping with the spirit of the project' (Walton, 2012, p133). If this were the case, Clive's financial donation would predictably lead to Deborah failing to contribute. This fact counts against making a financial donation, especially given the presence of a more publicly verifiable alternative that would avoid this outcome. Second, if 'one's only means of making a financial contribution is very secretive', then that too could predictably lead to Deborah failing to contribute (Walton, 2012, p133). This too counts against making a financial donation and in favour of mending broken playground rides.

These considerations suggest that, in the long run, (the harmful effects of) injustices are more effectively mitigated through the pursuit of public activities, which are capable of guaranteeing higher levels of assurance. This is because, by virtue of exhibiting certain properties – 'to wit, those which are suitably public and which garner wide support from a population' – it 'will be more conducive to prompting others to act in desirable ways' (Walton, 2012, p127). This lesson has implications for the content of our philanthropic duties. In particular, it reveals that we have reasons to prefer discharging our philanthropic duties through publicly verifiable activities, such as one's choice of career, rather than through more secretive means, such as making charitable donations. If correct, this argument generates a prima facie case in defence of the claim that citizens ought to be willing to pursue careers that mitigate (the harmful effects of) injustice.

The demandingness objection

The previous section sought to assemble a case in defence of extending the scope of philanthropic duties beyond merely making charitable donations, and to include a willingness to pursue careers that mitigate (the harmful effects of) injustice. This section is concerned with an objection to this conclusion, which focuses on its alleged over demandingness. Demandingness objections do not refer to a single objection, but rather to an eclectic set of objections. These objections are united by a shared structure: they all attempt to show that the demandingness of the requirements of a position count against the plausibility of that position. Of course, they could count against it in many ways, and each of these ways gives rise to a distinct demandingness objection. It is not possible to consider each version of the demandingness objection. Instead, this section proceeds by offering some quite general remarks that serve as a response to the set of demandingness objections. More precisely, the aim is to show

how the position defended in the previous section is – or, at least, may be amended to become – less demanding than initially appears. Establishing this will alleviate some of the concerns regarding the position's demandingness.

Though the duty to pursue careers that mitigate (the harmful effects of) injustice appears to be a very demanding one, there are at least two responses to this conclusion. The first response invokes the familiar distinction between *wrongdoing* and *blameworthiness*. While the argument of the previous section demonstrates that citizens who fail to pursue careers that mitigate (the harmful effects of) injustice engage in *wrongdoing*, this need not necessarily entail that they are *blameworthy*. The force of this point is captured neatly in a passage by G. A. Cohen:

> It is essential to apply principles of justice to dominant patterns in social behavior – that, as it were, is where the action is – but it doesn't follow that we should have a persecuting attitude to the people who display that behavior. We might have good reason to exonerate the perpetrators of injustice, but we should not deny, or apologize for, the injustice itself. (Cohen, 2000, p143)

Very often, our hostility to highly demanding moral principles reflects unease about the widespread adoption of 'a persecuting attitude'. As Cohen's remarks show, however, this unease does not give us reasons to resist highly demanding moral principles. This is because, in such cases, the affirmation of others' wrongdoing need not commit us to blaming them. We could consistently maintain that, though refusing to be willing to pursue careers that mitigate (the harmful effects of) injustice is wrongful, it need not in general be a blameworthy act.

In addition to this, there is a second, more concessionary response to demandingness objections to the position defended in the previous section. This response derives from the fact that it is in principle consistent with a duty to pursue careers that mitigate (the harmful effects of) injustice that citizens are permitted to pursue a fairly wide range of careers. This is because there is indeterminacy in how we understand the phrase 'careers that mitigate (the harmful effects of) injustice'. The point, in short, is that the demandingness of the duty will be sensitive to how we specify what constitutes a career that mitigates (the harmful effects of) injustice. If it is understood to include only those careers that *maximally* mitigate (the harmful effects of) injustice, then the duty will be highly demanding. However, if the duty is understood to include all those careers that *generally* mitigate (the harmful effects of) injustice, then it will be possible to discharge the duty through the pursuit of many more careers.

In essence, the demandingness objection prompts us to develop a definition of 'careers that mitigate (the harmful effects of) injustice' that avoids two extremes. First, it ought not to be defined so widely that it lacks any political purchase. This would be the case if it were to be defined such that the duty excludes only particularly harmful careers, such as, say, assassin or investment banker. Second, it ought not to be defined so narrowly that it generates overly demanding duties. This would be the case if it were to be defined such that the duty could be satisfied only by pursuing the single career that maximally mitigates (the harmful effects of) injustice. If a given specification is either overly or insufficiently demanding, then the appropriate response is simply to think either more or less expansively about the range of careers that can be said to satisfy the duty in question. Once this feature of this approach is appreciated, demandingness objections to the duty to pursue careers that mitigate (the harmful effects of) injustice would seem to lose their force.

The naïvety objection

Generally speaking, this chapter has cast philanthropy, and the duties deriving from its importance to the realisation of social justice, in a positive light. Philanthropy, let us remember, has been characterised as a tool for mitigating (the harmful effects of) injustice. It may be objected, however, that this chapter's analysis, and the ensuing conclusions, depend upon sociologically naïve assumptions. In particular, it may be objected that the arguments presented pay insufficient attention to the oppressive and unaccountable aspects of philanthropic relationships. Though this objection, which can be called the *naïvety objection*, applies to all approaches that cast philanthropy in a positive light, it is particularly acute for the version advocated in this chapter, which seeks to extend the scope of philanthropic duties to include a willingness to pursue careers that mitigate (the harmful effects of) injustice.

The naïvety objection comes in two forms. The first challenges the attractiveness of philanthropy by pointing out that philanthropists seldom practice philanthropy with the *intention* of mitigating (the harmful effects of) injustice. Rather, motivations for practicing philanthropy are varied (Anheier and Leat, 2013), and not always so morally unobjectionable. The analysis of philanthropy up until this point has been insufficiently sensitive to the fact that *voluntarily giving* one's time or money can re-entrench a sense of dependence and, by implication, reinforce social inequalities (Slim, 2002, esp. 4–5). This oppressive aspect of philanthropy is aggravated when the philanthropic act is motivated not by a concern for social justice, but instead by a concern for, say, power or social status. If correct, these conclusions would put pressure on the idea that philanthropy can serve as an *effective* tool for mitigating (the harmful effects of) injustice.

The second version of the naïvety objection focuses on the undue influence that some philanthropists are able to exert. The worry, here, is that even some well-motivated philanthropic ventures may lack the necessary democratic accountability to render them morally justifiable. As Robin Rogers points out, the claim that philanthropy can effectively mitigate (the harmful effects of) injustice 'is based on a rather flat assumption that what matters are results rather than process. Philanthropy, of course, is not the role of government and cannot be – because it is based on voluntary donation – representative' (Rogers, 2011, p377). This objection does not deny the effectiveness of philanthropy; rather, it challenges its legitimacy.

It is important to note that the two naïvety objections would seem to bite more forcefully against some types of philanthropic practices than others. Even if philanthropy always re-entrenches social inequalities and lacks democratic accountability, it is surely the case that some forms of philanthropy re-entrench social inequalities and lack democratic accountability more than others. It might therefore be thought that the crucial implication of the naïvety objections is not that we should condemn philanthropy as such, but instead that we should condemn only those forms of philanthropy that re-entrench social inequalities and lack democratic accountability to a greater degree.

Though this conclusion is intuitive, it ought to be rejected. This is because the justification that underpins this conclusion is insufficiently attentive to the distinction between *the moral status of an action* on the one hand, and *the moral status of recommending it* on the other. Whereas the two naïvety objections are capable of establishing that the philanthropist's act is wrongful, it need not follow from this that it would similarly be wrongful to recommend that the philanthropist act in this way. As an example of a case in which this result arises, let us consider the following gruesome case presented by Victor Tadros:

> I am standing on the shore of a lake and a boy is drowning out of reach. There is a boat on the shore and only one person can get in the boat. Unfortunately, though, I'm no sailor and if I try to rescue him I will almost certainly fail. You, an experienced sailor, are standing next to me.

> I encourage you to save the boy, but you are unwilling to do so. You are wearing a shiny new suit, and once you get out to the boy your suit will almost certainly get wet. I have a claw hammer and I could give it to you. That would allow you to save the boy without damaging the suit. But unfortunately you would have to jam it into his eye to pull him out. (Tadros, 2011, p161)

Even though it is clearly wrongful for you to save the boy with the claw hammer (rather than pull the boy out of the water in a way that will get your suit wet), I am surely required to recommend your wrongful action by giving you the claw hammer. The point of this example is not to show that the moral status of an action and the moral status of recommending it always diverge; rather, it is that they may diverge when the costs of failing to recommend an act are sufficiently great, as would be the case if the boy were left to drown.

Cases involving philanthropy often share a similar structure to this case. Though many philanthropic practices have properties that render them wrongful, it is not the case that we ought not to recommend them. This is because failing to recommend philanthropy may result in the incurrence of grave costs. This would be so if, for example, rather than being willing to engage in charitable giving and pursue careers that mitigate (the harmful effects of) injustice, philanthropists instead pursued more obviously self-interested goals. Even if certain forms of philanthropy are wrongful, it is surely better that citizens' financial and occupational efforts are invested in them rather than in serving other ends. It is important to issue a clarification in order to avoid a misunderstanding. The position defended in this section does not sanction an uncritical attitude towards philanthropy. That is, it is not the case that whenever philanthropy is wrongful it ought nonetheless to be recommended. The take home message of this section is only that the naïvety objections are insufficient to establish that philanthropy in general ought not to be recommended.

Social policy and the importance of philanthropists

This chapter has defended a duty to pursue careers that mitigate (the harmful effects of) injustice. This conclusion is, no doubt, strongly at odds with current practice and, for this reason, will strike some as unacceptably extreme. This worry is best understood not as one concerning the philosophical validity of this chapter's argument, but, instead, as one concerning the *political significance* of the argument. The worry, in a nutshell, is that the conclusions endorsed in this chapter are too radical to stand any meaningful chance of garnering political support and, for this reason, cannot serve any important political end.

There are at least three responses to this worry, all of which involve further clarification of either the argument developed in this chapter or its implications. The first is suggested by David Estlund's recent work (2011), which seeks to establish that, while 'ought' might imply 'can', it does not imply 'is likely'. Zofia Stemplowska and Adam Swift summarise the thought as follows: 'it would be odd for political philosophers to desist from the business of telling people what they should be doing just because they know they are not going to do it' (Stemplowska and Swift, 2012, p387). Even if citizens are not likely to be willing to pursue careers that mitigate (the harmful effects of) injustice, this should not provide a reason to let them off the moral hook. The veracity of the duty to pursue careers that mitigate (the harmful effects of) injustice must surely be independent of whether or not citizens are willing to discharge it.

The second response denies the empirical premise that citizens are unlikely to exhibit a willingness to pursue careers that mitigate (the harmful effects of) injustice. At first blush, this may seem to be an unpromising strategy to pursue. This is because a society in which citizens pursue careers that mitigate (the harmful effects of) injustice looks to be a very distant one. Within the context of career choice, the practice of acting self-interestedly looks to be strongly entrenched, and is a motive that would seem to be nearly impossible to displace. This dismissal is too quick, however. This is because, as Kwame Anthony Appiah (2010) has shown, there is a tremendous capacity for rapid transformations of moral behaviour. One of Appiah's central insights is that so-called *moral revolutions* can occur in remarkably short periods. Duelling, Chinese feet binding, and Atlantic slavery were all widespread practices that ended very suddenly, often within a generation or so (Appiah, 2010). He also notes that the law tends only to play a somewhat limited role in the development of moral revolutions; duelling, after all, was widely practiced for many years despite it being illegal to do so. This is significant for our purposes as it suggests that we should be much more hesitant to dismiss this chapter's conclusions on the grounds that a society in which citizens pursue careers that mitigate (the harmful effects of) injustice looks to be a very distant one. Instead, this worry simply prompts us to think harder about how we ought to bring such a society about. This leads neatly onto the final response.

The third response is much more concessionary than the previous two. This response develops by making explicit the implications of this chapter's argument for social policy. These are steps that, if taken now, would bring us closer to the goal of having a society in which citizens generally pursue careers that mitigate (the harmful effects of) injustice. In short, the kinds of social policies sanctioned by this chapter's argument are ones that aim at raising public awareness either about the demands that social justice makes upon citizens' career choices or about the extent to which citizens' choice of careers is capable of affecting others.

Conclusion

Though this end may be pursued in many ways, it would seem reasonable to conclude that *civic education* will play an especially important role in this regard. This could be achieved through the inclusion of citizenship classes as part of a national curriculum; the teaching of citizenship through other subjects, such as the study of literature, history, or geography; or through the fostering of a school ethos that aims at ensuring the citizens co-operate with their peers in a way that takes seriously others' interests (Clayton, 2006, pp144–5). The extent to which each of these practices should be pursued is dependent upon many complex empirical facts regarding each practice's effectiveness at ensuring that citizens take seriously the demands that social justice makes upon their choice of career.

The purpose of this chapter has not been to recommend that citizens pursue any particular career. Rather, it has been to advocate a particular model for how citizens should think about their own choice of career – namely, that they should use their career to pursue the mitigation of (the harmful effects of) injustice. The precise content of this demand of social justice is sensitive to empirical data in many ways. After all, it is a largely empirical matter as to which careers best mitigate (the harmful effects of) injustice. That is, it is to be empirically tested whether (the harmful effects of) injustice is best mitigated through the pursuit of a career in medicine or international development, or through the pursuit of a highly-paid career that enables one to make much more generous financial donations. These are the important social scientific questions to which we must now turn.

References

Anheier, H K and Leat, D, 2013, Philanthropic foundations: what rationales?, *Social Research*, 80, 2, pp449–72

Appiah, K A, 2010, *The honor code: how moral revolutions happen*, New York: Norton

Banerjee, L, ,2013, The impact of giving on the recipient: a summary, *Social Research*, 80, 2, pp587–90

Clayton, M, 2006, *Justice and legitimacy in upbringing*, Oxford: Oxford University Press

Cohen, G A, 2000, *If you're an egalitarian, how come you're so rich?*, Cambridge, MA: Harvard University Press

Estlund, D, 2011, Human nature and the limits (if any) of political philosophy', *Philosophy & Public Affairs*, 39, 3, pp207–37

Illingworth, P, Pogge, T and Wenar, L, eds, 2011, *Giving well: the ethics of philanthropy*, Oxford: Oxford University Press

Pogge, T, 2008, *World poverty and human rights*, Cambridge: Polity Press

Rogers, R, 2011, Why philanthro-policymaking matters, *Society*, 48, 5, pp376–81.

Singer, P, 1972, Famine, affluence, and morality', *Philosophy & Public Affairs*, 1, 1, pp229–43

Singer, P, 2010, *The life you can save*, New York: Random House Trade Paperbacks

Slim, H, 2002, Not philanthropy but rights: the proper politicisation of humanitarian philosophy, *International Journal of Human Rights*, 6, 2, pp1–22

Stemplowska, Z and Swift, A, 2012, Ideal and nonideal theory, in D. Estlund, ed, *The Oxford handbook of political philosophy*, Oxford: Oxford University Press, pp373–89

Tadros, V, 2011, *The ends of harm: the moral foundations of criminal Law*, Oxford: Oxford University Press

Walton, A, 2012, Consequentialism, indirect effects and fair trade, *Utilitas*, 24, 1, pp126–38

Part Two
Philanthrocapitalism and the process of commodification

FIVE

Philanthrocapitalism, biodiversity conservation and development

George Holmes

Introduction

The rising interest in new forms of philanthropy, particularly philanthrocapitalism, has led scholars to consider how biodiversity conservation is affected by these new ways of thinking about and doing philanthropy. The incorporation of capitalist discourse, practices, and motives within philanthrocapitalism have been analysed as part of wider moves towards neoliberal forms of conservation in which saving biodiversity is increasingly done using market mechanisms, and justified using market discourses. These analyses consider what philanthrocapitalism means for endangered biodiversity; what species are saved, how, and where; and what it means for social justice and people living near this biodiversity. Yet so far, these questions have not been examined empirically. This chapter examines philanthrocapitalism's role in the rise of privately owned nature reserves in southern Chile. In the last two decades such reserves, some totalling more than 300,000 hectares, have emerged as a major land use in Chilean Patagonia. Drawing on 40 interviews with owners and managers of private nature reserves, as well as other actors, this chapter considers how the discourses and practices of these private reserves reflect philanthrocapitalist ideas. Such an empirical analysis has profound implications for debates on the role of philanthropy and the private sector in biodiversity conservation worldwide.

Discussions of philanthrocapitalism have expanded rapidly in recent years, both within and outside of academia (see Edwards in Chapter 2). This new approach is characterised by a remarkable enthusiasm for integrating capitalism into philanthropy as a part of wider processes of neoliberalism. Various analyses have considered the origins, potential, and limitations of philanthrocapitalism, and its contribution to broader processes of capital accumulation and social change (Schervish,

2003; Bishop and Green, 2008; Edwards, 2008; Lorenzi and Hilton, 2011; Ramdas, 2011; Rogers, 2011; Holmes, 2012). Discussions on philanthrocapitalism have focused on issues such as poverty alleviation, health and education rather than environmental issues. At the same time, analyses of conservation and environmentalism have not adequately explored ideas of philanthropy (Holmes, 2012). The lack of mutual engagement is puzzling as recent years have also seen the rise of neoliberal forms of conservation, which demonstrate remarkable enthusiasm for integrating capitalism into conserving biodiversity. As the practice (rather than the discourse) of philanthrocapitalism, and its interactions with wider trends in capitalism and philanthropy, has yet to be subject to much empirical analysis, this chapter asks how neoliberal forms of philanthropy and neoliberal forms of conservation might interact, and what practices result. It does this by examining the emergence of privately owned nature reserves in southern Chile.

The chapter begins by defining philanthrocapitalism and neoliberal conservation, and identifying areas of synergy. It then explains how neoliberalism has engaged with the environment in Chile, before demonstating how several private nature reserves in Chile demonstrate philanthrocapitalism in practice. It then turns to the wider context of private and public conservation in Chile to demonstrate the potential and limitations of philanthrocapitalist environmentalism.

As philanthrocapitalism is relatively new, the academic literature exploring it is only just emerging. One weakness of this literature is that it has focused on the discourse and theory of philanthrocapitalism, rather than how it works in practice – though this perhaps reflects a principle critique of philanthrocapitalism: that its rise is as much hubris as a new form of philanthropic action (Schervish, 2003; Edwards, 2008; Lorenzi and Hilton, 2011; Ramdas, 2011; Rogers, 2011; Edwards in Chapter 2 of this volume). There is a need to understand how philanthrocapitalist projects work in practice, to understand the trend, its limitations, and consequences (Moody, 2008).

Philanthrocapitalism and its engagements with conservation

The meaning of philanthrocapitalism, and its distinction from other forms of philanthropy, is diffuse, ill defined and contested. Nevertheless, three key features are common across most accounts. First, whilst the great philanthropists of the 20th century made their fortunes through industry (Carnegie and steel, Rockefeller and oil, Ford and motor manufacturing), 21st-century philanthrocapitalism is most associated with donors who made their fortune at a relatively young age through the IT and finance industries. Their young age mean that philanthrocapitalists can guide their giving during their lifetime, rather than leaving a foundation to succeed them (Bishop and Green, 2008). Second, philanthrocapitalism considers that successful capitalists are better at improving the world than government, NGO bureaucrats, or others traditionally engaged in social change because they bring the aptitudes, skills, contacts, drive, and other features which made them successful in business, and apply them to philanthropy (Schervish, 2003; Bishop and Green, 2008; Edwards, 2008). Some enthusiasts refer to philanthropists as hyper-agents: individuals who have the abilities, persona or contacts to leverage large amounts of political or financial support for a cause, 'individuals who can do what it would otherwise take a social movement to do' (Bishop and Green, p48).

Philanthrocapitalists explicitly transfer the approaches, techniques, and strategies from their successful businesses into their philanthropy. These are frequently drawn from IT and finance, as philanthrocapitalists' fortunes often originate from these industries (Moody, 2008). For example, practices of venture capitalism in the IT industry – where an investor provides funding, guidance, and regular quantitatively-defined targets for small start-ups anticipating that a few of these will grow into large business – becomes venture philanthropy, where a donor invests in multiple small causes, providing guidance, targets, and encouragement to grow into larger organisations (Holmes, 2012). Third, philanthrocapitalism explicitly blurs boundaries between philanthropy and capitalism, arguing that integrating markets and profit motives into philanthropy will increase its efficacy and reach (Bishop and Green, 2008; Edwards, 2008; Lorenzi and Hilton, 2011; Holmes, 2012). Markets are expected to bring more dynamism, innovation, efficiency and money into philanthropy. Bishop and Green (2008) argue that for-profit microfinance can access more funding and is more successful than not-for-profit microfinance. Philanthrocapitalism is criticised for being hubristic, overly confident in its own transformative abilities, and focused on short-term quantitative targets and technical fixes rather than long term social transformation (Edwards, 2008, 2011; Bosworth, 2011; Rogers, 2011).

Changes in the engagement between capitalism and conservation in recent decades have been described by scholars as neoliberal conservation. Whilst this is a broad, heterogeneous trend, it is characterised by practices and discourses which place responsibility for governing endangered biodiversity on communities, and especially markets, rather than the state (Sullivan, 2006; Igoe and Brockington,

2007; Castree, 2008; Brockington and Duffy, 2010). Increasingly, the economic value of habitats and species for ecotourism, ecosystem services and other ways of paying to save nature is seen as key to their survival. New structures and regulations are created to support these markets, such as the accountancy rules of markets in ecosystem services like carbon sequestration (Castree, 2008). Capitalism is viewed not as threatening endangered biodiversity, but as essential to saving it, and biodiversity conservation is justified for its contribution to global economic growth (Brockington and Duffy, 2010). Neoliberal discourses dominate major conservation conferences, permeate the work of large conservation NGOs, multilateral organisations and donor agencies, and guide many individual conservation projects (Buscher, 2010; Corson, 2010; MacDonald, 2010; Holmes, 2011). Relevant to philanthrocapitalism, a central part of neoliberal conservation has been closer engagement between conservation organisations and corporations and the transfer of ideas, strategies and individuals from corporations into conservation organisations (MacDonald, 2010; Holmes, 2011).

Neither philanthrocapitalism nor neoliberal conservation represent radically new forms of philanthropy or conservation, but rather an extension and strengthening of long-held engagements with capitalism. Both are enthusiastic about the potential of capitalism to provide solutions, and both deepen and strengthen the involvement of capitalist ideas, discourses, practices and actors into philanthropy and conservation. Both extol their ability to find win–win solutions – to grow the economy whilst doing social good or conserving biodiversity. Examples of philanthrocapitalist conservation explored by Holmes (2012) include Silicon Valley venture philanthropists, who use their experience as venture philanthropists to invest in and grow small conservation projects, and NGOs who take over failing national parks in Africa and make them financially viable through commercial high-end ecotourism projects, using the business expertise. Critiques of philanthrocapitalist conservation are that it, like neoliberal conservation generally, positions capitalism as the solution to biodiversity loss rather than as a significant part of the problem. Second, philanthrocapitalist conservation projects are accused of land grabbing, privatising large amounts of land and resources at the expense of local people (Bedelian, 2012). Third, philanthrocapitalist conservation strategies may only provide partial solutions in certain places with certain forms of biodiversity, with limited wider potential (Holmes, 2012). For example, only certain types of places can support for-profit conservation, such as those with large numbers of species attractive to tourists (lions or elephants, rather than slugs and ferns), or which have tradable and valuable ecosystem services, such as forests storing large amounts of carbon.

Philanthrocapitalist conservation in Chile

There are good reasons for expecting to see considerable amounts of neoliberal conservation in Chile. Since the Pinochet dictatorship (1973–90), and continuing with ostensibly centre-left democratic governments, Chile is widely considered to be one of the countries where the neoliberal project was first tried and where it is most entrenched (Carruthers, 2001; Tecklin et al, 2011). Since the 1970s, state involvement in many areas has been greatly rolled back and reduced, with privatisations and reduced regulation, except where new markets have been facilitated in areas like education and water rights (Budds, 2004). Environmental regulation was first neutered during the Pinochet era, then subsequently redesigned explicitly to support, rather than regulate, market exports in natural resources seen as the key to economic growth (minerals, forestry products and fish) (Tecklin et al, 2011). For example, the Environmental Framework Law of 1994 (the main environmental law from which others derive) was written to ensure Chile complied with the environmental conditions of the North American Free Trade Agreement, to facilitate Chile's entry to the scheme, rather than by any environmental concern (Tecklin et al, 2011). Tecklin et al (2011) describe Chile's environmental legislation as 'market-enabling' rather than 'market-regulating', as its main concern is to support and expand, rather than tame, export markets. Regulatory bodies are weak and subject to agency capture by industry, and the environmental impact assessment system has been designed to fast track, rather than impede or reject, strategic infrastructure investments (Carruthers, 2001; Sepúlveda and Villarroel, 2012). Major dam, forestry or industrial projects have been pushed through by central government, despite social and environmental concerns, although public outcry over recent environmental catastrophes resulting from failures in legislation has led to some reforms (Sepúlveda and Villaroel, 2012). Compounding this, environmental movements have struggled to become effective political actors following the debilitation of civil society during the dictatorship society (Carruthers, 2001). Neoliberalism and the dictatorship have left other legacies that distinguish Chile from other Latin American countries. Chile has strict, clear, and widely respected private property rights, a legalistic culture which respects legal structures, and very little corruption. It could be reasonably concluded that Chile is particularly amenable to philanthrocapitalism and neoliberal conservation. Chile's four decades of neoliberalism, deeply embedded in the economy, political culture, and society, combined with a legalistic culture of strong individual property rights, market-facilitating regulations, and widespread use of market approaches to social goals such as education, provide fertile ground and wider support for such approaches. Additionally, Chile's deregulated, market-facilitating, environmental legislation, in combination with weak civil society, limit the potential for other forms of philanthropy and environmentalism.

The southern third of Chile is an ideal study area. It has historically been economically and politically isolated from the rest of Chile, partly because indigenous opposition and harsh terrain prevented effective state penetration until the late 19th century. It retains far lower population densities, although in recent decades forestry, fishery and hydroelectric power development have advanced southwards. Reflecting this, land prices have rapidly increased in recent years, averaging 20% per year (to be discussed later). It also contains high levels of biodiversity and spectacular landscapes, and occupies a place in the Chilean and global imagination as a harsh wilderness.

A particularly prominent form of conservation in Chile is privately owned protected areas (PPAs). These are nature reserves, national parks, which are governed not by states but by private organisations – such as corporations, NGOs or individuals. Globally, some PPAs are run as for-profit enterprises, such as game farms and safari lodges in southern and eastern Africa, whilst others have no commercial activity (Langholz and Lassoie, 2001). PPAs can form part of neoliberalism, as they provide an alternative to state-led conservation and therefore facilitate reduced state involvement in conservation, and they often have markets embedded throughout their structure and strategy (Holmes, 2012). Importantly, PPAs are not inherently neoliberal forms of conservation, and protected areas under state or community governance can also demonstrate neoliberal characteristics (Igoe and Brockington, 2007; Buscher, 2010). PPAs may be particularly amenable to philanthrocapitalist approaches because they offer opportunities for market-based or profit-orientated activities, and to transfer strategies, skills and attitudes from business into conservation (Holmes, 2012). An example of this is the African Parks Network, an NGO founded by businessmen including Dutch chemicals billionaire Paul Fentener van Vlissingen. African Parks Network take over all responsibility for managing and financing selected state parks in Africa – which are perceived to be failing – and running them as quasi-private protected areas, financed through high-end ecotourism. They are explicit that their approach is superior because it uses the business expertise of its staff and directors – the organisation's tagline reads 'a business approach to conservation' (www.african-parks.org).

The highest profile actor in Chilean PPAs is Douglas Tompkins, a US entrepreneur (founder of mountaineering firm The North Face and fashion chain Esprit) who began purchasing large areas of Patagonia in southern Chile for private conservation in the early 1990s. He has purchased over 6,370km^2 of Chile to be run as PPAs, although he has committed to donating all of this to the Chilean state on condition that they continue to conserve it. Tompkins owns a similar amount of land in southern Argentina. He has been subject to wideranging criticism of land-grabbing, neo-imperialism, having ulterior motives such as hidden goldmines, and undermining Chilean national security with the creation of the Pumalin private park (3,109km^2), which cuts Chile in half, stretching from the Pacific to the Argentine border (Bowermaster, 1995; Nelson and Geisse, 2001). Whilst Tompkins has the highest profile, there are over 300 other PPAs in Chile, equivalent to over 16,040km^2, or 2.12% of Chile's total surface area. They range in size from a few hectares to over 3,000km^2, with owners varying from international and national NGOs, millionaire and billionaire philanthropists, universities, forestry and tourism corporations, co-operatives and middle-class families to smallholder farmers (Maldonado and Faúndez, 2005). Some aim to produce profits; others to break even, whilst others are financed almost entirely by their (wealthy and not-so-wealthy) owners' largesse. This chapter is concerned with the first, and to some extent second, category, particularly ways in which these reflect philanthrocapitalism in practice. Specifically, it explores how Chilean PPAs are enacting philanthrocapitalist ideas, how capitalists, their ideas, practices, motives and strategies are integrated into protected area governance, and the extent to which these areas reflect the idea that conservation is done best through markets and profit. The next sections outline case studies that demonstrate these characteristics.

This study draws on grey literature, public documents, and academic literature on private conservation in Chile. Most data come from 47 semi-structured interviews conducted between September and December 2011. Seven interviewees represented public sector bodies, companies or NGOs with an interest in private conservation. The remaining interviewees were either owners of PPAs or representatives of individual corporations or organisations that owned PPAs (although some owners/representatives were also involved in civil society campaigns). Overall the owners interviewed had a total of 27 private protected areas and the representatives spoke for 20 areas. Areas ranged from a few dozen hectares to over 300,000. I also attended a number of events, such as a workshop on PPAs hosted by the Global Environmental Facility and a campaign launch by conservationists hosted by the Chilean parliament.

Patagonia Sur, the Cliffs Preserve, and for-profit conservation

The company Patagonia Sur (corporate motto: 'for-profit conservationists') is an interesting example of neoliberal conservation in southern Chile. It was founded in 2007 by Warren Adams, an IT entrepreneur who created one of the first social networking websites, later sold to Amazon.com for approximately US$100 million. While on a year-long global holiday, he visited and became enamoured with Chilean Patagonia. He created Patagonia Sur out of a desire to both conserve the region and to exploit the business potential there. The company draws upon the business experience of Adams and cofounders, who include Chilean IT entrepreneurs.

The company combines conservation with profit – as the land and development manager explained 'what we try to do is do conservation, but in a way that generates profit'. The company's strategy is to purchase property for conservation (they currently own six PPAs), to generate three revenue streams (with plans for more streams in future). First, they offer high-end ecotourism to Chilean and international visitors, including a tourist club offering discounted use of properties and exclusive opportunities for a one-off membership fee of US$40,000. Second, the company is creating limited real estate developments on the properties to market as second homes. With this, they are self-imposing strong legal restrictions on any development, modelled on US conservation easements, to give assurances that developments will remain strictly contained. Third, they aim to sell carbon credits based on new forests created by replanting degraded parts of their properties with native trees. These can be purchased through their website, and they have also entered agreements with Colgate University (Adams's alma mater) and Land Rover's Chilean dealerships to offset their carbon emissions. In addition, they are using knowledge of southern Chile's property market gained while building their property portfolio to create a real estate brokerage for others interested in investing in the region, but with loosely defined ethical standards on potential clients they would work with, excluding uses seen as anti-conservation. The multiple complimentary income streams are a deliberate strategy to give the company stability. For example, the tourism business is described by the land and development manager as "candy" to attract investors in the real estate and tourist club parts of the business, adding "you have to make them [potential investors] realise what is a special place and what is the difference between one place and any other place … if they identify with the place like they own it, it is different".

Patagonia Sur very explicitly links its conservation goals with its business goals and profit seeking. Its website asserts that the company 'presents an innovative business model that merges conservation and capitalism seamlessly and symbiotically' (www.patagoniasur.com). In Adams's view, southern Chile provides good investment potential because of increasing land prices – many interviewees commented on rocketing land prices, and while details are uncertain, Patagonia Sur's analysts suggest that they increased by 115% between 2006–11 (Jose Tapia and Muñoz, 2012) – and because of the potential of ecosystem services markets, particularly carbon offsetting (Dumaine, 2011). Adams argues that for-profit conservation has greater potential because it can leverage larger investments than other land conservation models: 'in place of donating a million dollars to a good cause, and the donor receiving a tax deduction, we put the investors money to good use, and in 10 years, give them back two million dollars' (San Cristobal, 2012) and that this has demonstrable effects: 'Our capitalism-conservation is absolutely protecting places that wouldn't be protected otherwise' (Pitts, 2012). Second, Adams argues that conservation needs the innovation and efficiency provided by business techniques. Third, he sees Patagonia Sur as a template for conserving other places which share southern Chile's features: cheap land, stable politics and property rights, and the potential for multiple, complimentary, income streams (Pitts, 2012).

A similar view of conservation and capitalism is reflected in the Cliffs Preserve, which opened in 2007. Like Patagonia Sur, it originated with a holiday taken by the founder to Patagonia, resulting in a desire to conserve whilst creating a business. The founder, Jim Anthony, a successful real estate entrepreneur in the US (who went bankrupt in 2012 during the US real estate market crisis), purchased a 4,000-hectare coastal property in northern Patagonia to operate as a for-profit PPA with high-end ecotourism lodges (approximately US$1,000 per person, per night, with a maximum capacity of 36). Unlike other PPAs with large amounts of native forest, the Cliffs preserve is dominated by plantation forestry and pasture, although with goals to restore native biodiversity. The attraction is the extensive coastline and luxury service. As with Patagonia Sur, the Cliffs represents an attempt to combine business with conservation, and to use profit motives to do good.

These two projects demonstrate the philanthrocapitalist ideas of combining business and philanthropy, and particularly in the case of Patagonia Sur, that for-profit conservation is better than not-for-profit conservation. They express ideals that the expertise, skills and attributes of the conservationists' prior business activities can make conservation more effective.

Karukinka, the Valdivian Coastal Reserve, and Huilo Huilo

This section explores three similar sites where conservation philanthropy is the most recent in a series of forms of capitalist exploitation and where philanthropy, capitalism and conservation are engaging in different ways to the cases discussed above. The first is Karukinka Natural Park (272,000 hectares), located on Isla Grande, Tierra del Fuego. Environmentalists see Karukinka as untouched wilderness, yet it has millennia of indigenous occupation, and has been integrated into global capitalism since sheep farming was established in the 1880s. Its origins lie in the 1994 purchase by Trillium (US timber corporation) of large tracts of sub-Antarctic nothofagus hardwood forest for US$26 million (Klepeis and Laris, 2006)[1]. Although Trillium saw their project as a pioneering example of sustainable logging, committed to maintaining areas unlogged and to selective logging, it was opposed by Chilean and international environmentalists. Some opponents argued against any kind of logging, despite any claims to sustainability made, because it would inevitably damage the fragile forest, and because it would open up the area to extensive exploitation. This was mixed with wider opposition to neoliberalism, to discontent over the relative political neglect of austral regions in Chile and to concerns that locals would see little benefit from logging (Klepeis and Laris, 2006; Saavedra et al, 2011). Due to poor management and the high cost of infrastructure development in such harsh terrain, the project faced financial difficulties and defaulted on loans. In 2002, Trillium's land in Chilean Tierra del Fuego was acquired by their creditors, Goldman Sachs (GS), who saw an opportunity for corporate philanthropy. GS donated the property to New York-based Wildlife Conservation Society (WCS), seeding a trust fund for the property with a US$1.5 million cash donation, supplemented by a US$6.6 million personal donation from GS's chairman. The actions of GS towards Karukinka should be considered alongside their decision to establish a Centre

---

[1]   Trillium also invested in the Argentinean portion of Isla Grande. This discussion only refers to their Chilean operation.

for Environmental Markets in 2005 to work in emerging markets in environmental services. WCS plan to part fund Karukinka though carbon credits, taking advantage of huge carbon stocks locked in the area's peat bogs. The park aims to self-finance through the trust fund and commercial activity. This case shows how conservation in southern Chile can be seen as the latest in a series of engagements between the natural world and global capitalism.

The case of the Valdivian Coastal Reserve is similar. The temperate forests in the Valdivian coastal mountain range have been a target for conservation NGOs, particularly the World Wildlife Fund (WWF), as they contain high levels of biodiversity and endemism yet are being converted into exotic tree plantations to supply the wood pulp industry. Following the bankruptcy of a 65,000-hectare forestry project, of which nearly 10% was eucalyptus plantation, WWF saw an opportunity to create a reserve to protect this. They formed a coalition alongside other international NGOs (The Nature Conservancy (TNC) and Conservation International) to purchase the property and created the Valdivian Coastal Reserve (Fishbein, 2010). The reserve is owned and administered by TNC, as WWF's statutes prevent it from owning land for conservation. The reserve aims to self-finance using a trust fund created by the sale of the property's eucalyptus plantations once these are matured.

A third example is Huilo Huilo Biological Reserve in the Andean foothills of Chile's Lake District, a 65,000-hectare property with a history of forest exploitation and lumbering. The owners, prompted by the economic decline of forestry, began converting the property into a PPA and tourist business in 2000. The first step was to create a development of several hundred properties within the forest to sell as second or retirement homes, followed by the establishment of three small hotels on the property and a small ski area to encourage year-round visits. The reserve maintains old forests while restoring previously logged areas and contains a captive breeding project for an endangered deer species. While the tourism operation makes a profit, it is not yet sufficient to finance the overall reserve. The strategy of creating limited housing developments within a broader conservation area – what Sepulveda (1998) calls 'conservation communities' – is relatively popular in Chile because it allows entrepreneurs to combine conservation, rural recreation and a profitable property investment.

These cases demonstrates two key features of philanthrocapitalist conservation. First, in Karukinka, corporate philanthropy may create business opportunities, as GS may be ideally positioned to take advantage of carbon market opportunities in Karukinka. Second, the three reserves reflect the idea that conservation and philanthropy should self-finance using markets and that they are enhanced by using capitalist ideas and practices.

Land investment, Patagon Lands and land brokerage

In the last seven years, there has been a rapid increase in land purchases by private individuals in southern Chile. Interviewees indicated that this has occurred as wealthy Chileans look to make secure investments in a region where land prices are increasing by approximately 20% per year; some interviewees suggested that Chilean investors have repatriated their capital following the global financial crisis. Data on this trend are slim, but notable purchases have included Tantauco park (114,000 hectares) on the island of Chiloé by credit card and aviation billionaire (and current Chilean president) Sebastian Piñera, and Futangue (12,500 hectares) by real estate magnate and sports minister Gabriel Ruiz-Tagle. Several other Chilean industrialists have purchased properties greater than 10,000 hectares (Burgos, 2009; De la Fuente, 2010). Interviewees commented on the 'fashion' amongst Chile's super-rich to purchase large properties in southern Chile. Whilst Tantauco is controlled by a foundation and Ruiz-Tagle has made numerous public commitments to permanently conserving his land, no other large-scale investors have indicated their intended long-term use for their properties.

Various companies have emerged to take advantage of this demand for land. The principle business of Patagon Land is land brokerage for people seeking to invest in southern Chile. Its founders are well-known Chilean business people and lawyers, and their initial client pool draws on their personal connections. Patagon Land aims to use in-depth knowledge of the region's property to offer investment opportunities to clients. Some directors are interested in conservation and are involved in the conservation easement law (discussed later) and the company encourages clients to incorporate environmental goals into their properties, such as creating PPAs or renewable energy generation. This is challenging because most clients are not motivated by conservation when choosing to invest. As Patagon Land's Conservation Director explained, clients are principally interested in reliable and profitable investments and in purchasing a property for family holidays, with minimal motivation for conservation. They have struggled to convince clients to embrace conservation. One way in which Patagon Land is trying to encourage conservation is by presenting clients with land management plans, outlining ways they could create conservation or alternative energy projects on their land and presenting their services as land managers to enact such a plan. They are also expanding to own properties themselves, creating an investment fund that will buy land in southern Chile, developing tourism, second homes and conservation projects. The fund promises a 12% annual return over a 10-year period. They see the newly-established Chilean carbon exchange as a source of profit through preserving forests or reforesting denuded properties. Various other brokerages sell land as an investment with a view to including conservation – such as Patagonia Sur – although Patagon Land is perhaps the largest and most ambitious. Patagon Land demonstrates philanthrocapitalism in action because it aims to combine business with conservation, to save Patagonia whilst making money, although to date is has been more successful as a business than as a conservation organisation.

Many of Patagon Land's directors, as well as individuals from TNC and Patagonia Sur, were involved in the campaign to create a conservation easement right (*derecho real de conservación*), which became law in 2012. This measure, based on US conservation easements, allows landowners to put voluntary permanent protection on their property, restricting uses for themselves and future owners of the property. The long-term goal is to replicate the US system, which grants owners tax breaks for private land conservation (Tepper and Alonso, 2010). The project was initiated by TNC (which has successfully established many conservation easements in the US) to boost conservation in the Mediterranean ecosystem of central Chile, which has high biodiversity and endemism but suffers substantial habitat loss to agriculture. Conservation there is difficult compared to further south because land is expensive and properties relatively small and fragmented, with significant competition for alternative land uses. At an event to launch the law, which had cross-party backing, supportive parliamentarians emphasised how it made conservation and economic growth compatible by providing new incentives to support activities such as ecotourism. The easement right does not in itself constitute philanthrocapitalist conservation, but it does encourage private sector involvement in conservation, particularly conservation-based businesses.

The case against a philanthrocapitalist turn in Chilean conservation

The cases explored above demonstrate some key characteristics of philanthrocapitalism in private conservation in Chile. First, key philanthropists operating there come from new industries such as IT and finance (for example, Warren Adams and Henry Paulson). Second, some projects represent for-profit conservation, sometimes with accompanying discourses that markets improve conservation. Business practices have infiltrated conservation, although venture philanthropy is not present here as elsewhere in conservation – Moody (2008) argues that venture philanthropy has rarely transferred from discourse into practice. Yet philanthrocapitalist approaches have made relatively little impact on Chilean PPAs. First, many initiatives do not involve philanthrocapitalist approaches, particularly the many small projects created by middle-class families, which almost exclusively aim to combine conservation ethics with creating places for family holidays. Many market-based activities are post-hoc additions to bring financial stability, rather than being integral to the project's design. For example, one owner of a 75-hectare property described how the expense of educating her children led them to create business activities by renting out cabins on the property to tourists:

> In reality you have to look for ways for it to self-sustain, so that the income that comes into this park can be used for its conservation and maintenance … I will feel satisfied and content if it also self finances and gives some benefits, but it is not the goal. (interview, December 2011)

Even large projects, such as Tantauco and Pumalin, make virtually no attempt to use markets to run their conservation work and are financed almost entirely through the largess of their owners. Second, the managers of some initiatives that display philanthrocapitalist features, such as Karukinka Natural Park and the Valdivian Coastal Reserve, did not invoke market mechanisms because they believed them to be more effective but because other options to finance their activity were absent. For example, the then-president of the Wildlife Conservation Society explained how Karukinka's strategy was determined by the conditions of Goldman Sachs's donation, stating: "there was no process of critically evaluating what options were available and deciding that this model was best launched with that programme. That was just the nature of the gift and the opportunity that was available to us" (interview, 13 May, 2011). He has also authored an editorial in the leading conservation journal sceptical of the hubris surrounding payments for ecosystem services schemes (Redford and Adams, 2009).

Third, whilst some organisations supporting private protected areas (such as international NGOs, the Chilean PPAs association and the World Bank's Global Environmental Facility) encourage PPAs to engage market mechanisms and actively promote PPAs' role in increasing Chile's economic growth, this is not from a conviction that such mechanisms make better conservation but from pragmatic desires to give such areas long-term financial stability and to access political debates that are dominated by questions of economic growth. As one well-placed interviewee, involved in lobbying for government support for private protected areas, put it:

> One of the things that has got the attention of the conservation world is that when you speak to politicians, who generally assess things as economists, you have to compete directly with these values. So a forestry company will say: 'listen, I can support GDP with so many millions of dollars, or the local economy with so many millions of dollars', and the conservation: 'I support three little frogs by conserving them'. So sadly you need to enter this logic of saying 'I conserve water worth so many millions of dollars'; 'I conserve rare things which might be worth something at some point, but we don't know their value.' (interview, November 2011)

In other words, they speak policy makers' language in order to gain influence, not because they believe in it. Fourth, some private protected areas' strategies and statements directly contradict philanthrocapitalist ideals. For example, several indigenous communities have created community protected areas, motivated by a desire to maintain cultural and livelihood autonomy rather than profit generation. Other PPAs are owned by universities for research purposes. Douglas Tompkins, by far the biggest player in Chilean private conservation (his foundations own approximately 40% of the area under private protection in Chile), is resolutely against using market principles in his conservation work. Despite his entrepreneurial successes, his projects contain virtually no market mechanisms, nor does he claim that his entrepreneurship makes him a better conservationist. Furthermore, he sees markets as threats, not opportunities, for conservation, and has publicly endorsed steady-state economic theory. Overall, although PPAs may appear well-suited to philanthrocapitalist approaches, very few could be described as philanthrocapitalist, and many directly contradict its key principles.

Philanthrocapitalism, PPAs and social justice

The case of Chilean PPAs has implications for social justice and philanthropy, both in Chile and beyond. First, PPAs reinforce private versus community land rights and the domination of large landowners by offering a private and market-based answer to the loss of a public good (biodiversity), sometimes with access restricted to owners or wealthy clients (such as The Cliffs and Patagonia Sur). This is important in Chile, where land ownership has historically been extremely unequal and where experiments with redistribution resulted in a backlash and the 1973 coup, leading to the imposition of neoliberal ideals, stronger private property rights and a further dismantling of community land ownership. Some large PPAs were agglomerated by purchasing land from multiple smaller landowners, although community protected areas represent a counter-current to this. PPAs in Chile work within the neoliberal system, reinforcing it rather than challenging it. They reinforce the place of markets in providing public goods, a contentious issue in Chile where water supply, education and other public goods are privatised and marketised, resulting in highly politically contentious inequalities of provision and social injustices.

More broadly, the case of Chilean PPAs offers lessons for general critiques of philanthrocapitalism and a reevaluation of its spread. Chile has many features that might make it a prime location for philanthrocapitalist practices: a large, dynamic, wealthy capitalist class and a deeply neoliberal economy and society, although it does have a relatively weak philanthropic culture and the Chilean tax code does not recognise environmental philanthropy as tax deductible, unlike culture or education. Furthermore, while Chile lacks the megafauna central to making African private conservation so profitable, it is still a desirable tourist destination and has considerable potential for carbon trading, making conservation potentially profitable there. Overall, there are sound grounds for considering southern Chile as fertile ground for philanthrocapitalist practices, yet they are relatively rare there and other forms of philanthropy dominate. This supports broader critiques (Moody, 2008; Holmes, 2012; Edwards, Chapter 2 in this volume) that while philanthrocapitalist practices do occur, and while they can be distinguished from other philanthropic practices, it remains largely hyperbolic and rhetoric and is yet to have a widespread impact on philanthropy. It puts arguments promoting and critiquing philanthrocapitalism and its implications for social justice in context, by demonstrating the extent to which philanthrocapitalist projects are being enacted, the form they take, the impacts they have and the limitations of philanthrocapitalism in action.

References

Bedelian, C, 2012, Conservation and ecotourism on privatised land in the Mara, Kenya: the case of conservancy land leases. *International Conference on Global Land Grabbing*, Department of Development Sociology, Ithaca: Cornell University

Bishop, M and Green, M, 2008, *Philanthrocapitalism: how the rich can save the world and why we should let them*, London: Bloomsbury

Bosworth, D, 2011, The cultural contradictions of philanthrocapitalism, *Society*, 48, 5, 382–8.

Bowermaster, J, 1995, Take this park and love it, *New York Times*, 3 September, www.nytimes.com/1995/09/03/magazine/take-this-park-and-love-it.html

Brockington, D and Duffy, R, 2010, Capitalism and conservation: the production and reproduction of biodiversity conservation, *Antipode*, 42, 3, 469–84

Budds, J, 2004, Power, nature and neoliberalism: The political ecology of water in Chile, *Singapore Journal of Tropical Geography*, 25, 3, 322–42

Burgos, S, 2009, Earth protected, *Capital*, 28 April, www.capital.cl/poder/la-tierra-protegida/

Buscher, B, 2010, Anti-politics as political strategy: neoliberalism and transfrontier conservation in southern Africa, *Development and Change*, 41, 1, 29–51

Carruthers, D, 2001, Environmental politics in Chile: legacies of dictatorship and democracy, *Third World Quarterly*, 22, 3, 343–58

Castree, N, 2008, Neoliberalising nature: processes, effects, and evaluations, *Environment and Planning A*, 40, 1, 153–73

Corson, C, 2010, Shifting environmental governance in a neoliberal world: US AID for conservation, *Antipode*, 42, 3, 576–602

De la Fuente, A, 2010, The new map of Conservation, *Que Pasa*, 11 June www.quepasa.cl/articulo/16_3546_9.html

Dumaine, B, 2011, Warren Adams: searching for profits and saving Patagonia, *Fortune*, 21 March, www.management.fortune.cnn.com/2011/03/10/warren-adams-searching-for-profits-and-saving-patagonia/

Edwards, M, 2008, *Just another emperor? The myths and realities of philanthrocapitalism*, New York: DEMOS; London: Young Foundation

Edwards, M, 2011, Impact, accountability, and philanthrocapitalism, *Society*, 4, 5, 389–90

Fishbein, G, 2010, Rafting in Valdivia: the Valdivian Coastal Reserve and beyond, in Levitt, J (ed) *Conservation capital in the Americas: exemplary conservation finance initiatives*, Cambridge: Island Press

Holmes, G, 2011, Conservation's friends in high places: neoliberalism, networks, and the transnational conservation elite, *Global Environmental Politics*, 11, 4, 1–21

Holmes, G, 2012, Biodiversity for billionaires: capitalism, conservation and the role of philanthropy in saving/selling nature, *Development and Change*, 43, 1, 185–203

Igoe, J and Brockington, D, 2007, Neoliberal conservation: a brief introduction, *Conservation and Society*, 5, 4, 432–49

Jose Tapia, M and Muñoz, M, 2012, Lands and Conservation values, *La Tercera*, 31 March, www.diario.latercera.com/2012/03/31/01/contenido/negocios/10-105142-9-tierras-en-aysen-duplican-su-valor-por-conservacionismo-y-proyectos-electricos.shtml

Klepeis, P and Laris, P, 2006, Contesting sustainable development in Tierra del Fuego, *Geoforum*, 37, 4, 505–18

Langholz, J and Lassoie, J, 2001, Perils and promise of privately owned protected areas, *Bioscience*, 51, 12, 1079–85

Lorenzi, P. and Hilton, F, 2011, Optimizing philanthrocapitalism, *Society*, 48, 5, 397–402

MacDonald, K, 2010, The devil is in the (bio)diversity: private sector 'engagement' and the restructuring of biodiversity conservation, *Antipode*, 42, 3, 513–50

Maldonado, V. and Faúndez, R, 2005, Counseling for base mapping data update private protected areas nationwide: final report, Biodiversity Program CODEFF / CONAMA, Santiago: CODEFF

Moody, M, 2008, 'Building a culture': the construction and evolution of venture philanthropy as a new organizational field, *Nonprofit and Voluntary Sector Quarterly*, 37, 2, 324–52

Nelson, M and Geisse, G, 2001, The lessons of the Tompkins case for environmental policy and foreign investment in Chile, *Environment and Development*, www.cipma.cl/web/200.75.6.169/RAD/2001/3_Nelson_Geisse.pd

Pitts, G, 2012, Cutting edge eco-tourism in Chile's last lonely wilderness, *Globe and Mail*, 21 April, www.theglobeandmail.com/life/travel/destinations/cutting-edge-eco-tourism-in-chiles-last-lonely-wilderness/article4101379/?page=all

Ramdas, K, 2011, Philanthrocapitalism: reflections on politics and policy making, *Society*, 48, 5, 393–6

Redford, K H and Adams, W M, 2009, Payment for ecosystem services and the challenge of saving nature, *Conservation Biology*, 23, 4, 785–7

Rogers, R, 2011, Why philanthro-policymaking matters, *Society*, 48, 5, 376–81

Saavedra, B J, Simonetti, J A and Redford, K H, 2011, Private conservation, the example that the Wildlife Conservation Society builds from Tierra del Fuego, in Figueroa, E (ed) *Biodiversity conservation in the Americas: lessons and policy recommendations*, Santiago: Ocho Libros Editores Ltda

San Cristobal, M, 2012, The business of private lands in Chile, *The Ciudano*, 4 March, www.elciudadano.cl/2012/03/04/49132/el-negocio-de-las-tierras-protegidas-en-chile/

Schervish, P, 2003, *Hyperagency and high-tech donors: a new theory of the new philanthropists,* Boston: Boston College

Sepúlveda, C and Villarroel, P, 2012, Swans, conflicts, and resonance: local movements and the reform of Chilean environmental institutions, *Latin American Perspectives*, 39, 4, 181–200

Sullivan, S, 2006, Elephant in the room? Problematising 'new' (neoliberal) biodiversity conservation, *Forum for Development Studies*, 33, 105–35

Tecklin, D, Bauer, C and Prieto, M, 2011, Making environmental law for the market: the emergence, character, and implications of Chile's environmental regime, *Environmental Politics*, 20, 6, 879–98

Tepper, H and Alonso, V, 2010, The private lands conservation initiative in Chile, in Levitt, J. (ed) *Conservation capital in the Americas: exemplary conservation finance initiatives*, Cambridge: Island Press

SIX

Philanthrocapitalism, 'pro-poor' agricultural biotechnology and development

Sally Brooks

Introduction

This chapter traces the evolution of philanthropic involvement in Global South agriculture from the 'scientific philanthropy' of the Rockefeller Foundation during and after the 'Green Revolution' era to the 'capitalist philanthropy' (Morvaridi, 2012a), or 'philanthrocapitalism' (see Edwards in Chapter 2), of the Bill and Melinda Gates Foundation (BMGF). Specifically, it focuses on two research initiatives: the Golden Rice project and drought tolerant (or 'water efficient') maize research. Comparison of the 'logic model' (Frumkin, 2006) informing these ventures highlights both disjunctures and continuities in terms of the theory of change and notions of scale and leverage that have informed their design. First, the belief in the inherent scalability of a solution based on genetics-led crop improvement remains unshaken, despite a professed shift in focus to the needs of smallholder farmers. Second, a theory of change combines the familiar 'technical fix' with a 'market fix' that would integrate smallholder farmers into commercial value chains. Third, this change model relies on a transformed understanding of leverage as 'connecting to' rather than 'correcting for' the market in the provision of public goods.

Most importantly, a focus on institutional challenges and innovations highlights as a key element of continuity the inseparability of questions of philanthropic 'giving' and capitalist accumulation. In each of the initiatives explored in this chapter, novel institutions developed for technology transfer and development assistance have served to prepare the ground for future accumulation in ways that may not be immediately obvious. In this context, these initiatives can be seen as institutional experiments that are already shifting debates about genetically modified ('GM') crops and their regulation, reframing questions of 'access' to technology in terms that valorise corporate 'donors' of proprietary technologies and bolstering the case for industry-friendly technology regulatory frameworks. Meanwhile, an emphasis on silver bullet solutions and institutions that 'connect to the market' is diverting attention away from the multiplicity of alternative approaches that respond to the conditions, needs and practices that constitute smallholder agriculture in diverse locations.

Philanthropy, agriculture, development

The relationship between US-based philanthropic foundations and agriculture in the Global South has a 70-year history. In 1943, the Rockefeller Foundation facilitated a US–Mexico agricultural development cooperation programme, which would later become the template for an international network of international agricultural research centres known today as the CGIAR (Consultative Group on International Agricultural Research[1]) system (Perkins, 1997). However, it was with the creation of crop research centres such as the International Rice Research Institute (IRRI) and International Maize and Wheat Improvement Centre (CIMMYT) in the 1960s that an intervention model – which identified increased production, or yield, as the overriding goal and genetics-led crop improvement as the solution – became firmly established (Anderson et al, 1991).

The mode of overseas development assistance pioneered by the Rockefeller and Ford Foundations during the 'Green Revolution' era continued in the tradition of 'scientific philanthropy', which sets out to address 'causes' rather than symptoms of poverty, as long as these can be addressed by science or education rather than major structural or societal change (Carnegie, 1889). Against the backdrop of the Cold War, for the US Government and its allies the core aim of the Green Revolution was to avert a 'red' revolution in Asia. In this context, the emphasis on a Green Revolution 'signal[ed] like a flag, that social change was not necessary, since the technical means in agriculture (evoked by "green") alone were supposed to solve the problem of hunger' (Spitz, 1987, p56). Thus, framing of the problem to be solved as one of production, not income, deftly steered the debate away from socioeconomic concerns and towards technical ones; while the identification of a solution embedded 'in the seed', with built-in

[1]   This term more accurately refers to the donor group that supports the network of research institutions. However, in everyday parlance 'the CGIAR' and 'the CGIAR system' refers to the network of research centres.

scalability, preempted discussion of issues of distribution and inequality (Anderson et al, 1991; Cullather, 2004).

The socioeconomic and environmental consequences of the Green Revolution have been extensively debated over the years (Griffin, 1979; Pearse, 1980; Glaeser, 1987; Lipton and Longhurst, 1989; David and Otsuka, 1993). Moreover, while primarily a public sector effort, there is no doubt that the widespread adoption, during the Green Revolution, of 'improved' seeds, chemical inputs and farm mechanisation served to open up agriculture in the Global South to capitalist investment (Cullather, 2004; Morvaridi, 2012b). In this context, the role of private philanthropy was understood as an intermediary one, positioned between the 'public' and 'private', acting to 'correct for' the market and ensure the new technologies qualified as 'public goods'.

In contrast, contemporary 'philanthrocapitalists,' such as the Bill and Melinda Gates Foundation (BMGF), see their role as bringing business principles to the development sector, 'extending leverage' through links with the private sector and so achieving 'impact at scale'. Rather than 'correct for' the market, they seek to '*connect to*' the market (Brooks et al, 2009a; Brooks, 2011). This paper illustrates this transition from scientific philanthropy to philanthrocapitalism through two case studies: first, the two-decades-long 'Golden Rice' project, which has bridged the two eras; and second, a more recent programme aiming to develop and commercialise drought tolerant maize varieties in Sub-Saharan Africa, whose design has drawn selectively on these early lessons.

Bridging 'old' and 'new' philanthropy: the case of Golden Rice

In the early 1990s, scientists based at the Swiss Federal Institute of Technology (ETH) secured funding from the International Program on Rice Biotechnology (IPRB), a programme established in the 1980s by the Rockefeller Foundation to support the development of biotechnology capacity and applications oriented to the needs and priorities of countries in the Global South (Evenson et al, 1996). While the majority of projects funded addressed, either directly or indirectly, the problem of yield, funding was also allocated to a project that sought to 'genetically engineer the pro-vitamin A pathway into the rice endosperm' (Potrykus, 2001). The justification for funding this research was that, while the likelihood of success was considered to be low, the potential benefits in public health terms would be significant, given that vitamin A deficiency was a priority concern for the international nutrition community (Mason et al, 2001). When the scientists achieved the transformation in their laboratory in Zurich in 1999, on the eve of the closure of the IPRB, the project was hailed as the IPRB's 'greatest achievement' (Normile, 1999).

In 2001, a lead article in Time magazine announced the discovery of what had become known as 'Golden Rice' with the assertion: 'this rice could save a million kids a year' (Nash, 2001). The article confirmed the project's status as 'poster child' in an increasingly polarised GM crop debate, as claims made for a technology still in the lab attracted contestation and controversy (BIOTHAI et al, 2001; Nestle, 2001). A significant and less well-understood dimension of the controversy was the transfer of the outputs of what had been public sector research, financed by governmental as well as philanthropic funding, to a private company, Syngenta, in exchange for assistance in negotiating unanticipated intellectual property restrictions, intensifying suspicion that Golden Rice would serve as a 'Trojan Horse' to gain public acceptance of GM crops more generally (Pollan, 2001). The inventors and their new sponsors, on the other hand, drew attention to the creation of a 'new type of public private partnership,' which would allow the free transfer of proprietary technology to public research institutions in Global South countries able to adapt and disseminate the new, nutrient-dense varieties to resource poor farmers (Potrykus, 2001).

In 2002, Golden Rice materials were transferred to the International Rice Research Institute (IRRI)[2] in the Philippines. A 'humanitarian board', initially comprising the Golden Rice inventors and donors and a Syngenta representative, had issued a 'humanitarian license' enabling IRRI and selected regional partners to begin the time-consuming and far less glamorous task of 'back-crossing' the Golden Rice 'trait' into *indica* varieties, using conventional plant breeding techniques. Ingo Potrykus and his colleagues at ETH had succeeded in transferring a gene containing beta-carotene, a precursor of vitamin A, into a *japonica* rice variety, which grows in temperate zones. Populations targeted by the Golden Rice project live in tropical environments, where *indica* varieties predominate. In parallel with this adaptive research at IRRI, scientists at Syngenta continued to work on *japonica* materials, and were twice successful in increasing the beta-carotene level in the grain (as well as removing the selectable marker gene), prompting IRRI and its partners to discard the results of earlier adaptive research and start again with the newly donated *japonica* materials. The research continued,

[2] IRRI is the CGIAR international crop research centre whose mandate focuses on rice research.

in a far from linear fashion, over several years, until, in 2008, IRRI scientists stablised germplasm ready for open field trials and preliminary nutrition studies (Al-Babili and Beyer, 2005; Brooks, 2010).

The BMGF began co-funding Golden Rice research in 2003, channeling funds through two major new initiatives – the CGIAR HarvestPlus Biofortification Program (HarvestPlus, 2004) and, under its 'Grand Challenges for Global Health' initiative, the 'ProVitaMinRice' Consortium – created to extend Golden Rice research to the development of rice enriched with multiple nutrients (BMGF, 2003). In their design, both programmes emphasised a genetic-led research approach which, it was envisaged, would have a large scale impact on micronutrient malnutrition across the Global South: part of a centralised vision that equated biofortification (an umbrella term for micronutrient-dense staple crops) with water fluoration: 'The [required nutrients] will get into the food system much like we put fluoride in the water system. It will be invisible, but it will be there to increase intakes' (Bouis, 2004). Here elements of continuity can be found with the scientific philanthropy of Carnegie, Rockefeller and Ford, in the attraction of 'silver bullet' solutions – technical, generic and inherently scalable – repackaged in the context of a contemporary target culture as a 'Grand Challenge' (Brooks et al, 2009a). Despite the lack of evidence at the time as to the effectiveness, or even the efficacy, of biofortification, the BMGF took a 'leap of faith' in committing substantial funding to a suite of biofortification initiatives, including Golden Rice (Brooks, 2010).

In 2011, the BMGF announced nearly US$20 million in new grants for biofortification projects, including funds to 'help in the development, testing and marketing of Golden Rice' (Nayer, 2011). Since then, the Philippines Rice Research Institute (PhilRice), in cooperation with IRRI, has carried out two seasons of field trials, which concluded in early 2013 (PhilRice, 2013). Meanwhile, the findings of a nutrition study carried out with a group of healthy children in controlled conditions have been published (Tang et al, 2012)[3]. With the field trials and preliminary nutrition studies completed, community nutrition studies to ascertain whether Golden Rice will indeed prove effective as an antidote to vitamin A deficiency in malnourished populations in 'real world' settings are now underway, overseen by a new project partner: Helen Keller International. These studies, together with further post-harvest research and preparation

---

[3]   Nevertheless, ethical concerns surrounding the study have generated further controversy.

for regulatory assessment, 'will take two years or more', according to a recent clarifying statement from IRRI (IRRI, 2013).

Nevertheless, a consistent theme running through Golden Rice project communications has been an emphasis on institutional constraints and achievements, which has diverted attention from the faltering progress of the research itself (Brooks, 2010). The celebration of the project as a 'new type of public private partnership' through which the inventors had secured assistance from Syngenta in negotiating the 'frightening number' of patents and material transfer agreements (MTAs) (Potrykus, 2001) is a case in point. In fact, this solution had been one of a range of options set out in a Rockefeller Foundation-commissioned 'freedom to operate' study which, interestingly, had drawn attention to the inapplicability of many of the patents in the countries targeted by the project (Kryder et al, 2000; Hindmarsh and Hindmarsh, 2002; Brooks, 2010). In the event, settlement on the 'humanitarian use' option preempted exploration of these alternative options. The agreement generated a series of new institutions: a 'humanitarian license', to allow the technology to be 'donated' by Syngenta, free of charge, to public research institutions and ultimately to farmers whose income was below a set level (US$10,000 per annum); a 'humanitarian board' to oversee the use of the license; and a 'Golden Rice Network' of public research bodies, coordinated by IRRI (as 'technology holder') and including several of its 'traditional' regional partners, though on markedly different terms (Brooks, 2010).

Juxtaposed against the success story of the institutionalisation of the 'humanitarian use' principle was a more negative story about the regulatory hurdles standing between the Golden Rice technology and its projected beneficiaries. Here the Golden Rice trajectory intersected with the contested politics of biosafety regulation, particularly in the Global South, where it has become the focus of broader public debates about GM technology and development – largely because it is one of the few remaining spaces where such debate can still take place (Van Zwanenberg et al, 2011). In this context, Golden Rice has been afforded a very different, 'virtual' identity in policy and public discourse, as a potent symbol of the thwarted promise of GM crops (Brooks, 2013). In contrast to its messy material reality as experimental material in the laboratory and greenhouse, Golden Rice was reconstructed as a proven technology and all but finished product, which, but for unnecessarily burdensome regulation and irrational opposition, would already be in farmers' fields and saving lives (Potrykus, 2010, 2012; see also Taverne, 2007; McVie, 2013). Some have even have gone so far as to state that regulatory 'hurdles' slowing down the dissemination of a lifesaving technology constitute 'a crime against humanity' (Potrykus, 2010, p466).

The dynamics and consequences, for downstream 'users', of a complex research trajectory in which a range of scientific and policy uncertainties have been shielded from view have been explored in depth elsewhere (Brooks, 2010; 2011; 2013). Crucially, fundamental questions regarding the efficacy and safety of Golden Rice both as a commercial rice variety and solution to vitamin A deficiency have yet to be unanswered. Nonetheless, as an institutional experiment in conditional intellectual property transfer, the institutional arrangements surrounding the Golden Rice project, which embed a particular model of technology transfer, have served as a template for the development of a more refined and thus far less contentious partnership: the Nairobi-based African Agricultural Technology Foundation (AATF).

Transferring the lessons: AATF as a model partnership?

Drought-tolerant maize is the Holy Grail for agricultural research in Sub-Saharan Africa (Brooks et al, 2009b). Breeding maize varieties for drought conditions has been a research priority in Sub-Saharan Africa for many years, beginning with early maturing 'drought escaping' varieties developed in the 1960s and 1970s (Heisey and Edmeades, 1999). From the 1980s onwards, the development of drought-tolerant (as opposed to drought-escaping) varieties became a priority for the International Centre for Improvement of Maize and Wheat (CIMMYT)[4], and in the 1990s scientists at CIMMYT's base in Zimbabwe developed a plant-breeding methodology which represented an important departure from the approach – up to that point entrenched within the CGIAR – of developing elite lines in 'optimal conditions'. Researchers in CIMMYT's 'Southern African Drought and Low Soil Fertility' (SADLF) project piloted a new breeding technology for a range of 'managed stress conditions', including – but not confined to – drought conditions, under what has been referred to as 'Africa's new smallholder maize paradigm' (McCann et al, 2007). This methodology was implemented on a wider scale under the 'African Maize Stress' (AMS) project (Banziger and Diallo, 2000): a project that was also innovative in other ways, for example in piloting the 'mother–baby' model that invited an (albeit limited) degree of farmer participation

---

[4] CIMMYT is the CGIAR international crop research centre whose mandate focuses on maize and wheat research.

in technology development (de Groote and Siambi, 2005; Sawkins et al, 2006).

In the early 2000s, two parallel research initiatives were funded by the BMGF. The first was the CGIAR-led programme 'Drought Tolerant Maize for Africa (DTMA)', and the other – headed by the newly-established public private partnership, the African Agricultural Technology Foundation (AATF) – was entitled 'Water Efficient Maize for Africa (WEMA)'. Their aim was to tackle the problem of breeding maize for drought conditions. While employing the maize-breeding methodology refined during the years of the SADLF and AMS projects, these new programmes differed from precursor initiatives in important ways: dispensing with the more context-sensitive and participatory aspects of the 'smallholder paradigm' that had been so positively evaluated (McCann et al, 2007). First, both the DTMA and WEMA were framed as responses to the impacts of climate change on African agriculture, and focused specifically on the problem of drought, not on the broader range of interrelated stresses and constraints faced by smallholder farmers that was formerly the case (Brooks et al, 2009b). Second, while precursor programmes had prioritised development of open pollinated varieties (OPVs), which allow farmers to save, exchange and replant seed from one year to the next, both DTMA and WEMA are designed around a package that includes newly developed hybrid maize varieties and commercial fertilisers. These were to be made available to farmers via a network of private providers, or agro-dealers, now cast as the de facto extension service in a model promoted under Africa's new 'Green Revolution': which was also the recipient of substantial funding from the BMGF (Odame and Muange, 2011). In this case, it was envisaged that a model, designed with Kenya's high-potential maize-growing zones in Western Kenya and the Rift Valley in mind, would 'trickle down' to the precarious mixed farming systems found in drought-prone areas to the east of the country. At the same time, the participatory element in the earlier programmes was eclipsed by a recasting of 'the farmer' as a consumer of predetermined technologies rather than as a partner in participatory technology development (Ashby, 2009; Brooks et al, 2009b; Scoones and Thompson, 2011).

The two programmes can be also contrasted with each other in important ways. First, the DTMA programme is, as mentioned earlier, a public initiative, although (as in the case of HarvestPlus) the CGIAR centres coordinating the programme act as brokers in a research consortium that includes both public and private sector actors. The WEMA initiative, on the other hand, is headed by AATF, a public–

private partnership whose *raison d'etre* is to facilitate transfer of patented technologies and whose design owes much to lessons learned from institutional innovations around the Golden Rice project (Interview, Golden Rice Humanitarian Board member, 29 May 2006). Second, while DTMA (in common with HarvestPlus) emphasises conventional plant breeding, WEMA follows the example of the Golden Rice project in securing patented, transgenic materials 'free of charge' from a private company, Monsanto, for back-crossing into locally-developed hybrid varieties. Interestingly, and again in common with HarvestPlus and Golden Rice, the DTMA and WEMA programmes are separate and distinct in theory but, in practice, intimately connected in multiple ways (see Brooks, 2010 and Brooks et al, 2009b for more extended discussion of these dynamics).

Thus far WEMA (and the AATF) has avoided the controversy courted by the Golden Rice project. First, the organisational image could not be more different. AATF presents itself very clearly as an *African* institution. Criticisms of the role of corporate interests and control, so heightened in Golden Rice debates, have been more muted, while managers of both WEMA and DTMA have been careful to manage expectations about when technologies can be expected to emerge from the pipeline (Brooks et al, 2009b). Nevertheless, the virtual identity of drought-tolerant maize as a symbol of technological promise (cf. Glover, 2010) has made itself felt in debates surrounding the design of biosafety regulatory systems in Sub-Saharan Africa. In this case, the use of WEMA project communications to advocate 'science-based' – read 'more permissive' – biosafety regulation (African Agricultural Technology Foundation, n.d.) suggests this is a role that has passed seamlessly from Golden Rice to the WEMA project. As concerns about the effects of climate change on African agriculture continue to escalate (Thornton et al, 2011; Vermeulen et al, 2011), the promise of drought-tolerant maize in maize-centred farming regions may, in the long run, prove to be a powerful lever in shaping regulatory instruments that are currently under development. Meanwhile, projects such as WEMA serve as an opportunity for continued experimentation and learning, by various actors, including the life sciences industry, in the conditional transfer of intellectual property rights and benefits.

Conclusion

One of the advantages that private philanthropists have over other international development actors, governmental and nongovernmental, is their independence from short-term incentives and pressures.

Private foundations are uniquely able to take a long-term view and take risks. Decisions by the Rockefeller Foundation to found IRRI, the first institution of its kind (Anderson et al, 1991), and to invest in the 15-year IPRB, which would lay the foundations for a global biotechnology research capacity in rice (Hindmarsh and Hindmarsh, 2002), are clear examples of this. Similarly, in the contemporary era, the BMGF has taken decisions to support not only the development of new technologies, but also 'new types of public private partnership', as exemplified by the Golden Rice project and AATF. In each case, an emphasis on institutional maneuvers enabling the transfer of proprietary technology (the appropriateness of which is not open to question) has helped to steer attention away from the not insignificant scientific hurdles both research projects still face, as well the relative merits of alternative approaches more responsive to local realities and needs. These developments have, in turn, created conditions in which the purported urgency of these projects is used as a lever to influence the design of technology regulatory systems in countries in the Global South.

The Asian Green Revolution, launched with the support of the Rockefeller and Ford Foundations in the 1960s, was a public sector effort that nevertheless played a key role in opening up Global South countries' agriculture to capitalist investment. Today, global attention is focused on an imperative to accelerate agricultural production in Africa. A 'New Alliance for Food Security and Nutrition', a major new US-led initiative which aims to 'help lift 50 million people in Sub-Saharan Africa out of poverty in the next 10 years by supporting agricultural development' was recently launched (USAID, n.d.), giving a key role to agribusiness corporations. These developments, alongside an increasingly high-profile presence of the BMGF and other philanthrocapitalists in development debates, are blurring the boundary between development aid and private investment yet further. It is important, therefore, to look beyond the 'win-win' rhetoric that surrounds the 'new philanthropy' and its defining role in global development: to critically examine the design and operation of philanthropic ventures *in practice* and ask who will be the winners and losers in the long term.

References

African Agricultural Technology Foundation, nd, *Combining breeding and biotechnology to develop water efficient maize for Africa (WEMA)*, concept note, African Agricultural Technology Foundation: Nairobi, www.aatf-africa.org/UserFiles/File/Wema-Concept-Note.pdf

Al-Babili, S and Beyer, P, 2005, Golden Rice – five years on the road – five years to go?, *Trends in Plant Science*, 10, 12, 565–73

Anderson, R S, Levy, E and Morrison, B M, 1991, *Rice Science and development politics: research strategies and IRRI's technologies confront Asian diversity (1950-1980)*, Oxford: Clarendon Press

Ashby, J A, 2009, Fostering farmer first methodological innovation: organisational learning and change in international agricultural research, in Scoones, I and Thompson, J (eds) *Farmer first revisited: innovation for agricultural research and development*, London: Practical Action Publishing

Banziger, M and Diallo, A O, 2000, Stress-tolerant maize for farmers in Sub-Saharan Africa, *Maize Research Highlights 1999-2000*, Mexico: CIMMYTBIOTHAI, CEDAC (Cambodia), DRCSC (India), GRAIN, MASIPAG (Philippines), PAN-Indonesia and UBINIG (Bangladesh), 2001), *Grains of delusion: Golden Rice seen from the ground*, Los Baños: MASIPAG

BMGF, 2003, Grand Challenge #9: Engineering Rice for High Beta Carotene, Vitamin E and Enhanced Fe and Zn Bioavailability, www.grandchallenges.org/ImproveNutrition/Challenges/NutrientRichPlants/Pages/Rice.aspx#ResearchObjectives

Bouis, H, 2004, Hidden hunger: the role of nutrition, fortification and biofortification, *World food prize international symposium: from Asia to Africa: rice, biofortification and enhanced nutrition*, 14–15 October, Des Moines, Iowa

Brooks, S, 2010, *Rice biofortification: lessons for global science and development*, London: Earthscan

Brooks, S, 2011, Is international agricultural research a global public good? The case of rice biofortification, *Journal of Peasant Studies,* 38, 1, 67–80

Brooks, S, 2013, Biofortification: lessons from the Golden Rice project, *Food Chain,* 3, 77–88

Brooks, S, Leach, M, Lucas, H and Millstone, E, 2009a, *Silver bullets, grand challenges and the new philanthropy*, working paper no 24, Brighton: STEPS Centre,

Brooks, S, Thompson, J, Odame, H, Kibaara, B, Nderitu, S, Karin, F and Millstone, E, 2009b, *Environmental change and maize innovation in Kenya: exploring pathways in and out of maize*, working paper no 36, Brighton: STEPS Centre

Carnegie, A, 1889, Gospel of wealth, *North American Review*, CCCXCI

Cullather, N, 2004, Miracles of modernisation: the Green Revolution and the apotheosis of technology, *Diplomatic History*, 28, 2, 227–54

David, C C and Otsuka, K, eds,1993, *Modern rice technology and income distribution in Asia*, Manila: IRRIDe

de Groote, H and Siambi, M, 2005, Comparing and integrating farmers' and breeders' evaluations of maize varieties in East Africa, in Gonsalves, J, Becker, T, Braun, A, Campilan, D, Chavez, H, Fajber, D, Kapiriri, E, Rivaca-Caminade, M, J. and Vernooy, R (eds) *Participatory research and development for sustainable agriculture and natural resource management: a sourcebook, Volume 3: DOING participatory research and development*, CIP-UPWARD/IDRC

Evenson, R E, Herdt, R W and Hossain, M, 1996, *Rice research in Asia: progress and priorities*, Wallingford: CAB International

Frumkin, P, 2006, *Strategic giving: the art and science of philanthropy*, Chicago: University of Chicago Press

Glaeser, B, 1987, Agriculture between the Green Revolution and eco-development: which way to go? in Glaeser, B (ed) *The Green Revolution revisited: critique and alternatives*, London: Allen and Unwin

Glover, D, 2010, Exploring the resilience of Bt Cotton's 'pro poor success story', *Development and Change,* 41, 6, 955–81

Griffin, K, 1979, *The political economy of agrarian change: an essay on the Green Revolution*, New York: Macmillan Press

HarvestPlus, 2004, *Breeding crops for better nutrition: harnessing agricultural technology to improve micronutrient deficiencies*, Washington DC: International Food Policy Research Institute

Heisey, P W and Edmeades, G O, 1999, Maize production in drought-stressed environments: technical options and research resource allocations, in *World Maize Facts and Trends 1997/8; Maize production in drought-stressed environments: technical options and research resource allocations*, Part 1, Mexico: CIMMYT

Hindmarsh, S and Hindmarsh, R, 2002, Laying the molecular foundations of GM rice across Asia, *Resource Book Volume 1,* Penang: Malaysia Pesticide Action Network

IRRI, 2013, Clarifying recent news about Golden Rice, Manila: International Rice Research Institute, www.irri.org/index.php?option=com_k2&view=item&id=12483

Kryder, R D, Kowalski, S P and Krattiger, A F, 2000, *The intellectual and technical property components of pro-vitamin A rice (Golden Rice): a preliminary freedom-to-operate review*, New York: International Service for the Acquisition of Agri-biotech Applications (ISAAA)

Lipton, M and Longhurst, R, 1989, *New seeds and poor people*, London: Unwin Hyman

Mason, J B, Lotfi, M, Dalmiya, N, Sethuraman, K and Deitchler, M, 2001, *The micronutrient report: current progress and trends in the control of vitamin A, iodine and iron deficiencies*, Ottawa: The Micronutrient Initiative/ International Development Research Centre

McCann, J C, Dalton, T J and Mekuria, M, 2007, Breeding for Africa's new smallholder maize paradigm, *International Journal of Agricultural Sustainability*, 4, 2, 99–107

McVie, R, 2013, After 30 years, is a GM food breakthrough finally here? *The Observer*, 2 February, www.theguardian.com/environment/2013/feb/02/genetic-modification-breakthrough-golden-rice

Morvaridi, B, 2012a, Capitalist philanthropy and hegemonic partnerships, *Third World Quarterly*, 33, 2, 1191–210

Morvaridi, B, 2012b, Capitalist philanthropy and the new Green Revolution for food security, *International Journal of Sociology of Agriculture and Food*, 19, 2, 243–56

Nash, M, 2001, Grains of hope, *Time Magazine*, 5 February, 38–46, www.content.time.com/time/magazine/article/0,9171,50576,00.html

Nayar, A, 2011, Grants aim to fight malnutrition, *Nature News*, 14 April, www.nature.com/news/2011/110414/full/news.2011.233.html

Nestle, M, 2001, Genetically engineered 'Golden Rice' is unlikely to overcome vitamin A deficiency; response by Ingo Potrykus, *Journal of the American Diabetes Association*, 101, 3, 289–290

Normile, D, 1999, Rice biotechnology: Rockerfeller to end network after 15 years of success, *Science*, 286, 5444, 1468–9

Odame, H and Muange, E, 2011, Can agro-dealers deliver the Green Revolution in Kenya?, *IDS Bulletin*, 42, 4, 78–89

Pearse, A, 1980, *Seeds of plenty, seeds of want: social and economic implications of the Green Revolution*, Oxford: Clarendon Press

Perkins, J H, 1997, *Geopolitics and the Green Revolution: wheat, genes and the Cold War*, Oxford: Oxford University Press

PhilRice, 2013, *Two seasons of Golden Rice trials in Phl concluded*, Neuva Ecija: Philippines Rice Research Institute, www.philrice.gov.ph/?page=resources&page2=news&id=211

Pollan, M, 2001, The Great Yellow Hype, *The New York Times Magazine*, 4 March, www.nytimes.com/2001/03/04/magazine/04WWLN. html

Potrykus, I, 2001, Golden Rice and beyond, *Plant Physiology*, 125, 3, 1157–61

Potrykus, I, 2010, 'Lessons from the humanitarian Golden Rice project: regulation prevents development of public good genetically engineered crop products', *New Biotechnology*, 27, 5, 466–72

Potrykus, I, 2012, Golden Rice, a GMO-product for public good, and the consequences of GE-regulation, *Journal of Plant Biochemistry and Biotechnology*, 21, 1, 68–75

Sawkins, M C, DeMeyer, J and Ribaut, J M, 2006, Drought adaptation in maize, in Ribaut, J M (ed) *Drought adaptation in cereals*, New York: Haworth

Scoones, I and Thompson, J, 2011, The politics of seed in Africa's green revolution: alternative narratives and competing pathways, IDS Bulletin, 42, 4, 1–23

Smith, R, 2009, The emergence of vitamins as bio-political objects during World War I, *Studies in History and Philosophy of Science Part C: Studies in History and Philosophy of Biological and Biomedical Sciences*, 40, 3, 179–89.

Spitz, P, 1987, The Green Revolution re-examined in India', in Glaeser, B, ed, *The Green Revolution Revisited: Critique and Alternatives*, London: Allen and Unwin

Tang, G, Hu, Y, Yin, S, Wang, Y, Dallal, G E, Grusak, M A and Russell, R M, 2012, Beta-carotene in Golden Rice is as good as beta-carotene in oil at providing vitamin A to children, *The American Journal of Clinical Nutrition*, 96, 3, 658–64Taverne, R, 2007, The real GM food scandal, *Prospect*, 140, 24–7.

Thornton, P K, Jones, P G, Eriksen, P J and Challinor, A J, 2011, Agriculture and food systems in Sub-Saharan Africa in a 4°C+ world, *Philosophical Transactions of the Royal Society*, 369, 1934, 117–36

USAID (nd), *The new alliance for food security and nutrition*, www.usaid. gov/unga/new-alliance

Van Zwanenberg, P, Ely, A and Smith, A, 2011, *Regulating technology: international harmonization and local realities*, London: Earthscan

Vermeulen, S J, Aggarwal, P, Ainslie, A, Angelone, C, Campbell, B M,Challinor, A, Hansen, J W, Ingram, J, Jarvis, A and Kristjanson, P, 2011, Options for support to agriculture and food security under climate change, *Environmental Science and Policy*, 15, 1, 136–44

Part Three
Philanthropy and social protection

SEVEN

Philanthropy and the politics of social policy

Ayşe Buğra

Introduction

During the last few decades, philanthropy has become an important and widely discussed social phenomenon throughout the world. The term philanthropy refers to a wide range of activities undertaken by many different types of non-governmental organisations (NGOs) as well as individuals. This chapter focuses on 'voluntary giving', which has social policy relevance, and uses the term to describe voluntary sector activities that involve the provision of social assistance and services.

The chapter asks four questions. The first concerns the way philanthropy complements the role played by other institutions in welfare provision. These other institutions include the state, the family and the market; but the main focus here will be on the relationship between philanthropic activities and state redistributive practices. The second question addresses the way in which philanthropy affects, and is affected by, prevailing normative attitudes towards social solidarity.

The third question focuses on the role of religion, which is often an important dimension of the voluntary sector: shaping philanthropic action and influencing social policy processes and institutions in different historical and social contexts. Finally, the fourth question is about the political implications of philanthropic activities, a question that is not unrelated to T. H. Marshall's (1964a) comment on the complementarity of civil, political and social rights.

These questions are pursued with reference to the recent developments in Turkey's social policy environment. After 1980, a large number of NGOs, many of which provide social assistance and services, were formed in Turkey.[1] This expansion of the voluntary

---

[1] In early 2010, 4,547 foundations and 86,031 associations were active in the country; in other words, 90,578 NGOs pursued their activities in different fields (TÜSEV, 2011: 61).

sector followed the country's entry into the global market economy, and coincided with the rise of political Islam.

The salience of religion in society and politics could not be seen as a phenomenon peculiar to Turkey or to Islamic countries generally. Globally observed in cultural trends in the post-1980 period included questioning of Enlightenment values and intense debates on 'post-secularism' or the 'return of public religion' (Levine, 1986; Casanova, 1994, 2008; Habermas, 2006). It is in this cultural context that philanthropy has acquired a new significance and its role, with regard to social policy, has changed.

However, in Turkey social policy reform and the changing role of philanthropy in the social arena were also shaped against the background formed by the country's old system of social protection whose inegalitarian character facilitated its dismantling and the legitimation of the emerging model of social solidarity. This new model has been developed by using a repertoire of institutions and practices informed by both religious traditions and the sociopolitical relations that characterised the welfare regime of the country in the past.

This chapter will develop a discussion on the place of philanthropy in social policy development during the administration of the Justice and Development Party (*Adalet ve Kalkınma Partisi*: AKP) since 2002. Since 19th- and 20th-century perspectives on philanthropy and public welfare are relevant for an analysis of contemporary approaches to social solidarity in Turkey, or anywhere, we will begin by revisiting earlier debates in order to provide a background to the Turkish case.

Perspectives on philanthropy: from poverty and compassion to equality and citizenship

In 1833, when he was still working on *Democracy in America*, Alexis de Tocqueville visited England where he witnessed and even participated in debates around the preparation of the Poor Law Amendment Act (or the New Poor Law) of 1834. The Act put an end to relief outside the workhouse and forced the beneficiaries of aid to renounce their basic liberties as members of the society in which they lived. This was one of the particularly radical changes made to institute the 19th-century self-regulating market society with the commodification of labour as one of its crucial characteristics;[2] but Tocqueville's position was even more radical. In his *Memoir on pauperism* written in 1835, he challenged the principle of public relief itself, which he found objectionable particularly because it tended to replace voluntary assistance: 'individual charity is almost unknown in a country of organised public charity' (Tocqueville, 1997, p62).

In contemporary capitalism – which replaced regulated, organised capitalism of the three decades following the Second World War – the ideas of Tocqueville have become widely appreciated and begun to influence the debates on the social foundation of economic and political regimes, as Gertrude Himmelfarb (1997) observed in her introduction to a new edition of the *Memoir on pauperism*.

As an article (written in an ironical tone) in *The Guardian* stated, 'The 19th century was the age of capitalism, the 20th the age of socialism. The 21st is to be the age of charity, or so we are given to hope' (Jenkins, 2006). Tocqueville would approve the increasingly important role of charity in the emerging 21st-century social policy environment. However, the changes observed in social policy processes and institutions hardly conform to the zero–sum relationship between private benevolence and public welfare found in *Memoir on pauperism*.

While several studies indicate that after 1990 there has been an important expansion of the voluntary sector throughout the world (OECD, 2003; John Hopkins University Centre for Civil Society Studies, 2004), we observe that public social expenditures have also increased in the same period. In fact, in four of the five countries where non-profit sector employment, as a percentage of the economically active population, was found to be the highest (Belgium: 10.9%; Ireland: 10.4%, US: 9.8% and UK: 8.5%) by the John Hopkins Comparative Non-Profit Sector Project, the share of public social expenditure in GDP was considerably higher in 2012 than in 1980. In the case of the fifth, The Netherlands (14.4%), there was no increase in public social expenditure but it was higher

---

[2]   In *The great transformation*, Karl Polanyi refers to the Poor Law Reform Act of 1834, the Anti-Corn Law Bill of 1846 and Peel's Bank Act of 1834 as marking a crucial moment in the legislative process which 'instituted' the self-regulating market economy (Polanyi, 1944, pp135–150).

than the OECD average in 1980 and in 2012.[3] The expansion of philanthropy appears to be neither the *cause* nor the *effect* of the retreat of the state as a welfare institution. But it is possible to say that the two institutions affect and reshape each other in a way that changes in different historical conjunctures.

In order to analyse the non-zero-sum relationship between the institutions that play a role in welfare provision, it might be useful to consider Esping-Andersen's (1990, 1999) influential contribution to the comparative analysis of welfare regimes and welfare regime transformation on the basis of the intercausal triad of state, market, and family, representing the three principles of social security provision: redistribution, exchange and reciprocity. Esping-Andersen limits the institutional realm of reciprocity relations to the family, and does not attempt to expand it to other relations involving different types of reciprocity. It might, nevertheless, be possible to incorporate voluntary associations in the same model – as institutional actors playing a role in welfare provision – on the basis of the principle of reciprocity. Such an attempt would be useful for an analysis of the way philanthropy articulates with other institutions in a given historical setting. It would also enable us to situate voluntary giving in the normative framework of social policy debate and to evaluate views concerning socially acceptable and morally justified types of inequality, which inform different approaches to private benevolence and public welfare provision.

The moral implications of reciprocity relationships – between the providers and the beneficiaries of social assistance and social services – can be interpreted in different ways. Tocqueville's total rejection of public charity is formulated in an argument that emphasises the superiority of traditional relations between people in unequal social positions to institutional arrangements based on the principle of formal equality. As he puts it:

> individual alms giving establish[es] valuable ties between the rich and the poor ... A moral tie is established between these two classes whose interests and passions so often conspire

---

3   For Belgium, Ireland, USA and UK the share of public social expenditures in GDP in 1980 and 2012 were 23.5% and 30%; 16.5% and 23.1%; 13.4% and 19.4%, and 16.5% and 23.9% respectively. For the Netherlands these figures were 24.8% and 24.3% for 1980 and 2012, while the OECD averages are 15.5% and 21.7% for these years (Johns Hopkins University Center for Civil Society Studies, 2004; OECD, 2013).

to separate them from each other, and although divided by circumstances they are willingly reconciled. This is not the case with legal charity … Far from uniting these two rival nations … into a single people, [legal charity] breaks the only link which could be established between them. It ranges each one under a banner, tallies them, and brings them face to face, prepares them for combat. (Tocqueville, 1997, pp60–61)

A society in which the only bond that exists between the rich and the poor is established by alms is necessarily an unequal society. But even this model of social solidarity can incorporate a notion of equality in the sense of equality of all before God:

The poor man who demands alms in the name of the law is…in a still more humiliating position that the indigent; he asks pity of his fellow men in the name of He who regards all men from the same point of view and subjects rich and poor to equal laws. (Tocqueville 1997, pp59–60)

In his discussion of the early notions of social solidarity, which preceded and prepared the historical background for the development of the modern notion of solidarity, Brunkhorst (2005) mentions the Christian concept of fraternity. This concept evokes the equality of all Christians before God and attributes a special significance to that equality, which transcends the significance and even the relevance of social inequalities. The protection of the weak and the poor is commanded on the grounds of this type of equality before 'Him' that Tocqueville compares to the formal equality of atomised individuals in modern societies.

In the 19th-century market economy, while traditional charity informed by religious sentiment continued, non-religious forms of 'modern philanthropy' also emerged. Himmelfarb (1991) writes that in late Victorian England these modern forms of philanthropy were instrumental in drawing attention to those types of poverty that could *not* be attributed to the irresponsibility of the poor. They thus entailed, at least implicitly, a criticism of the prevailing socioeconomic relations and called for systemic reform. She argues, however, that this reformist bent was different from the reforms demanded and realised through the steps taken towards the 20th-century welfare state, whose normative basis was shaped by an egalitarian emphasis. According to Himmelfarb, in an attempt directed at the unrealistic objective of equal services and benefits for all, the advocates of the welfare state 'relativised' and 'de-moralised' the problem of poverty, and left it unresolved.

It is true that those who contributed to the formation of the theoretical foundations of the 20th-century welfare state, T. H. Marshall in particular, defined the objective of social policy in terms of 'class abatement' rather than as 'merely an attempt to abate the obvious nuisance of destitution in the lowest ranks of society' (Marshall, 1964a, p106). There was a shift of emphasis from poverty to equality of citizenship status, which would be developed on the basis of civil, political and social rights. Marshall writes that in the past, public assistance to the poor was not necessarily rights-based and that private charity, which assumed the major part of the responsibility for dealing with the problem of indigence, often operated with the understanding that those who received help had no personal right to claim it. However, Marshall's objection to the old *humanitarian* way of dealing with indigence does *not* involve the denial of the significance of moral concerns about individual responsibility. As he puts it:

> Gracious condescension and the charitable dole are things of the past, and the perpetual aim today is to help others to help themselves – to offer a service which hopes for a response, not of gratitude but of effort to face life with new courage. (Marshall, 1964b, p351)

In the period when welfare state institutions were emerging and developing, the prerogative 'to help others to help themselves' was by no means solely relegated to the public authority. Many participants in the social policy debate, including those who made the most significant contributions to the emergence of a universalist approach to welfare provision, emphasised the importance of reciprocity relations that involved different types of voluntary giving. Titmuss (1970), for example, presents an analysis of the intercountry differences between the altruistic and market exchange-dominated systems of blood donation and attributes these differences to the nature of social institutions to draw attention to the potential of public welfare policies, guided by universalist principles, to foster solidaristic relations among civil society actors.

William Beveridge was undoubtedly one of the most important contributors to the development of welfare institutions based on universalistic principles. Nevertheless, in his report on *Voluntary action* (1948) he was very much in favour of voluntary sector activity in welfare provision. In fact, T. H. Marshall (1964b) was somewhat disturbed by the privileged role Beveridge assigned to the voluntary sector in social service provision and his argument against fiscal and regulatory measures that would restrict private resources devoted to philanthropy or interfere in the substance and methods of voluntary activities. The objections Marshall voiced against The Beveridge Report would be useful for an assessment of the social implications of the contemporary resurgence of philanthropy at a global level.

Equality is central to Marshall's position vis-à-vis voluntary action, with regard to social policy. He insists on the need to be watchful for *lingering* inequality in voluntary service provision by the privileged to the unprivileged. He draws attention to the problems of accountability and representation that inevitably emerge in the presence of different associations with different views about content and method of service delivery. He, thus, argues against Beveridge by insisting that it should be the public authorities that design the structure of taxes and determine the level and the allocation of resources for social service provision. He also argues that the voluntary sector should not try to compete but rather work in collaboration with the government, and accept being subjected to public regulation.

Partnerships between the state and the voluntary sector now appear to be a central characteristic of contemporary models of welfare governance (Jessop, 1999; Bode, 2006). Private business and international organisations – such as the World Bank – often advocate the articulation of the voluntary sector with other institutional components of the welfare provision. However, these approaches are shaped in a historical context that is quite different from that of welfare capitalism. Today, the social dislocations brought about by economic globalisation have put poverty alleviation onto the social policy agenda as a central objective dominating the concern with socioeconomic inequality. At the same time, religion has once again appeared as an important dimension of socioeconomic relations and as a key element in the realm of social policy where faith-based associations have acquired a new significance, at least in some societies (Dierckx et al, 2009; Göçmen, 2013). As might be expected, in this new environment partnerships between state and the voluntary sector are likely to operate in ways which are different from that envisaged by Marshall. In the particular case of Turkey, these global developments have led to the emergence of a social policy environment where the *logic of charity* extends beyond the voluntary sector and permeates welfare provision by the government in a way to undermine the *logic of equal citizenship*.

Changing welfare regime of Turkey and the discovery of charity in a new context

In Turkey, the expansion of the voluntary sector during the last few decades was, in part, related to widespread disillusionment with government action, which most people thought was neither just nor efficient. The formal security system introduced after the Second World War was of an inegalitarian corporatist type, which provided old age and health benefits differentiated according to the work status of the beneficiaries. At the same time, it excluded significant segments of the population employed in agriculture or in the urban informal sector; the excluded depended on family support in old age or during ill health. There were no institutional mechanisms of social assistance to the poor until the 1970s, when very modest income support was provided to the elderly and the disabled who did not have relatives to take care of them. [4]

The dismantling of this formal social security system - despite resistance from labour unions and professional associations - was legitimised not only by emphasizing the fiscal pressures it generated but also on the basis of its inegalitarian and exclusionary character (Buğra & Candaş, 2011). Nevertheless, in the new system of social protection, which replaced the old one, equality did not appear to be prioritised. The emphasis was, rather, placed on poverty, which took new forms in the liberal market economy. With the increasing pace of urbanisation that led to the weakening of the informal support mechanisms, the challenge of poverty required new responses, and the response came in the form of new institutions of social assistance and the increasing role of philanthropy in welfare provision.

In contemporary Turkey, where the increasing importance of religion as a public phenomenon eventually led to the electoral victories of Islamist political parties – first in the municipal and later in the general elections – capitalist development in a globalising economy made religion a central element of social policy change. Traditional Islamic instruments of charity, such as *zakat* (alms tax), *sadaka* (alms giving) and, especially, *waqf* (philanthropic foundation) – which originated in the country's Ottoman past – were remembered not only with nostalgia but also as models for new institution building.

The Directorate of Social Solidarity, currently the most important social assistance institution in Turkey, originated in an attempt to use the

---

[4] For information on Turkey's welfare regime and its ongoing transformation, see Buğra & Candaş (2011), Buğra & Adar (2008) and Buğra (2007).

waqf as a model of social solidarity. The Directorate was first established in 1986 as the Fund for the Encouragement of Social Cooperation and Solidarity to provide means-tested social assistance to the poor. The preamble of the law that established the Fund stated that:

> Islamic foundations, which are the most ancient and persistent institutions of the Islamic Turkish civilization of Anatolia and the most beautiful examples of cooperation and solidarity, are the most progressive institution of our times in fulfilling social, economic and cultural needs.
>
> It is to be expected that the vitality in Turkish foundations that is long missed would be regenerated through this law … The honour to serve the portion of society that is placed under the middle classes and who are without social security would be possible through the support of the charitable and self-sacrificing citizens alongside with our state.[5]

Until the late 1990s, the Fund did not have an important presence in the field of social policy, either as a regular welfare institution using public funds or as a public body regulating charitable donations from the benevolent. It is after a major economic crisis in 2001, and especially under the current AKP government, that the Fund has begun to play a significant role in assisting the poor. In 2004, it became the General Directorate of Social Assistance and Solidarity operating through over 900 local foundations, whose boards of directors are formed by local and central administrative authorities, elected representatives and philanthropists. The revenue comes from public funds and private donations, which have increased significantly over the years. In fact, the Directorate and the local foundations advertise to raise funds, thus blurring the boundary between the state and the voluntary sector.[6] It should be remembered that these developments have taken place in a context where religion appears as an important factor that influences the emergent welfare regime and the relationships between its institutional components.

Secularism was a central principle in the ideology of the Turkish Republic, and the founders of the Republic tried to introduce a particular interpretation of Islam as a rational, non-superstitious system

---

[5] Turkish Parliament (1986).

[6] The Directorate is not the only welfare institution that presents such a mixed source of revenue. The revenue of municipal government 'social funds' – a combination of public and private finance – is used to provide welfare and social services.

of individual faith, as an entirely private matter and not an instrument of politics. Paradoxically – but given the important place of religion in the Ottoman legal and political order, also quite unavoidably – the establishment of this secular version of Islam had to be realised by political intervention. The Directorate of Religious Affairs (*Diyanet İşleri Başkanlığı, DİB*) was established to oversee, coordinate and control religious practice (Parla & Davison, 2008).

However, throughout the single-party regime the budget and the staff of the DİB remained quite limited and started to be more important under the rule of the elected right-wing governments. Somewhat ironically, this organisation, created by Republican modernisers as a means to serve the objective of de-politicising and privatising religion, was used to affirm and enhance the place of Sunni Islam in public life under the rule of the AKP, a party representing a moderate version of Islamist politics. Since the AKP came to power in 2002, important steps have been taken by the government to expand the scope of the DİB's activities beyond the administration of mosques and religious courses to the administration of social services. With these changes, DIB became an important actor in prisons and other places of detention, old age homes and hospitals. At the same time, the Directorate became an active institutional partner of the Directorate of Social Services and Child Protection. The administration of the latter was changed to allow extensive collaboration with DIB and to include religious officials on the staff of social services. There is also extensive collaboration between DIB and the Ministry of Family and Social Policy.[7]

As important as these developments concerning the increasing significance of government-controlled religion in social affairs, is the way in which non-governmental organisations contributed to the shaping of the role of religion in society. As Wuthnow (1994) discusses in his study *Producing the sacred*, the place of religion in public life does *not* spontaneously stem from existing beliefs and values within a given cultural universe. Different actors operating through different organisations interpret and give meaning to these beliefs and values, thus shaping the way in which they are manifested in economic, political and social life. Insofar as Turkey is concerned, it would indeed be impossible to analyse the relationship between the rise of political Islam and the increasing significance of religion in public life without taking into account the role in this process of a myriad of non-governmental organisations, including those that carry out philanthropic activities independently or in collaboration with public welfare institutions or

[7] See DİB (2010).

social service administrations. Government– NGO collaborations are also carried out at the municipal level in activities that reach many people and sometimes closely affect their lives, as in the case of welfare provision.

The increase in the number of faith-based organisations, and the increasing significance of welfare provision, constitute an important aspect of the recent changes in Turkey's associational environment (Göçmen, 2011; 2014). Some of the most prominent organisations are situated in networks, bringing together different bodies active in different fields but sharing a common Islamic outlook. The Turkish Foundation of Voluntary Associations (*Türkiye Gönüllü Teşekküller Vakfı*, TGTV) – which has over 100 members – is a prominent example of such a network.[8] Under the umbrella of TGTV, there are charities and organisations involved in cultural activities and defence of human rights, as well as voluntary business associations. In fact, MUSIAD, a powerful business association with an Islamic outlook, played an important role in the establishment of the TGTV in 1994. This type of network formation between economic and non–economic actors is not limited to the case of TGTV. The faith-based Gülen network, whose power and influence has increased considerably alongside that of political Islam, is extensively engaged in philanthropy.[9] It is also involved in numerous media ventures and heads an important business confederation, TUSKON, which represents thousands of members. In such networks, as business people collaborate with NGOs 'devoted to just causes', they also develop good business relationships with each other. Thus, Islamic networks also serve economic interests while reinforcing cultural identity and nurturing a coherent ideological framework.

The current policy discourse, which has accompanied the institutional change that has been occurring in the field of social policy, is significantly shaped by this ideological framework. Government authorities, welfare administrators, representatives of charities and business associations all refer to Islamic notions of charity and underline the responsibility of Muslims to assist the poor. That the poor are entitled to a portion of the wealth created in society is also emphasised and, in this context, the Arabic word *hak* is often used. *Hak* could be

[8]   For detailed information about this association see: www.tgtv.org.

[9]   The network's most important philanthropic activities relate to education. It has hundreds of missionary schools around the world and also runs a nationwide charity called *Is there no one there?* (*Kimse yok mu?*), which developed from a programme on poverty and charity, broadcast by the Gülen-affiliated television channel *Samanyolu*.

translated as *right*, but its significance is qualitatively different from the concept of *right* as it is used in the debates on citizenship. *Hak* is rather a notion which is contingent upon the internalisation of moral values rooted in religion, with little differentiation between the duties of governmental and non-governmental actors. The Islamic discourse on the matter does not correspond to a secular set of legal provisions that define the content of rights, and the distribution of the responsibilities required for their exercise. Rather, people depend on the goodwill of others, whether the others are political authorities or representatives of philanthropic associations.[10] Redistributive justice is debated with little reference to the principles of taxation, but one occasionally encounters arguments that implicitly appeal to the principle of subsidiarity and suggest that, whenever possible, voluntary giving should replace government action, and engagement in philanthropic activity would often be more socially useful than the payment of taxes.[11]

The concept of equality is not absent in Islamic discourse on social policy-related problems and it echoes the parallel Christian notions of equality. Rich and poor are subjected to equal laws by God, and this should be sufficient to make the privileged concerned with the troubles of the unprivileged on a voluntary basis. The basic inequality between those who give and those who receive is not problematised; on the contrary, charitable deeds of good Muslims are guided by the Islamic proverb which says: 'the hand that gives is superior to the hand that receives'. However, redistributive policies that seek to eradicate talent- or effort-based inequalities, and deprive people of their rightfully-earned wealth, are clearly unacceptable. The following quotation from Fetullah Gülen reveals the priority attached to informal codes of behaviour informed by religious doctrine, as opposed to formal mechanisms that regulate socioeconomic relations:

> Taking from the rich to give to the poor does not bring about equality; on the contrary, it leads to the undermining of talent, loss of the desire of work, decline

[10] During field research conducted for a study on the relationship between employment and poverty in eight different cities, we noticed that the recipients of assistance from different sources were often not able to tell whether it came from public institutions or charities (Buğra & Keyder, 2008).

[11] See Ali Bulaç (2004; 2005).

of production and kills the laudable sentiments of love, respect, obedience and affection. Is it justice to take away the property of a human being who works in conformity with business ethics and thus acquires wealth in order to give it to a lazy individual who wastes his time in idle talk at the coffee house? … How would those who propose such justice deal with the inevitable hatred and animosity between those whose property is taken away by force to be given to the poor and the poor, who are thus turned into parasites? … Islam, with the fear of God guiding people, has adequately valued both capital and labour, has made wealth cease to be a fortune that keeps circulating in the hands of the rich and, generating the sources that feed the poor segments through the bridges built by alms, *zakat* and philanthropy, has assured the flow of wealth. (Gülen, 2010, p69)

Despite the emphasis on voluntary giving by devote Muslims, the presence of the government in the field of social assistance is now much stronger than before, and both the public funds spent on different forms of assistance and the welfare bureaucracy managing the system are much more important than in other periods of Republican history. Islamic philanthropy has not followed, or led to, the retreat of public welfare provision, but the latter has come to function in the same moral universe and is, in some ways, indistinguishable from the former. Islamic traditions of charity constitute a strong reference in fund raising, as well as in determining the 'deserving poor'.

Some people – such as members of the Roma community, who are regarded as lacking in morals by virtue of their lifestyle – could be excluded from the system even when they are in situations of extreme poverty for reasons obviously beyond their responsibility (Ekim Akkan et al, 2011). Women who do not have male relatives to take care of them are seen as *deserving poor par excellence*; but even their situation is assessed on *moral* grounds, rather than need.[12] This penetration of the logic of charity into the realm of public social welfare policy constitutes an obstacle to the development of a rights-based approach, which would enable the beneficiaries of assistance to participate in society as equal members. This, however, is not the only difficulty. Problems engendered by the welfare system can extend beyond the absence of social rights, to the very core of the political system.

Voluntary sector and political democracy in a polarised society

Two particular news items, which have been extensively covered by the Turkish media over the last few years, demonstrate how philanthropic activity can acquire political significance. The first news item concerns one of the members of TGTV, which has given much assistance to the poor: *Deniz Feneri* (the Lighthouse). This association developed out of a charity fundraising show on Channel 7, a TV channel close to the political parties situated within the Islamist movement. In 2008, a corruption scandal in Germany ended with prison sentences for several administrators of a charity and a television channel that had the same names.[13] The scandal involved the illegal use of donations made by Muslim residents in Germany to serve the interests of people in Turkish Islamic political circles, which were said to include some prominent AKP members.[14] A lawsuit was subsequently also filed in

---

[12] A research project undertaken for the Directorate of Social Cooperation and Solidarity by researchers affiliated with the Social Policy Forum is an interesting example (General Directorate of Social Assistance and Solidarity and Boğaziçi University, 2011). The project aimed to provide background information on the needs of poor women living alone, and, specifically, how regular income transfers are made available to them. The research project was conducted with women who were either divorced or widowed, but when the final report was published – with the objective of contributing to the formulation of a policy designed to assist women – only those who were widowed were included, the others were left out. The report was published in Turkish and in English by the Directorate, and the Turkish title makes it explicit that the programme only targeted women whose husbands had died: *Eşi vefat etmiş* kadınlar *için bir nakit sosyal yardım programı geliştirilmesine yönelik araştırma projesi final raporu* (Final report for the research project designed to develop a cash transfer programme targeting women whose husbands had died).

[13] See Ergin (2008).

[14] The relationship between Deniz Feneri and the AKP was covered in international media. For example, see Strauss (2008).

Turkey, at which point opposition parties claimed that the government had interfered in the judicial process, with the goal of protecting the defendants in the case.[15] In the course of the trial, the judges were replaced and the suspects were released. Then the prosecutors who filed the lawsuit against Deniz Feneri in Turkey were themselves sued on the grounds that they had abused their authority, but they were subsequently acquitted.[16]

The second development widely covered in the media tended to justify the concern about the role Islamic charity played in gaining electoral support for the AKP. Before the municipal elections held in 2009, in-kind assistance distributed to the poor had dramatically increased and changed to such an extent that the government was accused of trying to bribe voters. When in the Eastern town of Tunceli – where candidates from right-wing parties historically had little chance in elections – the local welfare administrators began to distribute consumer durables as social assistance to the poor, the Board supervising the electoral process intervened to stop the practice. Nevertheless, the decision of the Board was *not* heeded by the Provincial Governor, appointed by the government, and he was supported by the Prime Minister who declared, now famously, 'Charity is part of our culture'.

Notwithstanding these examples, which are significant in their implications for both social and political rights in the country, philanthropic activity in Turkey is not limited to Islamic networks. There are also associations of a secular character that sometimes, but not always, adopt a critical position against the social policy orientation of the AKP government. When the NGOs that are not in good terms with government authorities, they can risk serious marginalisation or even persecution, as in the case of the Association for the Protection of Secular Life (Çağdaş *Yaşamı Destekleme Derneği*: ÇYDD), which was established by Türkan Saylan, a professor of medicine, highly respected for the contribution she made to the eradication of leprosy in Turkey. ÇYDD was formed as a response to the rise of political Islam and has been supported by a large number of people, women in particular, who are concerned about the increase in religious conservatism and its implications for women's rights. It has been very active in the Kurdish region, where gender inequality is particularly severe, and has provided a large number of scholarships to girls enabling them to become economically independent. It is a rival, particularly, to the Gülen community, which is also active in the field of education, albeit

---

[15]   See Karapınar (2012).

[16]   See Türkaslan (2012).

with a different attitude to the emancipation of women. It is, therefore, not totally surprising that the Gülen-affiliated daily *Zaman* launched a particularly ferocious campaign against ÇYDD[17] and its founder, who was subsequently harassed by police who raided her house to investigate the association's *allegedly* subversive activities, at a time when she was terminally ill. After Saylan's death in May 2009, ÇYDD continued to face recurrent inspections and court trials for financial corruption or for providing support to Kurdish insurgents, despite which it managed to continue to raise funds and conduct its activities on a national scale, although recently one of its funding sources has been limited.

An important source of revenue for philanthropic associations in Turkey is the donations families and friends make during the funeral ceremony held at mosque courtyards. These donations were also important for the ÇYDD until religious authorities prevented the association from collecting donations on mosque premises. Although the Directorate of Religious Affairs denied that it had given an order to this effect, it did not make a statement *against* the ban, and left it to the discretion of those responsible for the management of individual mosques.[18]

Another example of such hostility faced by philanthropic associations that do not support the political orientation followed by the AKP government concerns Sarmaşık, which has been active in welfare and social service provision in the Kurdish city of Diyarbakır. In this city – where there is rampant poverty and related social problems – Sarmaşık has been closely cooperating with the municipal government ruled by the Peace and Democracy Party, which represents a large percentage of the Kurdish population. It has, therefore, been a rival to both the local Solidarity Foundation and the Islamic charities. In 2012, the association faced an investigation led by the governorship of Diyarbakır, which ended without any financial irregularities being discovered. However, a lawsuit was subsequently filed, enabling the investigation of an alleged relationship between the association and the illegal Kurdish separatist movement. As the trial continued, the collaboration

---

[17]   The accusations ranged from engagement in missionary activities to giving scholarships to people affiliated with Kurdish separatist movement PKK. See İşte ÇYDD›nin burs verdiği PKK'lı öğrencilerin listesi (Here is the list of the students affiliated with the PKK), *Zaman*, 18 April 2009; ÇYDD, bölücü hareketleri güçlendiriyor (ÇYD empowers the separist movements), *Zaman*, 3 August 2006; Türkan Saylan'a ağır ithamlar (Serious accusations against Türkan Saylan), *Zaman*, 16 April 2009.

[18]   On this see, for example, Bayer (2013).

between Sarmaşık and the municipal government was contested and the association was ordered to return funding it had received from the municipality for the provision of social services.[19] In the current context of welfare governance in Turkey, where partnerships between NGOs and government are commonplace, this Sarmaşık experience (which in effect bankrupted the association) prompted disturbing questions concerning how political interest could affect relations between the government and the voluntary sector.

The cases of Sarmaşık and ÇYDD also show that the voluntary sector does not constitute a homogenous arena but rather consists of actors with competing objectives and strategies, which are pursued in collaboration with or against government policy. In a polarised environment, this type of *competition* can easily turn into hostile rivalry, which the government may not view with neutrality.

Conclusion

In this chapter, I have discussed the role of philanthropy in social policy change by revisiting 19th- and 20th-century debates on the voluntary sector, and with reference to the changing place of benevolence in the contemporary system of social protection in Turkey. On the basis of this discussion, it is possible to make the following observations:

1. Rather than having a zero–sum relationship with the state redistributive process, philanthropy articulates with the public welfare policy in changing and society-specific ways.
2. Attitudes towards the voluntary sector are defined by the prevailing moral perspectives on social solidarity and ideas of legitimate and illegitimate forms of inequality. At the same time, philanthropic action contributes to the formation of a moral framework for the social policy debate. Religion is an important dimension of this interface between the social policy debate and voluntary sector activity.
3. The developments in Turkey support Marshall's point about the complementarity of civil, political and social rights. They not only show how charity can infiltrate formal social policy processes, but also draw attention to political outcomes that could result from this infiltration.
4. The case of Turkey contributes to the debate on the voluntary sector by suggesting that it is not appropriate to consider philanthropy as

[19] See Yavuz and Sunar (2012)

constituting an undifferentiated domain of activity, reflecting similar moral views, and resulting in a uniform impact on social relations and political processes. The balance of power between competing associations, and the nature of the sector's impact on a given society, is not independent of the prevailing dynamics of political relations.

References

Bayer, Y, 2013, *Fenere yol ver,* ÇYDD'yi *kuşat* (Let the Lighthouse pass, keep the ÇYDD under siege), *Hürriyet,* 17 January, www.hurriyet. com.tr/yazarlar/22379534.asp

Beveridge, W, 1948, *Voluntary action: a report on methods of social advance,* London: Allen and Unwin

Bode, I, 2006, Disorganized welfare mixes, *Journal of European Social Policy,* 16, 4, 346–59

Brunkhorst, H, 2005, *Solidarity: from civic friendship to a global legal community,* Cambridge: MIT Press

Buğra, A, 2007, Poverty and citizenship: an overview of the social policy environment in republican Turkey, *International Journal of Middle East Studies,* 39, 1, 33–52

Buğra, A and Candaş, A, 2011, Change and continuity under an eclectic social security regime: the case of Turkey, *Middle Eastern Studies,* 47, 3, 515–28

Buğra, A and Keyder, Ç, 2008, *Employment structure of the poorest sections of the urban population and subsistence methods,* www.spf.boun.edu.tr/ index.php/tr/spf-projeleri

Bulaç, A, 2004, *Kayıt dışının olumlu sonuçları* (Positive outcomes of informality), *Zaman,* 17 March, www.zaman.com.tr/ali-bulac/-kayit-disi-nin-olumlu-sonuclari_27014.html

Bulaç, A, 2005, *Sivil toplum* üzerine (On civil society), *Zaman,* 20 August, www.zaman.com.tr/ali-bulac/sivil-toplum-uzerine_203415. html

Casanova, J, 1994, *Public religions in the modern world,* Chicago: University of Chicago Press

Casanova, J, 2008, Public religion revisited, in de Vries, H, ed, *Religion beyond the Concept,* NY: Fordham University Press, pp101–19

Dierckx, D, Vranken, J and Kerstens, W (eds) 2009, *Faith–based organizations and social exclusion in European cities: national context reports,* Anwerp: University of Antwerp

Ekim Akkan, B, Deniz, and Ertan, M, 2011, *Poverty and social exclusion of Roma in Turkey,* Istanbul: Edirne Roma Association (EDROM), Bogazici University Social Policy Forum and Anadolu Kultur

Ergin, İ., 2008, *Deniz Feneri'nin Başkanı Gözaltında* (The director of the Lighthouse under arrest), *Milliyet*, 21 August, www.milliyet.com.tr/2007/08/21/guncel/gun08.html

Esping-Andersen, G, 1990, *Three worlds of welfare capitalism,* London: Polity Press

Esping-Andersen, G, 1999, *Social foundations of post-industrial societies,* Oxford: Oxford University Press

General Directorate of Social Assistance and Solidarity and Boğaziçi University, 2011, *Research project for the development of a cash transfer program for widowed women,* General Directorate of Social Assistance and Solidarity and Boğaziçi University

Göçmen, İ, 2011, The politics of religiously motivated welfare provision, unpublished PhD thesis, Cologne: Max Planck Institute for the Study of Societies, www.kups.ub.uni-koeln.de/4194/

Göçmen, İ, 2013, The role of faith-based organizations in social welfare systems: a comparison of France, Germany, Sweden and the United Kingdom, *Nonprofit and Voluntary Sector Quarterly*, 42, 3, 495–516

Göçmen, İ, 2014, Religion, politics and social assistance in Turkey: the rise of religiously motivated associations, *Journal of European Social Policy* 24, 1 92–103

Gülen, F, 2010, İnancın *Gölgesinde*, Istanbul: Nil Yayınları.

Habermas, J, 2006, Religion in the Public Sphere, *European Journal of Philosophy*, 14, 1, 1–25

Himmelfarb, G, 1991, *Poverty and compassion: the moral imagination of the late Victorians,* New York: Vintage Books

Himmelfarb, G, 1997, *Introduction to Tocqueville, A. de, Memoir on Pauperism*, Chicago: Ivan R Dee

Jenkins, S, 2006, The welfare state is waning. Bring on the philanthropists, *The Guardian*, 28 June, www.theguardian.com/commentisfree/2006/jun/28/comment.policy

Jessop, B, 1999, Changing governance of welfare: recent trends in its primary functions, scale, and modes of co-ordination, *Social Policy and Administration*, 33, 4, 348–69

Johns Hopkins University Center for Civil Society Studies, 2004, *Comparative data tables,* www.ccss.jhu.edu/publications-findings?did=308

Karapınar, T., 2012, *Deniz Feneri'nde Örgüt Bulunamadı* (No criminal organization found in the Lighthouse case), *Milliyet*, 10 April, www.milliyet.com.tr/deniz-feneri-nde-orgut-bulunamadi/gundem/gundemdetay/10.04.2012/1526134/default.htm

Levine, D H, 1986, Religion and politics in comparative and historical perspective, *Comparative Politics*, 19, 1, 95–122

Marshall, T H, 1964a, Citizenship and social class, in *Class, Citizenship and Social Development, Essays by T H Marshall*, New York: Doubleday and Company

Marshall, T H, 1964b, Voluntary Action, in *Class, Citizenship and Social Development, Essays by T.H. Marshall*, New York: Doubleday and Company

OECD, 2003, *The non-profit sector in a changing economy*, Paris: OECD Publication Services

OECD, 2013, *OECD social expenditure statistics: government social spending*, www.oecd-ilibrary.org/social-issues-migration-health/government-social-spending_20743904-table1

Parla, T and Davison, A, 2008, Secularism and laicism in Turkey', in Jakobsen, J R and Pellegrini, A, eds, *Secularisms*, Durham: Duke University Press, pp58–75

Polanyi, K, 1944, *The great transformation*, Boston: Beacon Press

Strauss, D., 2008, Turkey's AKP Tarnished by Graft Case, *Financial Times*, 2 October, www.ft.com/intl/cms/s/0/06656c8e-901b-11dd-9890-0000779fd18c.html#axzz3S5QDt42l

Titmuss, R M, 1970, Gift relationship: from human blood to social policy, New York: Pantheon Books

Tocqueville, A de, 1997 *Memoir on pauperism*, Chicago: Ivan R. Dee

Türkaslan, N., 2012, *Deniz Feneri Savcıları Beraat Etti* (Prosecutors of the Lighthouse case acquitted), *Milliyet*, 17 November, www.radikal.com.tr/turkiye/deniz_feneri_savcilari_beraat_etti-1108188

Turkish Parliament, 1986, *Proposed law on the encouragement of social cooperation and solidarity, and the report of the commission on plan and budget*, n454, 16.5.1986

TÜSEV, 2011, *Civil society in Turkey: the civil society index project between nations* Türkiye Ülke Raporu, İstanbul: TÜSEV

Wuthnow, R, 1994, *Producing the sacred: an essay on public religion*, Chicago: University of Illinois Press

Yavuz, R. and Sunar, S., 2012, *Sarmaşık Derneğine Darbe* (Sarmaşık association under attack), *Radikal*, 29 August, www.radikal.com.tr/turkiye/sarmasik_dernegine_darbe-1098555

EIGHT

Charity, philanthropy and development in Colombo, Sri Lanka[1]

Filippo Osella, Roderick Stirrat and Tom Widger

Introduction

Anthropologists take an ethnographic approach to understanding everyday experience, including practices of giving and receiving. There is an established anthropological tradition of interest in 'the gift' and how this relates to a wider understanding of the politics of exchange, both material and intangible. 'Charity' or 'philanthropy' can be viewed, in time-honoured Maussian tradition, as particular modalities of the gift, and in this chapter we aim to explore how anthropological understandings of the everyday politics of exchange can help us comprehend philanthropic activities, and, at the same time, how an analysis of philanthropy and charity can illuminate an anthropological understanding of exchange.

There is increasing interest in the role that philanthropy plays in the process of development, especially given the pressures on international donors and the changing architecture of international aid. The apparent rolling back of the state and rolling out of the market – engendered by global structural adjustments associated with the neoliberal consensus of the last 30 years – have projected charity and philanthropy as a viable alternative to state provisions in the Global South as well as in the North. While much research has been concerned with the activities of major philanthropic or charitable institutions, relatively little has been written about what might be called 'indigenous' charity: the activities and impact of charities and philanthropic individuals outside

1   This chapter is based on an ESRC/DfID-funded research project (ref. no. ES/I033890/1) concerned with charity, philanthropy and development in Colombo, Sri Lanka. This two-year project involved researchers from the Department of Anthropology at Sussex University and from the Centre for Poverty Analysis in Colombo.

the western world (see, for example, Copeman, 2009; Latief, 2010; Bornstein, 2012; Atia, 2013).

This chapter has three broad objectives: first, to map the 'philanthroscape' of Colombo; second, to understand how this 'philanthroscape' has changed in the postcolonial period; and third, to consider the developmental nature of philanthropic/charitable activity with regard to how it can support both civil society and the state to set or achieve their development agenda.

We see Sri Lanka as a suitable venue for exploring contemporary forms of giving, and the relationships between givers and receivers, for a number of reasons. According to the World Giving Index, the population of Sri Lanka is the eighth most generous in the world with regards to charitable giving, and the most generous nation in the Global South (Charities Aid Foundation, 2010). The country experienced a huge influx of international philanthropy after the 2004 tsunami, whil more recently, and somewhat controversially, global charities have contributed to the rehabilitation process following the end of the civil war. While these events have changed the texture of local forms of giving, Sri Lanka has long been exposed to international charitable efforts in the form of developmental assistance, in part as a legacy of the colonial period. At the same time, globalisation and economic liberalisation have seen the emergence of a dynamic business and manufacturing sector that is beginning to engage with corporate social responsibility projects, in addition to older interests in corporate philanthropy stretching back also to the colonial period. Finally, there is a large Sri Lankan diaspora – in Europe, North America and the Gulf countries of the Middle East, for instance – which supports charitable activities at 'home'.

Colombo is especially suited to this study because of its heterogeneous population. According to the 2012 census, the population of the Colombo Divisional Secretariat area is 40.7% Muslim, 33.4% Tamil and 25% Sinhala. This translates into a religious composition of 42% Islam; 22.3% Hindu, 19.1% Buddhist and 16.5% Christian.[2] Extensive comparative literature from Europe and North America indicates that religion is a major factor in determining the scale, meaning and style of charitable activities. The presence of four global religions in one urban

[2]   This is an almost complete reversal of the wider Colombo District and national demographic where Sinhala are the majority ethnic group and Tamil and Muslim are the minority, and Buddhism is the majority religion and Islam, Hinduism and Christianity are minority religions. Thus, for many people in Sri Lanka, Colombo is regarded as a Muslim city.

milieu provides a manageable context within which to understand the relationship between religious identities and charity, the circulation of practices between religious groups and the relationship between religious and non-religious organisations. The range of income and wealth differentials in Colombo allows us also to investigate the link between wealth and charity; comparative evidence demonstrates that, as a proportion of their income, the poor tend to give as much as the rich. Finally, contemporary Colombo has a mix of charitable organisations, some dating back to the colonial period and still focused on the philanthropic values of that era, particularly educational and health charities. At the same time, there are newer institutions concerned with various forms of community-based development interventions that have developed in post-Independence Sri Lanka and display novel approaches to philanthropy and charity. The interplay between the local and the global is particularly evident in Colombo, where both national and international charitable organisations are headquartered (such as CARE, Plan, Oxfam, Red Cross, World Vision and South Asia Partnership).

This chapter considers two surveys of the Colombo philanthroscape: household gifting practices and gifting by private and public sector organisations. A small survey was also conducted of charities in order to gauge the extent to which funds are collected from within Sri Lanka rather than from foreign donors. The household survey was conducted using a cluster sampling method and achieved a representative breakdown by ethnicity and religion: two of our key variables. In total, 747 households were interviewed. The organisational surveys were conducted using a snowball technique, and included 261 businesses, 39 public sector entities and 54 charities. Qualitative data was collected through formal and semi-formal interviews of donors and recipients of charity across communities defined by different ethnic/religious affiliation, as well as a number of case studies of specific charitable/ philanthropic interventions and projects.

The politics of philanthropy in Sri Lanka

Literature on charity in Sri Lanka is sparse, but there have been two surveys (Dutta, 2000; APPC, 2007) and a study of volunteering (IPID, 2001). However, those studies were conducted using small samples, and theoretical issues were not addressed. There is also a considerable literature on the role of NGOs in Sri Lanka (see, for example, Woost, 1997; Goodhand,1999; Stirrat, 2006), but this generally focuses on issues of efficacy rather than on the charitable and philanthropic aspects of those organisations. More useful perhaps is the historical literature, which relates the changing patterns of charity to politico–economic change (Seneviratne, 1999; Jayawardena, 2000). This indicates the emergence in the late 19th and early 20th centuries of novel forms of charity intervention, mostly based in Colombo and supported by an emerging local bourgeoisie of wealthy traders, planters and liquor contractors. As in the rest of colonial South Asia, modern philanthropy did not replace existing practices of religious giving, but by the early 20th century the two began to coexist. For example, many rich Muslim traders – who made substantial donations to enable the construction in 1892 of the first modern Muslim College in Colombo: Zahira College – also set up *awqaf* (religious trusts), which ran mosques and madrasas and supported the performance of religious rituals. After independence, properties continued to be endowed as religious trusts, with the purpose of supporting religious activities but also with the aim of securing a steady income to the donors' descendants and, in the case of wealthy planters and landowners, to maintain the allegiance of rural clients and labourers.

In contemporary Colombo, most people of all religious groups and classes (90% of the respondents to our survey) were engaged in charitable acts. Most donations of cash and in kind – primarily food – were small but regular, taking the form of gifts to beggars and poor neighbours and relatives. Larger but more irregular donations were also given to religious causes – temples, churches, and mosques – or to institutions catering for the poor and needy; for example, orphanages, elders' homes and the national cancer hospital. Levels of volunteerism are lower (50% of participants to the survey), but nevertheless represented a high level of participation in charitable activities. Mention should also be made of membership of charitable societies, through which, for example, volunteers assist in management of churches, temples and mosques, or assist in the distribution of material assistance provided by these institutions. In addition, people volunteer for organisations such as the Sri Lankan Red Cross, the Rotary, and local groups such as Sarvodaya and Lankaseva.

Although a general commitment to humanity and a desire to help others motivates donors, our data indicates that the primary purpose underlying much charitable activity is religiously defined. Thus, for Buddhists, *daane* (the giving of alms to monks) is connected to the pan-South Asian practice of religious gifting, and reflects what it means to be a 'good' Buddhist. Both rich and poor support monks and monastic institutions. But for some Buddhists the concept of *daane* has been extended to other forms of giving; for example, of food to the poor, grants to poor children for their education and food to orphanages and elders' homes, especially to commemorate death anniversaries and birthdays. Similarly, charity is seen as a an important activity by all Christian religious groups both in terms of gifts to support church organisations and donations of food, material assistance and educational help for the poor. For Muslims of various sectarian or organisational affiliations, charity is also a central aspect of religious orthopraxy. Whilst the annual giving of *zakat* is an obligation for those who hold wealth or assets above a certain amount, *sadaqa* is a form of meritorious giving practised by every Muslim. Christians, Muslims and Buddhists talk in terms of the religious 'merit' which accrues in the present or the afterlife from charitable acts. The conceptualisation and the perceived results of this 'economy of merits' are different from one tradition to another, but a similarity is that this kind of charitable giving seems to be more about the giver than the recipient.

For all religious traditions, the act of giving and the intention of the giver is most important, while the scale of the donation might be less significant. *Sadaqa*, for instance, can entail something as substantial as donation of money to build a hospital, or as insignificant as removing a stone from a footpath. In theory, what matters are the intentions of those who perform the action. But of course, in practice size does matter, and large donors use their charity as a means of making statements about their status – although this is perhaps less common today than in the past, when the colonial administration provided an avenue for the public recognition of donors' munificence by conferring honours and titles and large public donations were the ground for the assertion of political and religious leadership within ethnic/religious communities. In the past, rich Catholic benefactors, for example, were keen that their names appear on the church buildings, orphanages and schools they supported. However, today charity appears to be less ostentatious. Similarly there is an ongoing debate that reflects the growing concern of Muslims about the need for anonymous giving. Many respondents to our survey argued that 'the right hand should not know what the left does'.[3] Some donations are more public than others; anyway, anonymity is difficult because giving remains a highly

---

[3] Although most respondents explained this by citing from the New Testament: 'the left hand does not know what the right hand is doing' (Matthew 6:3), they referred to the following passage from the Qur'an: 'If you give alms openly, it is well, and if you hide it and give it to the poor, it is better for you; and this will do away with some of your evil deeds; and Allah is aware of what you do" (Al-Qur'an 2:271).

socially-embedded activity. People continue to personally give *zakat* and *sadaqa* to those with whom they have long-term relationships, and the work of foundations or projects of corporate social responsibility is strongly connected to the identification of the givers. This also relates to the question of whether charity should be a matter of individual choice or whether it should be organised: another issue of debate in contemporary Colombo.

Much charity in Colombo is informal, a matter of individual giving directly to the poor who, for example, congregate around shrines, temples, churches and mosques. Gifts of money or food to poor people begging on the doorstep or to poor relations are the most frequent forms of charity. However, religious organisations have made attempts to manage the distribution of charity in order to ensure that it goes to 'deserving causes' rather than being given as a whim by individual donors motivated by self-interest or status considerations. Efforts to manage charitable actions are most evident in the Catholic community: unsurprisingly, given the hierarchical organisation of the Church. Individuals are discouraged from giving to the poor outside churches and, instead, encouraged to channel their charity through parish-based organisations run by members of the laity. There are also profession-based organisations, for example associations of Catholic lawyers and Catholic teachers, which attempt to manage the charitable process. Muslims are equally concerned about relationships between individuals and giving. While some small Muslim communities – namely the Bohras and Memons – have developed a tradition of pooling charitable donations for projects to help community members, *zakat* committees have also begun to spring up amongst the mainstream Sunni majority. These are often informal groups of people connected through friendship, university education, profession or business who collect *zakat* and *sadaqa* for specific purposes; for example, the provision of educational scholarships, basic housing and sanitation and the support of (rural) employment schemes. The tsunami emergency was a catalyst for the emergence of more organised forms of charitable giving; but also evident is the influence of various strands of Islamic reformism whose orientation is more engaged and *systematic* forms of charity, given in the name of piety, community strengthening, and development.

Supporters of various reformist organisations argued that 'a poor Muslim cannot be a poor Muslim' and were hopeful that, with more coordination and planning, *zakat* and *sadaqa* would lift all Sri Lankan Muslims out of poverty. More generally, for reformist Muslims the intended outcome of organised forms of charity is eliciting specific moral dispositions of both givers and receivers to ensure that charitable activity works towards reinforcing and supporting community and religious life.

In contrast to the ordering of Catholic and Muslim charity is Buddhist and Hindu philanthropy. Large charitable organisations exist, for example the All Ceylon Buddhist Congress and the All Ceylon Hindu Congress – and their respective Young Men's and Young Women's Associations – which use funds collected locally for charitable endeavours, principally running orphanages and elders' homes, scholarship programmes and projects designed to improve the quality of life in their communities. These are modelled on Christian organisations and came into existence in the late 19th century in direct response to the perceived threat of Christian proselytisation that took place on the back of colonial expansion (a threat which continues to motivate some Buddhist charitable giving today). The majority of Buddhist charities in Colombo are dependent on overseas, often non-Buddhist, donors. For example, the Foundation of Goodness raises funds principally from the international cricketing fraternity, while until recently Sarvodaya's largest donors were Jewish synagogues in the US and the UK. Overseas Buddhist organisations have also sponsored temple-based foundations, such as the Mahabodi Society, which runs small community development and education projects, and post-tsunami organisations, like SUCCESS and Red Lotus (the latter established as a Buddhist response to Red Cross and Red Crescent). It is increasingly clear that the Sinhala Buddhist diaspora are channelling funds through local 'social service' organisations in order to promote a nationalist agenda. Buddhist giving tends not to be framed by institutional framework, but is instead directed by the practice of *daane*. As a result, there is debate about whether temples are more deserving than orphanages or elders' homes, or an ad hoc desire to help the poor, sick, and needy.

Currently charitable giving is undergoing a transformation. The increased influence of small numbers of vociferous extremist Sinhala-Buddhist organisations has made Christian and Muslim minorities sensitive to criticism of their economic success and their particularistic orientation. As we have seen, much charitable activity in Colombo takes place within the ambit of individual religious traditions, enabling Catholics to benefit from Catholic donors, Buddhists from Buddhist donors, Muslims from Muslim donors, and so on. This in-group charitable orientation is most obvious when, as the result of donation, religious buildings are constructed. But it is also clear that *individual* acts of charity tend to link givers and recipients within the same community. This has led to accusations that certain groups (most notably Christians

143

and Muslims) have gained unfair advantage over the Buddhist majority by virtue of their ability to mobilise economic resources for the benefit of their communities as a whole through charity and philanthropy.

There is a continuing tension between particularistic and universalistic approaches to charity and a continual questioning as to whether charity should be aimed at 'our own' or a broader humanitarian constituency. The extent to which broader humanitarian goals are adopted often appears to depend on the degree to which local organisations are dependent on, or linked to, external agencies and their particular practices and agendas.

With regard to the Christian groups, the tendency to focus on humanity – or 'the poor', undifferentiated by religious affiliation – is perhaps most evident amongst long established Protestant (not Evangelical) groups. This, in part, can be seen as a reaction to the way western missionaries used charity as a means for encouraging conversion. But it is also a reaction to the strong links between Sri Lankan Protestant organisations and their secular Western partners. Similarly although Caritas, the global Catholic development charity, is primarily funded by organisations close to the Catholic Church, it is also moving towards a less particularistic focus, in part because of its reliance on funds from external agencies (both religious and secular) and its need to present itself as 'Sri Lankan' rather than narrowly Catholic. The situation is more complex amongst Muslims in that *zakat* must be given by Muslims to Muslims, and there is donor concern about the 'real' identity of doorstep beggars. Rumours are rife that there are professional beggars trying to pass themselves off as Muslims in order to receive *zakat* during *ramzan*. The same restrictions do not apply for *sadaqa*, and we have found a number of foundations associated to prominent Muslim businessmen which extend their charitable activities to anyone in need, regardless of religious or ethnic affiliation.[4] In practice, though, charity follows specific geographical trajectories, whereby donations in kind or cash tend to move from Colombo to the donors' natal or ancestral villages, reproducing particularism and long-term patronage relationships.

There is resistance to discourses seeking to promote more 'modern' forms of charity. First there is an obvious class dimension to giving, evidenced by middle-class concern about beggars, who are seen as a

---

[4]   For example, providing shelter and education to tsunami orphans, running medical camps for war refugees, and (in one case) channelling *sadaqa* through a corporate social responsibility (CSR) programme operating medical clinics across Colombo.

nuisance, bothering 'respectable' households with incessant demands and giving communities a bad name. Survey respondents argued that giving to beggars increases their dependency and does not foster long-term solutions to poverty. The view was that the poor should be 'helped to help themselves' through *systematic* intervention and support aimed at changing cultural orientation as much as improving economic conditions. This neoliberal penchant for *fostering* an entrepreneurial spirit amongst the urban and rural poor has particular purchase amongst young professionals and educated businessmen, although it finds little favour amongst bazaar traders and shopkeepers, for whom giving to beggars (often on a daily basis) is seen as means to further one's luck and success in business. While our respondents agreed that coordinated and organised charity is more effective, many felt a commitment to supporting individuals or families with whom they have long-term personal relations. The boundary between charitable giving and patronage is porous, and, as one Muslim bazaar trader put it, "I just don't like someone else giving away my money!"

Finally, 'what to give' remains an unresolved question, especially for Muslims. For some Muslims the main focus is the act of giving itself: either the fulfilment of a religious obligation (*zakat*) or a merit-filled pious act (*sadaqa*), which concerns only the giver. Cash, in this case, is deemed to be the most appropriate form of donation. For others, however, givers should be concerned with the transformation of the lives of those who receive charity, and, thus, donations should address specific needs; for example, providing appropriate sanitation or building low-cost housing. In practice, however, donors are seldom fixed on one form of giving alone, preferring instead to spread their donations. The most common practice is to continue responding to demands from individuals – not only beggars, but also those unable to meet the expense of medical emergencies, life-cycle rituals, education and utilities bills – and to support religious institutions, whilst giving a proportion of one's donations to various religious and non-religious charitable organisations.

Charity and other forms of giving

We have argued that the motive for giving is most frequently presented in terms of piety: part of being a good Catholic, Buddhist or Muslim. The act of giving is not simply a reflection of specific moral and religious concerns, but also helps constitute people as ethical subjects. More generally, though, motivations are subtle, multiple and often overlapping. There is evidence that, in the past, the big philanthropic donors – who established schools, hospitals and orphanages and gave substantial amounts of money to religious institutions – were partially engaged in a process of 'purification of their wealth', with an eye on acquiring merits in this life and the afterlife. Contemporary successful entrepreneurs couch their charity in terms of Corporate Social Responsibilty and see no great divide between their productive activities and those concerned with redistribution of wealth; both are governed by a common morality, or at least *linked moralities* (see later). Current debates concerning the anonymity of charity notwithstanding, we should *not* assume that altruism and self-interested instrumentality are necessarily at odds. Charitable giving is often conceived as producing immediate material benefits as much as spiritual rewards.

However, ideas of religious merit might articulate with other considerations when it comes to charitable giving. Charity is often couched in kinship obligation – the aim being to help one's poor or less fortunate relations, and by extension also one's clients and employees – or in terms of an inchoate feeling that the poor should be assisted. There are also issues of identity and community formation at stake. Membership of charitable organisations offers access to social networks and the various social benefits generated by these networks. Thus in the Catholic world, participation in young people's groups (for example, for young lawyers and doctors) creates the opportunity to meet others outside the individual's immediate circle. Many formal or informal charitable organisations have grown up around these professional friendships, and of course Rotarian Clubs and Lions Clubs are as much about networking and friendship as they are about assisting the poor and needy. And, as mentioned earlier, charitable giving supports projects of community building and strengthening. In this sense what charitable actions encourage are the creation of shared identities and shared values, which are only partly the result of the charitable acts themselves.

Our research also found that the motivations and intentions of those who make charitable donations might not be shared by those who receive them. For some, being a recipient is in effect a means to securing a livelihood, precarious as it might be. Time and again the same beggars are found outside the major shrines, churches, temples and mosques, or entering shops on the same day each week. In some areas there are organisations that ensure some equity of access to the best pitches. Without doubt, the best charity as far as the recipients are concerned is that which is given without conditions, and, of course, money is preferred over donations in kind. What is resented most are attempts by the giver to impose particular moral rules as a condition of the donation. Some distinction has to be made between the recipients of small-time charity and those who receive greater largesse. For instance, those who receive educational assistance or housing appear to be more positive about the moral demands of the donors than are wayside beggars or those who receive specific handouts during the ceremonies of the various religious groups. Moreover, donations that the givers categorise as acts of charity may be seen by the recipients as the fulfilment of obligations towards clients or kin that the latter have the prerogative to expect and demand. Whether the giver is moved by humanitarian concerns, religious piety, economic self-interest, political calculation or a combination of these makes little difference to recipients, who have to rely on the help of others to make ends meet and to deal with unpredictable emergencies.

So far we have stressed the religious and relational orientations of charity in Colombo, reflecting the dominant discourse in the field. Yet it has to be remembered that there is also a long history of a more 'secular' attitude towards charity. This goes back to the 19th-century establishment of friendly societies, organisations orientated towards assisting 'fallen women', the Eye Donation Society and international organisations such as the Red Cross. More recently there has been a growth in the number of 'trusts', often established by politicians who claim to support the poor and the marginal but also use them to reward their political followers. Grants to students or donations to support a local school or hospital might secure the loyalty of potential voters in a particular locality. Once more, the boundary is blurred between charity as a humanitarian activity and using charitable acts as an instrumental means of creating loyalties, dependencies and patronage.

Self-interest and benevolence are even more intricately intertwined in the field of corporate social responsibility, evidenced – amongst other ways – by the interesting interaction between religious ideals and the logic of contemporary 'philanthrocapitalism (for a critique of philanthrocapitalism, see Chapter 2 by Edwards). Formal Coproate Social Resposibility (CSR) projects are run by large Sri Lankan and Colombo-based international companies such as HSBC, Unilever, Ceylon Tobacco (owned by British American Tobacco (BAT)) and Dialog. International companies design local programmes under the auspices of parent company global sustainability aims, but at times, when applied in the local Sri Lankan context, the objective is not entirely clear. For example, Unilever – which is globally committed to improving personal hygiene – promotes hand washing and tooth brushing, and Ceylon Tobacco, in line with BAT's global efforts, focuses on agrarian development: helping to train farmers in agricultural and business skills. While the orientation, organisation and rhetoric of these companies are reflective of global discourses on CSR and sustainability, in practice corporate giving often does not move beyond a trite 'schoolbooks and bicycles' approach. Although Sri Lankan companies do also stress strategic value and sustainability, they use less of the globalised language of CSR, preferring instead a more emotive language of care for the wellbeing of fellow Sri Lankans. These initiatives are much more engaged in education and health, and in some cases they are closely connected to the government, with interventions designed to rehabilitate post-conflict areas.

An especially important feature of Sri Lankan private sector philanthropy is the political context within which it operates. In the post-conflict environment,[5] an increasingly combative Sinhala Buddhist nationalism (Ali, 2014) and the growth of anti-Muslim sentiment has made doing business in Colombo potentially dangerous, especially for the Muslims who own some of Sri Lanka's largest companies. It seems that private companies and public limited companies (PLCs) are responding to this by engaging in different forms of philanthrocapitalism through processes that might be better understood as 'philanthronationalism'. Our study identified four kinds of approaches to CSR projects:

1. 'Collaborative': where projects are conducted in direct partnership with government agencies, including the Army, and seek to engender specific nationalist functions and goals.
2. 'Reactive': where projects are launched with the intention of relieving specific nationalist threats.
3. 'Assimilative': where projects display overtly nationalist commitments in the face of anti-nationalist/anti-patriotic suspicion, and so attempt to appease nationalist fears.
4. 'Passive': where projects pay lip service to nationalist sentiments, with no explicit nationalist objectives.

[5]   The war between Tamil separatists and the Sri Lankan state is generally considered to have begun around 1983 and finally ended with the defeat of the separatist LTTE in 2009. The conflict led to widespread destruction of property and infrastructure plus large-scale issues concerning a displaced population and resettlement issues. For a discussion of the unfolding of the conflict see, for example Spencer, 1990; Woost and Winslow, 2004; Thiranagama, 2011). These issues are presently being addressed by various state and non-state parties, although there is widespread disagreement as to the effectiveness and motivations underlying elements of the relief effort.

It is in the charitable activities of major Sri Lankan companies and PLCs that the global language and tools of CSR are more fully hybridised and tailored to accommodate local concepts and practices of charity and philanthropy. LankaComm, for instance, is a group of companies that, amongst other activities, produces and imports herbal pharmaceuticals and medical products to the island. Its CSR programme, CommClinic, focuses on the provision of free outpatient healthcare and cheap medicines on a social enterprise model in five Colombo slums. The aim is to make health charity sustainable: too often charities run health camps but do not provide any follow up. To date, CommClinic has treated more than 50,000 patients. The success of the project lies in its apparent ability to appeal to poorer patients' desires to experience what they see as the convenience and customer-orientated characteristic of the private sector at an affordable price. The LankaComm case also underscores the complex layering of indigenous CSR programmes. Thus the LankaComm chair explains that the project helps him to discharge his desire – as a Muslim – to give *sadaqa* and so gain religious merits. For the CSR team the project fits the wider philanthrocapitalist 'win-win' model of social enterprise, which has produced a remarkably successful programme worthy of global advertisement. For the paid clinic staff, the project is viewed as a social service for the poor, and one that is more socially and morally engaged than regular healthcare. For patients, the clinics are variously understood as a way of getting healthcare akin to that provided by private facilities or, alternatively, as a second choice to private facilities. However, it was clear that for those living under the poverty line the only option was still the wholly free government service, as even CommClinic's subsidised medicines were too expensive.

Conclusions

Historical literature on charity indicates that its nature changes over time. Charity in 16th-century Europe is very different from philanthropy in the 19th or 20th centuries, as discussed by Cunningham in Chapter 1. In crude terms, the shift is from an 'organic' concept of the social – in which those deemed to be members of society have rights – to a context in which humanity and the individual become the *key values* (, 2012). In Europe, scholars have linked the shift from medieval and early modern charity to 19th- and 20th-century humanitarian philanthropy to the transformation of the *bourgeois self* (Owen, 1965; Jones, 1969; Haskell, 1985; Mollat, 1986; Cunningham and Innes, 1998; McCloskey, 1998; Adam, 2004; Baader, 2004; Lässig,

2004). The histories of Jewish charities in Germany and the United States stress ways in which they lost their specific *Jewish nature* and became increasingly concerned with bourgeois values and interests (Baader, 2004; Lassig, 2004). But these processes of change have taken place at different speeds and not always according to predictable teleology. So bourgeois philanthropy has coexisted with other forms of philanthropy where socially embedded practices have prevailed: a model of personalised patronage distinct from the alleged universalistic tendency of the bourgeoisie. Comparable processes have been noted in colonial and postcolonial South Asia, where colonial modernity changed the conceptualisation of charity and the nature of both givers and receivers (Haynes, 1987; White, 1991; Joshi, 2001; Sharma, 2001; Palsetia, 2005; Birla, 2009). In Sri Lanka, however, the complexities have been even greater than in Europe and North America. Different models of philanthropy and charity associated with different imaginings of the social, forming complex relationships, mean that in the Colombo context 'traditional' and 'modern' forms of philanthropic activity might not simply coexist (Haynes, 1987) but rather *interact* and work 'through each other' (Copeman, 2009, p4). Our research suggests that while we can ask questions about the motivation behind charitable acts, we also have to recognise the complexities of the context in which the giving takes place. As we have indicated, similar acts have very different significance in different contexts, and the same act of charity can be understood very differently depending upon the social positioning of the givers and receivers (Osella & Osella, 1996; Bourdieu, 2000).

Frequently, philanthropic and charitable acts are seen as being opposed to self-interested economic activities (see for example Mauss, 1925). This has created problems for mainstream economic theorists who analysed philanthropic activities on the grounds that altruism fits uneasily with mainstream economic thinking (Buchanan, 1975; Sugden, 1982, 1984; Bag, 2008). While not directly addressing issues of charity and philanthropy, the work of various economic sociologists suggests how deeply embedded in moral and ethical principles is the world of contemporary capitalism (Callon, 1998, 2007; Mitchell, 1998, 2005; Fourcade, 2007; Fourcade & Healy, 2007). At the same time, research has underscored that the market and its ideology might be closely imbricated with religiosity and religious practice (Comaroff & Comaroff, 2000; Feillard, 2004; Haenni, 2005; Marshall, 2009; Osella & Osella, 2009; Rudnyckyj, 2010). Our data on charitable and philanthropic practices in Colombo suggests a research agenda focused on understanding *how* the complex, fragmentary and at times contradictory elements of diverse moral economies relate to one another. This represents a shift towards focus on the everyday working of the economies of morality.

Religion appears to play an important role in various forms of giving, although in different modalities. For instance, Lässig (2004) writes of the 19th-century German *nouveau riche* as having to 'cleanse themselves of the "stink" of new money' (see also Hirschman, 1977). Many writers link the motives for charitable giving to the demands of particular religious traditions. There is an extensive literature examining the role of Christian charity in the search for salvation (Rosenthal, 1972; Henderson, 1994; Psotles, 2001; Boyd, 2002; Nichols, 2007). This can be paralleled with literature examining the role of charity in other religious traditions, for instance the philanthropic activities of Sir Moses Montefiore (a Jewish English financier and banker; see Green, 2005) and Sir Jamsetjee Jejeebhoy (an Indian Parsi merchant; see Palsetia, 2005). There is perhaps less literature on Muslim and Buddhist practices. The transformative nature of charitable and voluntary actions is quite clear: making saints out of sinners; absolving the giver of the taint of evil; transcending the material world (Ziliak, 2004) or, more generally, creating pious subjects. But this transformative effect is not limited to the world of the *religious* giver. The literature on more secular philanthropists – for example biographies of Rockefeller and Carnegie, not to mention the hagiographical literature on the new philanthropists (Handy, 2007) – is also replete with references to the transformative power of giving. The transformative impulse is not limited to the giver; what philanthropy aims to do, in many cases, is also transform the receiver. This is a major theme in 19th-century British philanthropy, which stresses the potentially transforming impact of giving (to the 'deserving poor') and the danger that this might *not* lead to changes for recipients (Himmelfarb, 1992, 1995).

The same theme runs through much of contemporary development philanthropy, the dream being that acts of charitable giving (including volunteering) will change not only the material but also the moral and spiritual nature of the recipients (Bell, 2000; Stirrat, 2008). The data we have presented suggests a *bigger* shift – across different religious traditions – towards more engaged attention to the transformative role of charitable giving. This leads to debates concerning definitions of the *deserving* objects of intervention and what it takes to achieve their *upliftment*. These changes are produced through circulation of ideas within and between religious traditions, as well as through a *dialogue* with the orientations and practices of international development organisations.[6] Accountability, sustainability, empowerment and participation have become currency in the language of both formal and informal local charitable organisations, just as the global discourse of corporate social responsibility has penetrated the private sector. We have argued that these novel orientations, which give rise to hybrid forms of charity, might be resisted or resignified by donors and receivers alike.

This leaves us with our last point: the vexed question of the relationship between charity, philanthropy and development. Our data identified the fragmentation of charitable practices in Colombo: a complex universe of individual givers, trusts, foundations and formal and informal groups/organisations operating oblivious of each other. Lack of transparency and trust, political ambition, competition for status and patronage are some of the shortcomings of an otherwise extensive network of charity. To that must be added the problems of replication and oversupply, whereby health and education programmes overshadow any other charitable intervention. The endless drawbacks marring local forms of charity and philanthropy lend support to those respondents in Colombo who tirelessly argue that charity can become a means for development only when it is anonymous, organised, planned, coordinated and administered efficiently. Different conceptions of what 'development' means notwithstanding, what is missing in these arguments is that much of charitable giving in Colombo and Sri Lanka more generally, while not concerned with engendering *lasting* transformation of the economic and moral practices of receivers, does potentially provide forms of everyday social protection. Access to monetary help in emergencies or the certainty of receiving gifts and handouts on religious festivals or for lifecycle rituals provide a lifeline for those whose livelihoods are, at best, precarious. Organised and coordinated charity might lift people out of poverty, something that cannot be achieved through informal giving; but perhaps it is oblivious to the everyday predicaments and compelling needs of the most vulnerable and marginal who rely on regular charity from individual donors. Finally, the emergence and increased importance of middlemen or gatekeepers (for example, parish priests, imams, school teachers, development workers and social activists), who mediate and enable access to organised forms of charity and philanthropy, suggests that the politics of giving can never be dissociated from the production and reproduction of social hierarchies and power relations.

[6]   The presence on the island of international development organisations increased substantially since the 2004 tsunami, but has begun to wane since Sri Lanka achieved 'middle-income status' in 2010.

References

Adam, T, 2004, *Philanthropy, patronage and civil society*, Bloomington: Indian University Press

Ali, A, 2014, Political Buddhism, Islamic orthodoxy and open economy: The toxic triad in Sinhalese–Muslim relations in Sri Lanka, *Journal of Asian and African Studies*, 49, 3, 298-314

APPC, 2007, *The measure of giving in Asia-Pacific: Sri Lanka*. Report compiled by the Asian Pacific Philanthropy Consortium, available at http://kordantnews.typepad.com/files/measure-of-giving-in-asia-pacific-sri-lanka.pdf

Atia, M, 2013, *Building a house in heaven: pious neoliberalism and Islamic charity in Egypt*, Minneapolis, MN: Minnesota University Press

Baader, M B (ed) 2004, Rabbinic study, self-improvement, and philanthropy: gender and the refashioning of Jewish voluntary associations in Germany, 1750-1870, in Adam, T (ed) *Philanthropy, Patronage and Civil Society*, Bloomington: Indian University Press, pp163–78

Bag, P K and Roy, S, 2008, Repeated charitable contributions under incomplete information. *Economic Journal*, 118, 525, 60–91

Bell, M, 2000, American philanthropy, the Carnegie Corporation and poverty in South Africa, *Journal of Southern African Studies*, 26, 3, 481–504

Birla, R, 2009, *Stages of capital: law, culture, and market governance in late colonial India*, Durham: Duke University Press

Bornstein, E, 2012, *Disquieting gifts: humanitarianism in New Delhi*, Standford, CA: Stanford University Press

Bourdieu, P, 2000, *Pascalian meditations*, London: Polity Press

Boyd, R, 2002, The Calvinist origins of Lockean political economy, *History of Political Thought*, 23, 1, 30–60

Buchanan, J, 1975, The Samaritan's dilemma, in Phelps, E (ed) *Altruism, Morality and Economic Theory*, New York: Russell Sage Foundation

Callon, M, 1998, Introduction: the embeddedness of economic markets in economics, in Callon, M, ed, *The laws of the market*, Oxford: Blackwell, pp1–57

Callon, M, 2007, What does it mean to say that economics is performative? In MacKenzie, D, Muniesa, F and Siu, L (eds) *Do Economists Make Markets? On the Performativity of Economics*, Princeton, NJ: Princeton University Press

Charities Aid Foundation, 2010, *World Giving Index*, available at www.cafonline.org/pdf/WorldGivingIndex28092010Print.pdf

Comaroff, J and Comaroff, J L, 2000, Millennial capitalism: first thoughts on the second coming, *Public Culture*, 12, 291–343

Copeman, J, 2009, *Veins of devotion: blood donation and religious experience in North India*, London: Rutgers University Press

Cunningham, H and Innes, J (eds), 1998, *Charity, philanthropy and reform from the 1690s to 1850*, Basingstoke: Macmillan

Dutta, R, 2000, Philanthropy and resource mobilisation in Sri Lanka: a mapping exercise, Colombo: The Asia Foundation

Fassin, D, 2012, *Humanitarian reason: a moral history of the present*, Berkeley, CA: University of California Press

Feillard, G, 2004, Insuffler l'esprit du capitalisme à l'Umma: la formation d'une éthique islamique du travail en Indonesie, *Critique Internationale*, 25, 93–116

Fourcade, M, 2007, Theories of markets and theories of society, *American Behavioral Scientist*, 50, 1015–34

Fourcade, M and Healy, K, 2007, Moral views of market society, *Annual Review of Sociology*, 33

Goodhand, J, 1999, Sri Lanka: NGOs and peace-building in complex political emergencies. *Third World Quarterly*, 20, 1, 69 –87

Green, N, 2005, mystical missionaries in the hyderabad state: Mu'in Allah Shah and his Sufi reform movement, *The Indian Economic and Social History Review*, 42, 2, 187–212

Haenni, P, 2005, *L'islam de marché*, Paris: Seuil

Handy, C, 2007, *The new philanthropists: the new generosity*, London: Heinemann

Haskell, T, 1985, Capitalism and the origins of the humanitarian sensibility (parts 1 and 2), *American Historical Review*, 90, 2, 339–61; 90, 3, 547–66.

Haynes, D, 1987, From tribute to philanthropy: the politics of gift giving in a western Indian city, *Journal of Asian Studies*, 46, 2, 339–360

Henderson, J, 1994, *Piety and charity in late medieval Florence*, Oxford: Oxford University Press

Himmelfarb, G, 1992, *poverty and compassion: the moral imagination of the late Victorians*, New York: Vintage

Himmelfarb, G, 1995, *The de-moralisation of society: from Victorian virtues to modern values*, New York: Knopf

Hirschman, A, 1977, *The passions and the interests: political arguments for capitalism before its triumph*, Princeton, NJ: Princeton University Press

IPID, 2001, *Volunteerism in Sri Lanka*. Report compiled by The Institute for Participatory Interaction in Development, available at www.worldvolunteerweb.org/fileadmin/docs/old/pdf/2002/02_03_18LKA_VolunteerResearch.pdf

Jayawardena, K, 2000, *Nobodies to somebodies: the rise of the colonial bourgeoisie in Sri Lanka*, Colombo: Social Scientists' Association

Jones, G, 1969, *History of the law of charity, 1532-1827*, Cambridge: Cambridge University Press

Joshi, S, 2001, *Fractured modernity: making of a middle class in colonial North India*. Delhi: Oxford University Press

Lässig, S, 2004, Bürgerlichkeit, patronage, and communal liberalism in Germany, 1871–1914, in T Adam (ed) *Philanthropy, Patronage and Civil Society. Experiences from Germany, Great Britain, and North America*, Indiana, IN: Indiana University Press, 198–218

Latief, H, 2010, Health provision for the poor Islamic aid and the rise of charitable clinics in Indonesia, *South East Asia Research*, 18, 3, 503–553

Marshall, R, 2009, *Political spiritualities: the Pentecostal revolution in Nigeria*, Chicago: Chicago University Press.

Mauss, M, 1990 [1925], *The gift*, London: Routledge

McCloskey, D N, 1998, Bourgeois virtue and the history of P and S, *The Journal of Economic History*, 58, 2, 297–317

Mitchell, T, 1998, Fixing the economy, *Cultural Studies*, 12, 82–101

Mitchell, T, 2005, the work of economists: how a discipline makes its world, *European Journal of Sociology*, 46, 297–320

Mollat, M,1986, *The poor in the Middle Ages*, New Haven: Yale University Press

Nichols, T, 2007, secular charity, sacred poverty: picturing the poor in renaissance Venice, *Art History*, 30, 2, 139–169

Osella, F and Osella, C, 1996, Articulation of physical and social bodies in Kerala, *Contributions to Indian Sociology*, 30, 1, 37–68

Osella, F and Osella, C, 2009, Muslim entrepreneurs in public life between India and the Gulf: making good and doing good, *The Journal of the Royal Anthropological Institute*, 15 (Special Issue), 202–221

Owen, D, 1965, *English philanthropy 1660-1960*, London: Oxford University Press

Palsetia, J, 2005, Merchant charity and public identity formation in colonial India: the case of Jamsetjee Jejeebhoy, *Journal of Asian and African Studies*, 40, 197–217

Psotles, D, 2001, Small gifts, but big rewards: the symbolism of some gifts to the religious, *Journal of Medieval History*, 27, 23–42

Rosenthal, J T, 1972, *The purchase of Paradise: Gift giving and the aristocracy, 1307-1485*, Toronto: University of Toronto Press

Rudnyckyj, D, 2010, *Spiritual economies: Islam, globalization, and the afterlife of development*, Ithaca, NY: Cornell University Press

Seneviratne, H L, 1999, *The work of kings: the new Buddhism in Sri Lanka*, Chicago, Chicago University Press

Sharma, S, 2001, *Famine, philanthropy and the colonial state*, Delhi: Oxford University Press

Spencer, J (ed) 1990, *Sri Lanka: history and the roots of conflict*, London: Routledge

Stirrat, Jock, 2006, Competitive humanitarianism: relief and the tsunami in Sri Lanka, *Anthropology Today*, 22, 5, 11–16

Stirrat, R L, 2008, Mercenaries, missionaries and misfits representations of development personnel, *Critique of Anthropology*, 28, 4, 406–425

Sugden, R, 1982, On the economics of philanthropy, *Economic Journal*, 92, 341–50

Sugden, R,1984, Reciprocity: the supply of public goods through voluntary contributions, *Economic Journal*, 94, 772–87

Thiranagama, S, 2011, *In my mother's house: civil war in Sri Lanka*, Philadelphia, PA: University of Pennsylvania Press

White, D, 1991, From crisis to community definition: the dynamics of eighteenth-century Parsi philanthropy, *Modern Asian Studies*, 25, 2, 303–320

Woost, MD, 1997, Alternative vocabularies of development? 'Community' and 'participation' in development discourse in Sri Lanka, in Grillo, R D and Stirrat, R L (eds) *Discourses of development: anthropological perspectives*, New York: Berg, pp229–254

Woost, M and Winslow, D (eds) 2004, *Economy, culture and civil war in Sri Lanka*, Bloomington and Indianapolis: Indiana University Press

Ziliak, S T, 2004, Self-reliance before the welfare state: evidence from the charity organization movement in the United States, *The Journal of Economic History*, 64, 2, 433–461

NINE

Philanthropists, civil society and international development

Rachel Hayman[1]

Introduction

Philanthropists, philanthropic foundations and corporate foundations are increasingly influential within international development. They are also working more closely with, or through, international and local non-governmental organisations (NGOs) to deliver projects and programmes of work in developing countries. However, while the overall goals of philanthropic foundations and NGOs working on international development issues may be the same – promoting social development and, particularly, improving the lives of the poor and vulnerable – the approaches, values, and structures utilised differ. This creates positive synergies and new opportunities for collaboration and innovation, but it also creates tensions between different approaches and worldviews.

This chapter explores the roles of philanthropic foundations in international development relative to NGOs, civil society and social justice. It is based on research, organisational development and capacity-building work by the International NGO Training and Research Centre (INTRAC) over several years. The research progressed iteratively, starting from an interest in opening up debate on what NGOs know, or think they know, about philanthropic foundations – and vice versa – and evolving into deeper reflections on the roles of philanthropic foundations in supporting civil society in developing countries.

The chapter first highlights the changing global context which is bringing philanthropic foundations and NGOs closer together in international development. The backdrop to the rising importance

[1]   Head of Research, International NGO Training and Research Centre (INTRAC), rhayman@intrac.org. This chapter draws on working papers and conference reports produced by various authors from INTRAC which are publicly available from: www.intrac.org/resources.php

of philanthropic foundations is one of economic and social change in many countries in the Global South. Second, it delves into knowledge of philanthropic foundations in international development, particularly among NGOs. Information on the work of philanthropic foundations in development is limited, and weak mutual understanding exists between them and NGOs, even those linked by funding relationships. Tensions emerge around the perception of philanthropists as taking a technical approach to development and around the weight some philanthropists carry in development policy agendas. The third part of the chapter therefore interrogates how philanthropists engage with social justice issues, and notably the development of civil society, with an emphasis on Sub-Saharan Africa.

I conclude with a reflection on two different lenses through which philanthropic foundations working in international development can be viewed, and how this might explain some of the tensions between NGOs and philanthropists; but also offer a way of moving forward into more constructive collaborative relationships. On the one hand foundations are donors, providing a source of financing for development in similar ways to public donors, although they can function according to different sets of rules and norms. They are funders of activities aimed at poverty reduction and social justice, and some have a profound interest in the broader societies with which they engage through their funding. On the other hand, foundations sit in a hazy space between the private sector and civil society, and can also be analysed through a civil society, social actor lens. For NGOs and other civil society organisations involved in development, this blurred role can also mean that philanthropists are potentially allies, competitors or even opponents.

Philanthropy and NGOs in a changing global environment

Private giving has always been an important source of financing, which predates public funding for international development (OECD, 2003). Many well-known NGOs trace their origins to private individuals who donate money to an array of charitable causes domestically and worldwide. Some private foundations have a long-established presence in the international development field, for example the Ford Foundation or the Wellcome Trust. Others are more recent, for example the Bill & Melinda Gates Foundation or the Sigrid

Rausing Trust.[2] However, philanthropists and private foundations have been largely invisible in the analytical literature on international development assistance, particularly in Africa. So while the literature on aid, development agencies and NGOs in Africa is vast, very little of it engages with the role of private foundations beyond the impact of the high-profile, controversial or politically charged activities of very large philanthropic organisations or celebrities (see Kharas, 2007; Nickel and Eikenberry, 2010; Morvaridi, 2012).

This is beginning to change. In recent years there has been a surge of interest amongst development scholars and practitioners in expanding understanding of philanthropic foundations, and particularly the 'new' philanthropists (see Edwards, Chapter 2). For example, the UK House of Commons International Development Committee published an influential report on private foundations in 2012 following a consultation process (International Development Committee, 2012). The same year, the Nuffield Foundation produced its in-depth research on foundations (Pharaoh and Bryant, 2012). Foundations themselves are trying to push thinking within their own circles. For example, through its work on *A funder conundrum* (Association of Charitable Foundations et al, 2012), The Diana, Princess of Wales Memorial Fund encouraged private foundations to consider where they located themselves, vis-à-vis bringing about systemic social change. They asked foundations whether they saw themselves just as grant givers or whether they closely engaged with the work of their grantees in 'Funder Plus' relationships, meaning that they might support the needs of the grantees, be active agents of change, engage stakeholders, build expertise and seek to influence public opinion, policy and behaviour (Association of Charitable Foundations et al, 2012). Academic literature in this field is beginning to expand slowly, and the number of forums within which foundations and NGOs can interact is increasing. An example of this is the Bellagio Initiative:[3] an 18-month collaborative

[2]   The Ford Foundation took an international interest soon after its creation in the 1950s (www.fordfoundation.org/); the Wellcome Trust likewise has supported international work throughout its long history (www.wellcome.ac.uk/). The Bill & Melinda Gates Foundation and Sigrid Rausing Trust were both founded in the mid 1990s (www.gatesfoundation.org/; www.sigrid-rausing-trust.org/).

[3]   The Bellagio Initiative, spearheaded by the Institute of Development Studies, the Resource Alliance and the Rockefeller Foundation, brought together policymakers, academics, opinion leaders, social entrepreneurs, activists, donors and practitioners from over 30 countries in a series of reflections on the future of international development (see www.bellagioinitiative.org/).

reflection on the future of international development, which included private and public donors, NGOs and development scholars. The final report stated: 'a radically different cast of players' was creating a 'new ecosystem for international development and philanthropic efforts' (Bellagio, 2012, p6). The report emphasised the attempts to overcome the 'gulf' between different development actors (Bellagio, 2012, p6).

The growing interest is partly borne of a changing global environment that profoundly affects international development. From the 1980s to the early 21st century, the international development landscape was dominated by OECD donors and international NGOs. However, the last five to ten years have seen the rise of new donors, the growing presence of large private funds and the emergence of new, less structured social movements pushing for change. These new actors have challenged dominant norms and brought new opportunities for civil society funding. Cooperation between countries in the South (known as south–south cooperation) is growing, and challenging the often top-down systems of support flowing from north to south. Many developing countries are also experiencing considerable growth, which translates into reduced poverty, new resources for state provision of services, strengthened national policy environments and more vocal regional institutions. On the other hand, these countries also often face growing inequality, environmental challenges, rapid urbanisation, a large youth population which places a strain on social services and employment structures, and potential conflict over new resources – including from external investors.

Public aid to these middle- and lower-middle-income countries from OECD countries is diminishing (World Bank, 2014). This is having a knock-on effect for international NGOs, which have relied heavily on public aid to fund their work, and this in turn is affecting local organisations that have been supported by NGOs for many years (INTRAC, 2012a). The roles of international NGOs are shrinking: a situation that is evident in Latin America, many parts of Asia and some parts of Africa, such as South Africa and Kenya. At the same time, new tensions are surfacing between local and international NGOs over voice, legitimacy vis-à-vis local institutions, financing, staffing and accountability to citizens (Malunga, 2012).

While growth is opening up spaces for different forms of collaboration between state–private and civil-sector actors in some countries, in others civil society space is increasingly squeezed (Tiwana and Belay, 2010). This has included clampdowns on the activities of international NGOs and legislation limiting civil society organisations to a mainly service delivery role. Even in emerging economies the changing funding environment is altering the role of civil society, risking conformity to government agendas or its transformation into a subcontract service provider (Tandon and Brown, 2013; PRIA, 2012). In many countries, even those with reasonable democratic institutions, civil society demands for a voice and space continues to be resisted by governments and power holders. Sustainability of local civil society, which has long relied on external funding in these contexts, is no longer a given.

In a context in which public aid for civil society and international development is diminishing, an important alternative source of funding for development work comes from private foundations. We are now seeing new forms of interaction amongst local philanthropists and civil society organisations, and new support bodies and intermediaries are emerging to facilitate dialogue and debate amongst philanthropists and NGOs. For example, in South America there is the Argentine Network for International Co-operation (RACI);[4] and in Africa, organisations like TrustAfrica and the African Grant Makers' Network (Moyo, 2010). Corporate social responsibility is also becoming more popular in emerging economies. In India, for example, in 2012 the government was working on legislation that would require companies to spend a certain percentage of their profits on corporate social responsibility projects.

Philanthropy, NGOs and development[5]

In our work with foundations and NGOs we have been struck by the limited mutual knowledge and understanding that exists between them. Despite their close connections through funding arrangements, it appears that traditional international development actors and private donors inhabit two separate worlds so far as their approaches and language are concerned. This has bred an environment of misperception and lack of mutual respect, with limited space for frank exchange, sharing and learning.

A fundamental problem is the sheer diversity of philanthropic foundations, which makes generalisation impossible and offers an opaque picture of philanthropic giving. Most foundations and private philanthropic donors focus on giving at a local or national level, and only a limited number support giving to international development

---

[4] See www.raci.org.ar/?lang=en

[5] Much of this section is drawn from Pratt et al (2012) and Fedeler and Hayman (2012)

(Sulla, 2006). Existing research suggests that much of the money from private philanthropic donors who do engage in international development is channelled through NGOs, rather than government or multilateral agencies (Stoianova, 2012). That said, there are also a small number of supranational philanthropic entities that work closely with foundations, multilaterals and governments. The Global Fund to Fight AIDS, Tuberculosis and Malaria, for instance, is a private–public partnership with funding from both government and philanthropic sources.[6] However, it is generally difficult to determine exactly how much money is going to what, from whom and through whom; it is equally difficult to access aggregate funding data in order to secure an overview of the level of funding by private philanthropic donors for international development. Analysis of such data is complicated because of the variety of definitions of a foundation, which differ across legal and cultural contexts. In some cases the definition even includes government-funded or publicly funded foundations. However, it is known that foundations fund a wide range of development activities: from emergency response to activist and advocacy funding, niche projects with particular target groups and healthcare systems.

Estimates of giving by philanthropists and private foundations for international development are unreliable, ranging from US$22.2 billion to US$52.5 billion in 2010 (International Development Committee, 2012). As noted above, foundation funding for international development is a niche area, representing a small proportion of overall foundational spending. Philanthropic giving is also dwarfed in international development figures by public flows, private investment and remittances. However, philanthropic flows are growing. The OECD estimates that philanthropic giving has increased by 128% since 2000 (Neophytou, 2013, p18). As Wickstead stated: 'At the beginning of the century philanthropic flows to developing countries were insufficient to warrant a line in the OECD/DAC's list of financial resource transfer. They now account for about half as much as [Overseas Development Aid] – a massive shift' (Wickstead, 2013, p14).

The increase in foundations located in developing countries, and particularly emerging economies, is important; but again the true extent is difficult to assess, as they are often informal and personal or remain undocumented or public. In Latin America, institutional philanthropy is beginning to grow, particularly in Argentina, Brazil, Ecuador, Guatemala and Mexico (Ambrose, 2005). There are a number of new, increasingly professional philanthropic foundations, including

---

[6] See www.theglobalfund.org/en/

the Tata Foundation in India, Adream in China and new Islamic foundations in the Gulf States, based on the tradition of *zakat*. There are also increasing numbers of wealthy philanthropists in emerging economies (International Development Committee, 2012). Sub-Saharan Africa is seeing unprecedented growth in local philanthropy (Moyo, 2010), but once again research is limited. Philanthropy here consists of a mixed picture of foundations established by high net worth individuals (HNWIs); former politicians, building on networks and influence; celebrities from the worlds of sport and music; individuals from the African Diaspora; and community-based agents raising funds within the population.[7] Likewise, Christian, Islamic and other religious foundations are increasing on the continent (Sy and Hathie, 2009; Moyo, 2010).

Giving is not the exclusive domain of the wealthy in Africa: there is online giving and public giving, including for emergencies in other parts of the world; social investment and public–private partnership; venture philanthropy and impact investing, and endowment building. Grassroots associations are increasingly forming private foundations and grant-making bodies as an alternative to – or in collaboration with – existing public and private development agencies. This manifests itself in collaborative partnerships such as the African Grantmakers Network. The most recent manifestation of what Sy and Hathie (2009) call institutional African philanthropy combines traditional relational transfer models with slightly more vertical ways of functioning. The largest pan-African and regional philanthropic organisations are involved both in horizontal philanthropy and in partnership with non-African foundations and donors. These externally supported African bodies play a significant role within the philanthropic landscape in Africa, acting as grant givers, collaborative organisations and intermediaries between external and indigenous philanthropic endeavours.

In addition to African foundations and hybrid bodies there is also a plethora of external foundations supporting development activities in Africa. They provide grant funding directly to local organisations, government departments and quasi-government bodies and institutions,

---

[7]   Wilkinson-Maposa et al. (2006) and Moyo (2011) describe community-based philanthropy as a 'horizontal' form of giving in that it emerges out of long-standing traditions of redistribution within the community. It is built around interpersonal relationships and community mobilisation. They differentiate this type of giving from top-down, vertical forms of giving, which often include external or foreign actors. See also Fedeler and Hayman (2012, p5).

and also through the intermediary of international NGOs or other bodies.

Challenges in collaboration between philanthropists and NGOs

Compounding the poor knowledge about philanthropic foundations among development NGOs are clashes around styles, expectations and attitudes. Approaches to management, planning, staffing and salaries, accountability chains and reporting may differ significantly and can create tension. This is especially difficult for larger NGOs, which are funded by different sources and thus have different reporting requirements and implementation styles across their portfolio. NGOs can feel both threatened and frustrated when foundations imply they are not efficient or effective because they have not managed to solve development problems despite decades of trying (Pratt et al, 2012).

This latter point reflects the greatest contention that emerges within the literature, and it resonated in many of our discussions with NGOs. There appears to be an entrenched perception that foundations, and particularly the 'new' philanthropists (see Edwards, Chapter 2), focus on finding *technical* solutions to clearly identified problems. This is uncomfortable for many actors who have moved towards a more holistic approach to development. Foundations, being private, can act outside of national or local politics and 'get things done'. In this way they are similar to NGOs in previous decades, which were flexible and able to move quickly, ignoring or working around their own and other governments (OECD, 2003; Hailey 2011; International Development Committee, 2012). The concern of those who take a more holistic view is that a preference for technical and vertical solutions has led to an overreliance on one-dimensional interventions. There has been a return to single-issue projects providing equipment or technology, for example, vaccinations, new water systems or bed nets. This technical investment approach does not go down well with those NGOs who have pursued a more participatory, socially-embedded approach to development over the last 30 years. Their approach has, rather, sought to enable empowerment, ownership, capacity building and sustainability. An overly narrow focus can deflect consideration of less technical developmental issues and mean that structural and political root causes are overlooked. But the technical fix approach seems to be emerging once again in the discourse of NGOs and donors, in part as a result of the current focus on evidence and demonstrable impact. For example, the UK's Department for International Development increasingly emphasises numbers of children in school or vaccinated or bed nets distributed as an indicator of aid outcome (DFID, 2011), and Christian Aid's Nets Now campaign focuses on the provision of bed nets as a means of saving lives.

A further issue that emerges is the influence of philanthropic foundations on development discourse and policy, despite their positioning outside of public accountability systems: a charge which can equally be levied at NGOs that do not receive public funding. NGOs have long used a range of advocacy and lobbying techniques to attempt to push policymakers and governments in particular directions on international development. Certain philanthropists adopt similar tactics. The concern among NGOs is that foundations may shift strategies in line with the changing interests and priorities of their founders or benefactors. Funding strategies may then depend on the interests of a few key individuals and decisions may not be transparent, evidence-based, or systematic (see Ostrower, 2004; also Edwards, Chapter 2). It could be argued that, as private organisations using their own resources, philanthropic foundations are entitled to make their own choices. But large foundations with economic and therefore political leverage may exert tremendous influence on the direction of aid and which issues are on the development agenda (Kapur and Whittle, 2010). This is particularly the case when private foundations accumulate so much power and influence – or 'philanthropic governing capacity' (Nickel and Eikenberry, 2010) – that they can single-handedly define, direct and execute development programmes, relying on their own rules and resources (Schervish, 2003).

The above implies the entrenched position that sets philanthropists and NGOs apart from each other in international development. Develtere and De Bruyn propose that private philanthropic donors constitute a 'fourth pillar' of development aid; an epistemic community separate from that of traditional development actors – a role which is often ignored by researchers (Delvetere and DeBruyn, 2009).

These issues were reiterated during a workshop with a group of international NGOs, philanthropic and private foundations and African organisations that support civil society and philanthropy in London in October 2012 (INTRAC, 2012b). There was considerable diversity within the room in terms of approaches and perspectives, even amongst a relatively small gathering (around 40 different organisations were present). For example, several participants were engaged in vertical relationships with funders, intermediaries, local partners and beneficiaries, often on specific projects. Amongst these, there was often an absence of in-depth understanding of the context in which projects were being undertaken and a limited understanding about partner organisations at different levels in the relationship. Like traditional donors, foundations often face the difficulty of finding suitable and capable local partners, which affects where they are able, or willing, to work. This leads to risk avoidance, use of international rather than local intermediaries and collaboration with strong existing partners rather than finding the most appropriate local partners to work with who have the possibility to bring about real change.

On the other hand, there were participants who had a broader interaction with the contextual environment in which they were working: the result of collaboration with other institutions and acquisition of an understanding of the connections and relationships surrounding development work, and of how their funding affected the wider local landscape. Participants in the workshop further highlighted challenges to building stronger engagement between foundations, international NGOs and local civil society in Africa. They noted a lack of spaces for networking, hearing others' experience, learning how to support civil society and gaining information about the issues civil society organisations faced in Africa. They raised concerns regarding the difficulty of bringing disparate funders, grantees and others together for dialogue in a meaningful way, beyond the funder–grantee relationship.

Supporting social justice and civil society: beyond the stereotypes

Our workshop discussions reiterated the problem of generalisation across a large and often opaque set of philanthropic foundations. However, it also provided greater insights into whether philanthropic foundations are able to leverage social change in developing countries – because of their origins, approaches and relationships – in ways that international and local NGOs cannot. There seems to be a demand coming out of African civil society and philanthropy support organisations for a stronger focus by philanthropic foundations on social justice and institutional change, away from technical assistance and service delivery (Moyo 2010, 2011, 2012; Malunga, 2012). But can philanthropic foundations utilise their business profiles, financial muscle and independence from public institutions and external donors in order to address the major structural problems in African countries? In principle, the new HNWIs are well positioned to champion policy agendas for change in Africa. But there is a tendency for HNWIs, who largely come from the private sector, to be reductionist and seek solutions for social challenges in the business models that have made them successful, rather than taking a broader view of social change (Fedeler and Hayman, 2012). However, this is not evident across the board. In seeking to unpack the perception amongst NGOs about philanthropic foundations taking a largely technical approach to international development, our research examined a small number of case studies of African and non-African foundations that appear to be actively seeking to tackle social justice questions through their work.[8] We examined how these foundations were tackling: mobilisation of community resources and promotion of sustainability beyond donor funding – particularly external funding; building capacity of local people and organisations; partnerships, collaborative relationships and networks, fostered to advance projects – including the promotion of cross-regional learning and sharing with other foundations and donors; and, finally, awareness-raising and advocacy activities – including engagement with policy-makers, government institutions, and international networks. The research demonstrated that amongst this group of foundations there was a common desire to tackle social justice, governance and policy-related matters. The African Women's Development Fund (AWDF), for example, encourages women to engage in national debate. Trust Africa works, among others, to strengthen civil society in politically sensitive environments. Both the Tony Elumelu Foundation and the Mo Ibrahim Foundation aim to improve institutional governance and political leadership.[9]

The external foundations active in social policy processes in Africa that we explored all considered themselves to be removed from explicit political engagement, working more to catalyse change through their activities and support for local civil society organisations. Rather than being apolitical, vertical implementers, these foundations actively attempt to shape and influence the policymaking spheres in different ways. African philanthropists seem to be explicit about their social

[8] The desk-based study looked at the Kenya Community Development Fund; the Tony Elumelu Foundation; the Mo Ibrahim Foundation; the TY Danjuma Foundation; Trust Africa; the African Women's Development Fund; the Southern Africa Trust; the African Grantmakers Network; the East Africa Association of Grantmakers; the Oak Foundation; the Diana, Princess of Wales Memorial Fund and the Baring Foundation (Fedeler and Hayman, 2012).

[9] See www.tonyelumelufoundation.org; Blair Elumelu Fellowship Programme: www.tonyblairoffice.org/africa/pages/blair-elumelu-fellowship; www.moibrahimfoundation.org/; the African Women's Development Fund: www.awdf.org/ and Trust Africa: www.trustafrica.org/en/component/k2/item/31

justice objectives, whereas non-African foundations are more likely to be implicit agents of sociopolitical change, providing support for local organisations and institutions to take action.

These represent a tiny number of examples from a very broad field, but they caution against over-generalisation and anecdotal statements. Moreover there are signs of other shifts relative to the role of philanthropic foundations in international development, for example with regard to monitoring and evaluation, accountability and transparency. Many foundations are now seeking to establish a clearer picture of what they are funding and what the outcomes are. While a 2004 study found that less than half of US foundations formally evaluated projects they had funded (Ostrower, 2004), in recent years many foundations involved in international development have taken steps towards ensuring better impact evaluation (Picciotto, 2011), which INTRAC has also experienced through its wider work with foundations. Likewise, some larger foundations are also making an effort to improve their accountability and transparency, for example by using the International Aid Transparency Initiative.[10] Moreover, philanthropic foundations are being encouraged to think more profoundly about their roles. The *Funder conundrum* materials (Association of Charitable Foundations et al, 2012) challenge funders to reflect on where they place themselves within a spectrum. At one end are the hands-off givers, who aspire to help people through the provision of grants for often technical projects, while at the other are funders who are social (political) actors aspiring to change the world, and using their funding as a tool in this process. The final report of the Bellagio Initiative recommends more political engagement in development by philanthropic foundations, calling on them 'to accept the political nature of the development policy process and to get involved in it' and to 'move away from a technocratic development agenda to one which recognises that the challenges of protecting and promoting human wellbeing on a global scale will inevitably entail difficult political debates and challenging political trade-off' (Bellagio Initiative, 2012, p16).

---

[10]   While donors and NGOs are the main development actors who publish information through IATI, more foundations and private sector actors are beginning to do so. Private foundations listed in the registry in 2013 included The William and Flora Hewlett Foundation and the Stars Foundation (see: www.aidtransparency.net/). In 2014, Grantcraft also produced a new resource on transparency amongst private foundations (see GrantCraft, 2014).

Nevertheless, the role of philanthropic foundations in social policy-related issues should also be treated with caution. The issues raised by Edwards (Chapter 2) about the legitimacy of philanthropic foundations and their influence are extremely salient. Philanthropic foundations engaged in political and policy processes need to be subject to intense scrutiny and held to account. Even the most horizontal type of philanthropic organisation or network, which aims to give voice to its beneficiaries and grantees and not dictate agendas, is driven by organisational imperatives and power dynamics. Other development actors – public institutions, official aid agencies and local and international NGOs – have been subjected to extremely critical analyses of the impact of their work, including the intended and unintended consequences of their actions and how they understand and engage with governance institutions in Africa at local, national and international levels. Such analysis has been limited, to date, on philanthropic foundations.

Conclusion

The global context for international development is changing profoundly. New opportunities and issues are altering approaches to addressing poverty, inequality and human rights. Different sets of actors are emerging and working together in ways that are challenging the norms of a donor-led international development system, which has long been dominated by western donors and international NGOs. The evidence is clear; local and international private donors – including philanthropists, philanthropic foundations and corporate foundations – are becoming increasingly important in the development funding landscape.

Our research highlights that lack of knowledge about philanthropic foundations – their activities, motivations, approaches and politics – affects the relationships between NGOs and foundations. While some NGOs are keen to engage with foundations that can offer new funding opportunities and innovative partnerships, many civil society practitioners are profoundly sceptical about philanthropists working in international development. One possible explanation for this could be the unclear place that philanthropists occupy in the international development sphere. Many foundations focus almost exclusively on the delivery of services to poor and vulnerable populations, either directly or through project grants to NGOs or local organisations. Their work is primarily technical and largely ambivalent to the broader dynamics of the societies in which they are engaged. For grant-seeking NGOs, such foundations are essentially donors, providers of funds through vertical channels. These philanthropic foundations can therefore be analysed through a lens similar to that used to analyse donors. Although they function according to different sets of rules, because of their money source, they share a great many similarities. Donor-based analysis entails reflection on the development theory behind the approach, the politics of the aid, and the systems and structures for grant making, monitoring and reporting. For civil society organisations that are recipients of these funds via a vertical chain-like system, which may be multi-layered and involve several intermediaries, the relationship will be one of grantor–grantee. The overarching issue for philanthropic foundations, when viewed through this lens, is whether they are considered to be 'good' donors: which, so far as the civil society organisations in receipt of funding are concerned, would tend to be related to how they engage with partners, what demands they make in terms of reporting and monitoring, and how reliable they are as funders.

The research also identified some concern amongst NGOs that philanthropic foundations are operating as their potential competitors in international development, moving into operational and advocacy space that they have long occupied in both poor communities and international arenas. Some of the criticisms of, and scepticism about, private philanthropic donors may stem from fears that new, independent grantors will *displace*, rather than complement, traditional development actors. From this perspective, philanthropic foundations in international development could be viewed through a civil society lens, as civil society actors in their own right who use, or could use, their financial clout to engage in deeper systemic social change. This resonates more closely with the thrust of the conclusions from Bellagio and the *Funder conundrum* initiatives, and would respond to the demand coming out of developing countries – which our research identified – that external actors should recognise that change is afoot and work with emerging civil society movements to get beyond service delivery. Philanthropic foundations occupy a hazy area between the market and civil society – just as many NGOs occupy a hazy space between civil society and government – and there are different schools of thought as to where they precisely sit in relation to civil society. The research highlighted a number of foundations that consider themselves to be active civil society actors: explicitly engaging with social policy, tackling governance and political issues, and supporting the development of a healthy and strong civil society as an end in itself.

In terms of relationships between philanthropic foundations and NGOs in this domain, the ideal scenario is one of philanthropists as *allies* aiming towards a common goal through their different approaches – not necessarily, but potentially, in collaboration. At the same time, there is a risk of over-assuming the positive influence of philanthropists. A concern that emerged in the research related to the limited knowledge of the political connectedness of some local philanthropists in developing countries. This could be significant for development, if philanthropic or corporate foundations are closely tied into a system that is repressing civil society or undermining social justice through economic activity. From this perspective, philanthropists could well be seen as *opponents* of NGOs.

As the role of private foundations increases in international development, there is a profound need for greater mutual understanding between foundations and NGOs. Even when they are connected by funding relationships, our research reveals weak communication and misperceptions. Relationships are often far from easy and the foundation landscape is a complex minefield for many NGOs. It can be extremely hard to approach foundations, and barriers to communication and engagement are extensive. On the other hand, participants in our research were overwhelmingly keen to identify opportunities to share, learn and reflect. The bigger question, perhaps, is how NGOs and foundations act upon new knowledge gained when they interact, particularly in response to the shifting international development context.

References

Ambrose, N, 2005, *Global philanthropy: emerging issues and strategic planning,* Arlington: Council on Foundations, www.cof.org/files/ Documents/Family_Foundations/Family-and-Global-Philanthropy/ Overview-of-Global-Philanthropy-COF.pdf

Association of Charitable Foundations, 2012, *A funder conundrum: choices that funders face in bringing about positive social change*, London: DP Evaluation and The Diana, Princess of Wales Memorial Fund, www.theworkcontinues.org/page.asp?id=1791

Bellagio Initiative, 2012, *Human wellbeing in the 21st century: meeting challenges, seizing opportunities*, www.bellagioinitiative.org/wp-content/ uploads/2012/09/BELLAGIO_WELLBEING_SPREADS.pdf

Delvetere, P and DeBruyn, T, 2009, The emergence of a fourth pillar in development aid, *Development in Practice*, 19, 7, 912–22

DFID, 2011, *Summary of DFID's work in Rwanda 2011–2015*, London: Department for International Development, www.gov.uk/ government/uploads/system/uploads/attachment_data/file/67385/ rwanda-2011-summary.pdf

Fedeler, K and Hayman, R, 2012, *Beyond the apolitical: private foundations and transformative development in sub-Saharan Africa*, policy briefing paper no. 33, Oxford: INTRAC

GrantCraft, 2014, *Opening up: demystifying funder transparency*, New York, NY: Foundation Center

Hailey, J, 2011, NGO funding and private philanthropy, *ONTRAC*, 49, 1–4

International Development Committee, 2012, *Private foundations: thirteenth report of session 2010-2012*, www.publications.parliament. uk/pa/cm201012/cmselect/cmintdev/1557/155702.htm

INTRAC, 2012a, *Aid withdrawal, partnership and CSO sustainability in a time of global economic change: workshop conclusions and recommendation*, Oxford: INTRAC, www.intrac.org/data/files/Aid_withdrawal_ workshop_conclusions_18_Dec_2012_FINAL.pdf

INTRAC, 2012b, *Supporting civil society in Africa: building 'deep vertical' and 'broad horizontal' partnerships among private foundations, NGOs and civil society organisations: Workshop conclusions and recommendations*, Oxford: INTRAC, www.intrac.org/resources.php?action=resource&id=754f

Kapur, D and Whittle, D, 2010, Can the privatization of foreign aid enhance accountability?, *Journal of International Law and Politics*, 42, 4, 1143–80

Kharas, H, 2007, *The new reality of aid. Brookings Institute*, Washington DC: Brookings Bloom Roundtable

Malunga, C, 2012, *Challenges and dynamics of civil society strengthening in Africa*, paper presented at the workshop 'Supporting civil society in Africa: innovative and effective collaboration between philanthropic foundations, NGOs and civil society organisations', London, October 2012.

Morvaridi, B, 2012, Capitalist philanthropy and hegemonic partnerships, *Third World Quarterly*, 33, 7, 1191–210

Moyo, B, 2010, Philanthropy in Africa, in Anheier, H K and Toepler, S, eds, *International ncyclopaedia of civil society*, part 16, pp1187–92

Moyo, B, 2011, *Transformative innovations in African philanthropy*, The Bellagio Initiative, www.bellagioinitiative.org/about-us/what-is-the- bellagio-initiative/commissioned-papers/.

Moyo, B, 2012, *Philanthropy and civil society in Africa*, paper presented at the workshop 'Supporting civil society in Africa: innovative and effective collaboration between philanthropic foundations, NGOs and civil society organisations', London, October 2012.

Neophytou, M, 2013, A new age for philanthropy, *The Networker*, 103, 18.

Nickel, P M and Eikenberry, A M, 2010, Philanthropy in the era of global governance, in Taylor, R (ed) *Third sector research,* New York: Springer, pp269–79, www.springerlink.com/content/r0g36p5g10h83832/

OECD, 2003, Philanthropic foundations and development cooperation, *DAC Journal*, 4, 3, Paris: OECD Publications

Ostrower, F, 2004, *Attitudes and practices concerning effective philanthropy: survey report,* Washington, DC: The Urban Institute Center on NonProfits and Philanthropy

Pharaoh, C and Bryant, L, 2012, *Global grant-making: a review of UK foundations funding for international development,* London: The Nuffield Foundation, www.nuffieldfoundation.org/sites/default/files/files/NUF1272_Global_grantmaking_FINAL_18_01_12.pdf

Picciotto, R, 2011, Where is development evaluation going?, in Rist, R, Boily, M H and Martin, F, *Influencing change: building evaluation capacity to strengthen governance,* Washington, DC: The World Bank, pp195–206

Pratt, B, Hailey, J, Gallo, M, Shadwick, R and Hayman, D, 2012, *Understanding private donors in international development,* policy briefing paper no. 31, Oxford: INTRAC

PRIA, 2012, *Civil society @ crossroads. Shifts, challenges, options?* New Delhi: Society for Participatory Research in Asia (PRIA)

Publish What You Fund, 2013, *Aid transparency index 2013*, http://ati.publishwhatyoufund.org/2013/

Schervish, P G, 2003, *Hyperagency and high-tech donors: a new theory of the new philanthropists,* Boston: Social Welfare Research Institute, www.bc.edu/content/dam/files/research_sites/cwp/pdf/haf.pdf

Stoianova, V, 2012, *Private funding: an emerging trend in humanitarian donorship,* Wells: Global Humanitarian Assistance Development Initiatives

Sulla, O, 2006, Philanthropic foundations, actual versus potential role in international development assistance, note for the *Global development finance report,* Washington, DC: World Bank Development Prospects Group (DECPG) International Finance Team

Sy, M and Hathie, I, 2009, *Institutional forms of philanthropy in West Africa,* Ottawa: International Development Research Centre, www.idrc.ca/EN/Programs/Donor_Partnerships/Documents/Institutional-forms-of-Philanthropy-SY-HATHIE-Formatted.pdf

Tandon, R and Brown, D, 2013, Civil society at crossroads: eruptions, initiatives and evolution in citizen activism, *Development and Practice*, 23, 5–6, 601–8

Tiwana, M and Belay, N, 2010, *Civil society: the clampdown is real: global trends 2009–2010,* Johannesburg: CIVICUS

Wickstead, M, 2013, Philanthropy, NGOs and international development: what next?, *The Networker*, 103, 1–3,14

Wilkinson-Maposa, S, Fowler, A, Oliver-Evans, C and Mulenga, C F N, 2006, *The poor philanthropist: how and why the poor people help each other*, Cape Town: Compress

World Bank, 2014, Country and Lending Groups, http://data.worldbank.org/about/country-and-lending-groups

TEN

Social justice, liberalism and philanthropy: the tensions and limitations of British foundations

Balihar Sanghera and Kate Bradley

Introduction

This chapter examines the nature of British social justice philanthropy, which can be described as a loose social movement of charitable and community foundations and grantmakers that seeks social change by tackling the root causes of social inequalities and problems.[1] In exploring how charitable and community foundations understand the values and beliefs that shape their grant-making portfolios, the aim is to offer a critical insight into the limitations of foundations and grantmakers to achieve social change, and to examine the normative dimensions of their activities. The chapter will argue that financialised foundations are inherently problematic, partly because their income is unearned and undeserving.

[1]   This project was funded by the Economic and Social Research Council, UK (Award No: RES-5693-25-0003/007). Our thanks to the participants at the Social Justice Philanthropy Conference, London and the New Philanthropy and Social Justice Symposium, Bradford for their suggestions and advice. We would like to express our gratitude to the interviewees for their time, guidance and patience. Emily Robinson also deserves our appreciation for arranging the interviews. The usual disclaimers apply.

Within philanthropy studies, we make an intervention in two debates. The first debate is whether foundations are a public good. Some scholars (such as Rabinowitz, 1990; Craig, 2005; Leat, 2007; Cohen, 2008) argue that foundations are a force for public good, supporting a thriving civil society, giving voice to disadvantaged and vulnerable groups, upholding basic liberties, tackling discrimination and ensuring fair opportunities. In addition, they provide goods that the state and the market cannot or will not offer. But critics (including Prewitt et al, 2004; Illingworth et al, 2011) argue that foundations and grantmakers face serious questions of legitimacy and accountability, namely, what is the legitimacy of private money to shape public policy, and what regulatory mechanisms ensure that foundations' activities benefit the public? They also suggest that the net impact of foundations can be negative, taking into account the effects of the loss of tax revenues to subsidise charities and the harm arising from the speculative and non-ethical nature of their endowment. We will suggest that foundations are defensive on questions of public interests, legitimacy and accountability, drawing attention to how legal guidelines and regulatory controls provide public safeguards.

The second debate involves scholars in critical philanthropy (Raddon, 2008; Eikenberry, 2009; Nickel and Eikenberry, 2009), who criticise forms of philanthropy that affirm existing power relations and structures, arguing instead for a transformative model of philanthropy (see Edwards in Chapter 2). In addition to traditional philanthropy, 'new' or entrepreneurial philanthropy, which entrenches markets and business as a way to address global problems, has also faced criticisms. Sandberg (2012) and Eikenberry (2009) note that new philanthropy reflects the dominance of neoliberal governmentality, in that foundations strategically use for-profit organisations to deliver social services, and employ business models to manage operations and to assess social impact and effectiveness. Furthermore, marketised philanthropy celebrates commodification and the market. Consider how charities ask individuals to buy fairtrade products to end poverty in Africa, or use celebrities (such as Angelina Jolie) to advocate for more equitable international trade relations (Nickel and Eikenberry, 2009). But scholars in critical philanthropy do not adequately explain how alternative forms of philanthropy can deliver transformative outcomes, and what their normative criteria for social change and justice are. Our research will show that while the rhetorical language of the social justice philanthropy movement reflects beliefs in human rights, equality and empowerment, foundations and grantmakers face internal and external constraints in their pursuit of social transformation.

In addition, we engage with issues in political philosophy, by examining the nature of foundations' understandings of social justice and the tensions and limitations of liberal egalitarianism. According to liberal social justice, a fair and just society has three important features: basic liberties and rights for all; equal opportunity to ensure a level playing field; and support for the most disadvantaged members in society. Liberals are neither economic utilitarians nor egalitarians, arguing instead that disparities in economic rewards provide incentives for innovation and growth, and that economic inequalities are morally acceptable as long as the least fortunate members benefit from them (Rawls, 1999). An important feature of liberalism is that civil society organisations (such as foundations and charities) aim to regulate, rather than eliminate, economic and social inequalities produced by capitalism, promoting and advocating social and economic inclusion, formal and fair equal opportunities and a plural civil society (Baker et al, 2004). But contemporary writers (such as Fraser, 2009; Sen, 2009) point out two serious limitations to liberal social justice. First, liberals largely focus on getting social institutions right, often neglecting to assess individual behaviour and motivations. Second, social justice tends to be confined to individual territorial states, thereby failing to consider how globalisation problematises the nation-state. We will argue that although foundations and grantmakers largely operate within a liberal social justice framework, it is inadequate for just and fair procedures and outcomes, and we will suggest how the liberal framework can be improved upon.

This chapter is divided into six sections. The first section will provide some contextual information about the charitable and community foundation sector, and discuss the extent of social justice grantmaking in the UK. In the next section, we will briefly describe the research design of our study on foundations and grantmakers. The third section will examine how liberal ideas of social justice and legitimacy can account for the values that underpin foundations' programmes and goals. In the fourth section, we will discuss why foundations and grantmakers are often reluctant to use the concept of 'social justice' to describe their activities. The fifth section will investigate some of the tensions and limitations of foundations' pursuit of progressive activities. Finally, we will make some concluding remarks.

Research design and methods

We conducted 34 semi-structured interviews with executive directors or senior project managers of charitable and community foundations and grantmakers. Each interview lasted on average 1.5 hours, divided into two parts: the first part asked the interviewees to describe the history of their organisations and to outline their current strategic themes and priorities; in the second part they explained the use, or lack of use, of the concept of 'social justice' in their organisations. In addition, further interviews were conducted with 16 participants from the first round, either via Skype or emails, to collect extra information.

The study was not a survey of the UK foundations, but rather an examination of foundations that are motivated either to a large or small extent by social justice issues, including human rights, poverty, social exclusion and disadvantaged communities in the UK or overseas. Our sample consisted of three distinct groups. First, 25 self-proclaimed progressive grant-making foundations were chosen, as were those foundations that had social justice elements in their programmes. These charitable foundations either have their own private endowment to fund their charitable activities, or rely upon their founders' annual donation to distribute funds to other charities. Some foundations, such as Leverhulme and the Wellcome Trust, were excluded because they do not pursue a social justice agenda. Second, prominent community foundations working on social change and justice issues were included in the sample. They differ from charitable foundations because they do not have a sizeable endowment, but instead attract and manage donations from philanthropists, corporate donors and the state in order to support local community causes and local regeneration. Third, large charitable grantmakers were selected, to enable examination of the values underlying their activities. They differ from the first two groups in that they rely upon public donation and the National Lottery to make grants to good causes and charities. While these three groups of philanthropic foundations and grantmakers overlap in how they operate and what they give to, their sources of funding (namely, private endowment, philanthropic donations, public donation and the National Lottery) differ. As we shall see, the nature of their funding can limit how effectively they pursue progressive agendas. Our sample ranged from established foundations and grantmakers with professional trustees and staff to relatively new foundations with living donors and family as trustees. We shall also see how the nature of the board of trustees can influence the direction of foundations' activities and grantmaking.

Charitable and community foundations in the UK

The Association of Charitable Foundations (ACF) estimates that there are approximately 10,000 independent trusts and foundations in the UK, giving £2.4 billion in grants each year to voluntary and community organisations (ACF, 2014). Foundations and trusts play a crucial role in funding the voluntary sector and in developing a thriving civil society. Because their endowment gives them a degree of independence, foundations and trusts are able to support innovative and risky projects, as well as to fund causes that lack popular and political support. It is worth noting that local authorities and central government often ask charities to provide services (such as social care and drug rehabilitation) to the local community (ACF, 2007). Community foundations support local community causes, and their role is to manage donor funds and to develop an endowment as well as to make grants to charities and community groups, linking local donors with local needs. ACF (2014) estimates that there are 46 community foundations across the country, which distributed £60 million in grants.

ACF (2007) reports the total grant-making expenditure of the top 500 charitable foundations and grantmakers rose from £746 million in 1994/5 to £2.72 billion in 2004/5. The report categorises the causes that the top 500 foundations and grantmakers list as their preferred funding areas into social care, health, education, arts and culture, environment, international, faith-based and other/general. It is difficult to know the extent of social justice grantmaking because the ACF does not capture data under the category of 'social justice', and what constitutes a social justice project is open to interpretation.[2] Furthermore, it is difficult to interpret the extent of social justice. For instance, the education category would include grants made to support scholarships, which would not be considered social justice grantmaking unless they were specifically targeted to those who would otherwise not be able to continue their education. Similarly, health projects can range from purchasing equipment for hospitals, which would not be considered a social justice project, to providing better information on health care in low-income areas, which would be a social justice project. To our knowledge, there has not been a study to review the grants from a representative sample of foundations and grantmakers to ascertain how much social justice grantmaking currently occurs in the UK (see Community Foundations of Canada, 2003, for information on the situation there). In reviewing grants of charitable and community foundations in the US, Jagpal and Laskowski (2010) show that social justice grantmaking expenditure averaged US$3 billion annually between 2008 and 2010, representing 15% of the total grantmaking expenditure in that period. They also report that

---

[2] Our thanks to Stephen Pittam for this point.

most sampled grantmakers spend less than 5% of their grantmaking on social justice projects.

According to ACF (2007), the top ten foundations and grantmakers in the UK include the Big Lottery Fund, the Wellcome Trust, Cancer Research (UK), the British Heart Foundation, Comic Relief, Christian Aid and the Gatsby Charitable Foundation. Of these, only Comic Relief and Christian Aid can be considered as social justice charitable grantmakers, because of their extensive work to tackle child poverty and social inequalities in developing countries. Comic Relief's vision is to create a just world by addressing the root causes of poverty and injustice. In contrast, Wellcome Trust's vision is to support the brightest minds in biomedical research and medical humanities. While the Gatsby Charitable Foundation has a programme on improving the income of the poor in Africa (15.4% of its total grantmaking expenditure), over half of its funds are allocated to science (55.3%), with arts receiving 12% and science and technology education getting 9.8% (Gatsby Charitable Foundation, 2012). Big Lottery Fund's vast annual budget and coverage of different causes from sports to wildlife allow it to undertake some social justice grantmaking. For instance, it operates the International Communities programme, which in 2011/12 made 16 grants worth £6.9 million to UK organisations to deliver projects in disadvantaged communities overseas (Big Lottery Fund, 2012). So while Big Lottery Fund is not a social justice grantmaker, some of its activities involve social justice.

Despite the lack of reliable survey data on social justice grantmaking, we can safely assume that it does occur in a variety of forms, differing due to whether social justice is the primary goal or one of many. For instance, there are some endowed foundations and trusts (such as the Joseph Rowntree Charitable Trust and the Soros Foundations) and publicly-funded charitable grantmakers (such as Comic Relief) that are dedicated to addressing poverty, inequalities and injustices in the UK and overseas. But for most, like the Gatsby Charitable Foundation and the Big Lottery Fund, social justice programmes comprise a small percentage of their total grantmaking expenditure.

Liberalism, social justice and philanthropy

In our study, we found that charitable and community foundations and grantmakers do enact liberal values. Many charitable foundations promote better civil rights for marginalised groups, tackling racial discrimination and religious intolerance and supporting the rights of asylum seekers and political prisoners in the UK as well as overseas.

Some foundations have educational programmes that encourage greater equality of opportunity and social mobility, providing financial support to students from low-income backgrounds and assisting schools in deprived areas. Most community foundations and grantmakers focus on social cohesion and financial inclusion, giving to charities that address youth unemployment, urban regeneration and start-up businesses in low-income communities. Charitable foundations and grantmakers give grants to charities that assist vulnerable groups who lack resources and the power to make demands upon the state. Such vulnerable groups include sex workers, abused children, the elderly and people with mental health difficulties.

Despite their privileged, elitist and undemocratic status, legitimacy is unproblematic for endowed and community foundations, in part because the state and charity law permit them to use their private resources for public benefit in ways that do not challenge the political legitimacy of the state or the economic legitimacy of the market (Prewitt et al, 2004). The state confers legitimacy upon foundations that address issues that otherwise would be neglected or underresourced. In return, the state subjects them to minimal accountability and regulatory checks. To have legitimacy, charitable and community foundations need not do their job well, be cost-effective or bring about significant social change, but rather satisfy the utilitarian public benefit test, as legislated by Parliament and administered by the Charity Commission (Cohen, 1983). The public benefit test is not prescriptive, allowing foundations to choose and devise their own goals and programmes, fostering autonomy, independence, choice and pluralism. The Charity Commission expects foundations to demonstrate their intention to satisfy the public benefit test and to document their activities in annual reports (Morgan, 2012). Foundations tend to slide from legal to moral legitimacy, though the latter does not necessarily follow from the former. Indeed, there are many forms of legal but immoral action in society, such as rentier activities.

Should restrictions be placed upon charitable foundations' agendas, their autonomy and independence, as well as the liberal political economy, would be undermined. Charitable foundations are protective of their autonomy, resisting government controls over their particular goals and agendas. While charitable foundations can deflect controls over substantive issues, accountability is stronger around procedural issues of transparency, fiscal responsibility and administrative efficiency (Prewitt et al, 2004). Foundations must satisfy a minimal accountability test by returning annual accounts as well as following the Charity Commission's recommendations on good practice, such as making information about their grantmaking criteria accessible on their websites, reviewing long-term strategies and programme priorities and evaluating grantees' perceptions.

In our study, charitable and community foundations were not troubled by their privileged and undemocratic status, arguing that they are regulated by charity law, are accountable to the Charity Commission and have as much legitimacy and autonomy as other organisations (such as corporations and universities) operating in a liberal, democratic civil society. They cherish their ability to 'speak truth to power' and to take risks too dangerous or costly for the state. To assess their administrative process and programme effectiveness, most foundations conduct surveys of their grantees' perceptions and have external evaluations of their programmes. To ensure transparency, most foundations publish annual reports describing the public benefit of their major activities and events. While foundations are undemocratic, many of them operate an open and responsive grantmaking application scheme, allowing 'the community' to define their own needs. In cases of established and professional foundations, programme priorities are based upon extensive consultation and research; for example, evidence-based needs. Despite their uniquely privileged status, their ability to project their private vision of the public good into the public arena is limited, as corporations, trade unions, lobbyists and other groups with special interests have more resources and power for social change.

Rejecting the 'social justice' label

Although charitable and community foundations in our study pursued a liberal agenda of social justice, most do not describe their programmes and grantmaking in terms of social justice. This may seem puzzling at first, but there are four reasons for this. First, the term 'social justice' would imply that foundations are obligated to pursue social justice, having a duty to society to address issues of basic liberties and social inequalities (Rawls, 1999). In our study, most living donors and family trustees were not motivated by impartial feelings of just obligations, but rather personal interests and connections to particular causes.

Second, the term 'social justice' would imply that grantmaking portfolios and programme priorities are open to critical scrutiny, debate and reason, possibly reflecting deliberations under 'the veil of ignorance' (Rawls, 1999); but in practice, the decision-making process often lacks impartiality, involving trustees' personal interests and connections. Furthermore, some charitable foundations operate a closed application process, which restricts the participation of charities and NGOs. Instead, trustees and staff invite applications on the basis of social connection and reputation.

Third, the term 'social justice' can have radical or left-wing political connotations associated with egalitarianism and redistribution of wealth (Baker et al, 2004). The term suggests that social and economic inequalities are structural, requiring reforms to basic institutions (Lester, 2011). But many charitable and community foundations and grantmakers believe themselves to be neutral, in that they shy away from overtly political ideologies and engage instead with advocacy and campaigns around normalised and taken-for-granted liberal values and causes that are enshrined in charity law (Cohen, 1983; Luxton, 2009; 2012; Morgan, 2012). In addition, some established charitable foundations believe that their grant-making is scientific and evidence-based, evoking the positivist ideals of objectivity and neutrality, not political bias and ideologies (Sealander, 2002).

Fourth, the term 'social justice' has multiple and contentious meanings that can confuse and discourage the public (see Ruesga and Puntenney, 2010 for different meanings of 'social justice'). In our study, most charitable and community foundations and grantmakers believed that the term 'social justice' could alienate their audience, and suggested that the public, donors and trustees preferred less contentious and more neutral terms, such as 'social change', 'poverty', 'community development' or 'human rights' (see Mayer, 2008 on how the term 'social change' can create suspicions and animosity in the US). Established foundations and grantmakers are particularly careful in how they engage with their key stakeholders through publications, the social media and public events, guarding their reputation against needless controversy (Carson, 2003).

Tensions and limitations of foundations' progressive agendas

To recap, so far we have argued that the charitable and community foundations and grantmakers in our study implicitly focus on issues of liberal social justice, and achieve legitimacy and accountability by satisfying both the utilitarian public benefit test and the procedural accountability test that preserve their choice, autonomy and independence. We have also suggested some reasons why foundations do not name their activities as 'social justice.' Now, we will discuss several tensions and limitations to foundations' pursuit of social justice issues and progressive agendas.

First, lack of ethical investment is a significant tension within most charitable and community foundations. They primarily focus on distributing the income from their endowment or philanthropic donations, having little ethical consideration to how the income is accumulated. Endowed foundations aim to maximise financial returns by investing in unit trusts that offer acceptable risks (Jenkins, 2012). Community foundations attract philanthropic and corporate donations from financial and commercial investments, such as hedge funds and alcohol production. But left-leaning liberals, such as Adam Smith, John Stuart Mill and John Rawls, argue that a just and fair society requires that private property ownership be more equal and dispersed rather than heavily concentrated in the hands of elites (Rawls, 1999; Fleischacker, 2003). In addition, Sayer (2012) notes that financial investment in unit trusts, bonds, loans and hedge funds involve social relations that are speculative and parasitic, contributing little towards productive capital and economic wellbeing. The financialised nature of the philanthropy sector means that foundations siphon off surplus produced by workers in the real economy, so that the income derived from their investments is unearned and undeserving. Furthermore, some foundations are enmeshed in the immoral economy of rent extraction, such as interest (also called usury), rent and capital gains. Eight of the foundations in our study had their origins in unproductive rent extraction – a form of legal corruption (Sayer, 2015). Clearly, the beneficial outcomes of foundations' grantmaking can be countered by the harmful and unjust effects of concentrated property ownership and parasitic financial capital. In our study, some foundations expressed unease about the sector's investment policy, suggesting that the net impact could be negative. Some established foundations have a slightly different investment approach to their endowment, operating a policy of ethical screening that prohibits investment in harmful industries such as tobacco, arms manufacturing and petroleum. Some also have a small percentage (less than 10%) of their endowment in mission-related and social investments, which generate a lower return than commercial ventures (Jenkins and Rogers, 2013). While mission-related and social investment are seen to be more ethical and socially responsible, they face similar usury issues of being unearned and undeserving.

Second, the lack of grantmaking programmes on international social justice issues represents another tension, accounting for only a small amount of grantmaking in this area. Many established charitable foundations limit their mission statements and grantmaking to domestic causes and particular regions and cities in the UK. In part, they are constrained by the historical legacy of their founders' inherent sympathy and moral concern for local and familiar causes (Core and Donaldson, 2010; Forman-Barzilai, 2010). Pratt et al (2012) estimate that 5% of the total foundation grantmaking expenditure from the UK is spent internationally. In our study, when international grantmaking occurs it is often to countries (such as South Africa and Ireland) that have close cultural links to the UK. For relatively new foundations, mission statements and grantmaking programmes are more outward looking, but the target countries (such as India, Eastern Europe, Israel and Zimbabwe) often have close affinities to living donors and family trustees (Pharoah and Bryant 2012). As several scholars (such as Singer, 1972; Smith, 1976; Boltanski, 1999; Fraser, 2009; Sen, 2009) note, social justice and humanitarianism require impartial ethical reasoning that gives greater attention to global inequalities and suffering.

Third, charity law and the Charity Commission prohibit foundations from engaging with issues of political ideologies and political party campaigning (Morgan, 2012). They also cannot be primarily interested in advocacy and campaigns that demand changes to laws and government policies, or which raise public awareness with the aim of changing laws and policies (Luxton, 2009; Breen, 2012). Foundations face severe constraints on what issues they can become involved in and how they can tackle structural inequality and injustice. In our study, charitable and community foundations dismissed ideas that class inequality or capitalism were partly responsible for poverty, unequal educational opportunities, environmental damage, crime and other forms of injustice and suffering. To acknowledge these effects would make the foundations advocate for a change to basic institutions and laws, including private property ownership (Lester, 2011). While the Charities Act 2011 and the Charity Commission encourage political advocacy and campaigning that are secondary to the foundations' primary motivation of public benefit, such as alleviating poverty or advancing education, most foundations have been reluctant to take advantage of this opportunity. The reticence can be partly explained by trustees' lack of political risk-taking and institutional habits and routines that have not evolved to encompass the new legal and political possibilities.[3]

Fourth, most foundations tend to ignore the concentrated levels of wealth and power of the super-rich, elites and global corporations, whose activities significantly affect the resources and opportunities for others in society (Rogers, 2012; Sayer, 2012). For example, the super-rich and large corporations can indirectly affect economic growth

---

[3]   We are grateful to Gareth Morgan for making this point.

and expenditure on vital public services through speculative financial capital and tax havens (Sayer, 2015; Shaxson, 2011). In failing to address issues of unequal power and wealth, foundations cannot complement their existing grantmaking programmes to produce more stable and lasting solutions to poverty, deprivation and exclusion (Rawls, 1999). Notwithstanding this general failure, some established charitable foundations in our study did make grants to research institutes and think tanks examining alternative forms of capitalism and governance. A few foundations also fund charities and commission reports to support campaigns to change rules on tax havens, tax avoidance, high pay and executive bonuses. These campaigns have become normalised and acceptable issues of contestation as a result of austerity cuts, research on income and wealth disparities and a network of protest groups, such as UK Uncut and the Occupy movement. But most foundations are reluctant to fully engage in a radical discussion of unequal power and wealth, deeming this to be 'too political', partly because trustees are too cautious and conservative and they fear a backlash from the right-wing media and conservative think tanks (Carson, 2003).

Fifth, despite claims of being independent, charitable foundations and grantmakers are socially embedded in ways that shape their activities and programmes. For example, some foundations and grantmakers express dismay at how the right-wing media, such as the *Daily Mail*, sometimes scrutinise their activities and publish sensational stories about their grants to animal rights or youth offenders charities, rather than to veterans or heritage charities (Deacon et al, 1995). They then receive letters from newspaper readers complaining about their programmes, and a few even send malicious packages. To rebut charges of left-leaning bias in their programmes, foundations and grantmakers balance their portfolios with grants to traditional and conservative charities. In addition, trustees often constrain the foundations' progressive priorities, distancing themselves from the term 'social justice.' In our study, most trustees are described as being conservative with a small 'c', many coming from business and elite backgrounds (Bond, 2012). The social networks that many trustees belong to lack social diversity and are removed from the everyday experiences of the poor and the marginalised. In many cases trustees are self-recruiting through invitation only by existing board members, though more professional and established foundations hire a recruitment agency to appoint trustees.

Sixth, charitable and community foundations recognise that their programmes and the size of their grants are insufficient to achieve social change when compared with larger and more powerful corporate actors such as local authorities, corporations and trade unions (Prewitt et al, 2004). Furthermore, most foundations express doubt about the impact of their programmes on social change and public policy, given that social inequality and suffering are complex and enduring problems and that programme effect has a long time lag. But nevertheless, they tend to make strong rhetorical claims about social change and justice in annual reports and strategic reviews, perhaps believing that social change is the basis of their legitimacy (Prewitt et al, 2004). As we have seen, there are several reasons why foundations lack the capacity to pursue social justice projects and progressive grantmaking.

Conclusion

To conclude, we have critically examined the implicit values of social justice, legitimacy and accountability that underpin charitable and community foundations' and grantmakers' programmes and priorities. Neoliberalism has significantly enriched and financialised foundations, creating huge wealth, almost all of it unearned and undeserving. As normative institutions, foundations are inherently flawed. While they possess the capacity for social change and justice, they have internal features and occupy structural positions within the polity that produce tensions and limitations to their pursuit of progressive issues.

In many ways foundations are a product of, and reflect, a (neo)liberal political economy, and they cannot be otherwise unless we change the nature of our politics, which cannot be called democratic any longer, but rather plutocratic. Nevertheless, foundations have some scope for better engagement and bolder activities and grantmaking that can address pressing political and structural issues. Not to do so means that they only partly accomplish the goals and aspirations of a liberal social justice, as envisaged by Adam Smith, John Stuart Mill and John Rawls. We have alluded to how a better social justice can be achieved: for example, through less parasitic endowment and sources of philanthropic donations; more international social justice programmes; bolder political risk-taking and advocacy work, a reduction in the concentration of power and wealth and more socially diverse trustees.

By engaging with liberal thinkers such as John Rawls, we have suggested how liberalism can be productively used in a left-leaning critique of the privileged class. Liberal ideas of social justice and legitimacy can be pragmatically employed to create a good society that requires a change to basic structures of private property ownership and political power. Indeed, Rawlsian liberalism calls for a duty of justice and a socialised and democratic production system, rather than just settling for charity and regulation of the worst excesses of capitalism.

References

ACF, 2007, *Grantmaking by UK trusts and charities*, www.acf.org.uk/uploadedFiles/Publications_and_resources/Publications/0416B_TrustAndFoundationBriefingPaper.pdf

ACF, 2014, *Giving trends: top 300 foundations 2014 Report*, www.acf.org.uk/uploadedFiles/Foundation_Giving_Trends_2014.pdf

Baker, J, Lynch, K, Cantillon, S and Walsh, J, 2004, *Equality: from theory to action*, 2nd edn, Basingstoke: Palgrave Macmillan

Big Lottery Fund, 2012, *Annual report and accounts 2011–12*, www.biglotteryfund.org.uk/annual_report_accounts2012.pdf

Boltanski, L, 1999, *Distant suffering: morality, media and politics*, Cambridge: Cambridge University Press

Bond, M, 2012, Business and the Big Society, in *Philanthropy and a better society*, Centre for Charitable Giving and Philanthropy, London: Alliance Publishing Trust, pp68–72

Breen, O, 2012, Too political to be charitable? The Charities Act 2009 and the future of human rights organisations in Ireland, *Public Law*, 2, 268–87

Carson, E, 2003, *Reflections on foundations and social justice*, www.spfund.org/Portals/0/PDFs/Reflections%20on%20Foundations%20and%20Social%20Justice.pdf

Cohen, H, 1983, Charities: a utilitarian perspective, *Current Legal Problems*, 36, 241–58

Cohen, R, 2008, Philanthropy and the role of social justice, in Kass, A, ed, *Giving well, doing good: readings got thoughtful philanthropists*, Bloomington: Indiana University Press, pp28–33

Community Foundations of Canada, 2003, *Potential and limitations of social justice grantmaking: Report II*, www.cfc-fcc.ca/documents/SocJust.ENG.PotentialR2.pdf

Core, J and Donaldson, T, 2010, An economic and ethical approach to charity and to charity endowments, *Review of Social Economy*, 68, 3, 261–84

Craig, G, 2005, Delivering social justice through philanthropy, *Alliance Magazine*, 10, 2, 22–7

Deacon, D, Fenton, N and Walker, B, 1995, Communicating philanthropy: the media and the voluntary sector in Britain, *Voluntas*, 6, 2, 119–39

Eikenberry, A, 2009, Refusing the market: a democratic discourse for voluntary and nonprofit organisations, *Nonprofit and Voluntary Sector Quarterly*, 38, 4, 582–96

Fleischacker, S, 2003, *On Adam Smith's wealth of nations: a philosophical companion*, Princeton: Princeton University Press

Forman-Barzilai, F, 2010, *Adam Smith and the circles of sympathy: cosmopolitan and moral theory*, Cambridge: Cambridge University Press

Fraser, N, 2009, *Scales of justice: reimagining political space in a globalizing world*, New York: Columbia University Press

Gatsby Charitable Foundation, 2012, *Annual report and accounts 2011–12)*, www.gatsby.org.uk/en/About-Gatsby/~/media/Files/About%20Gatsby/Gatsby%20Annual%20Review%202011.ashx

Illingworth, P, Pogge, T and Wenar, L (eds) 2011, *Giving well: the ethics of philanthropy*, Oxford: Oxford University Press

Jagpal, N and Laskowski, K, 2010, *The philanthropic landscape: the state of social justice philanthropy*, www.ncrp.org/files/publications/PhilanthropicLandscape-StateofSocialJusticePhilanthropy.pdf

Jenkins, R, 2012, *The governance and financial management of endowed charitable foundations*, London: Association for Charitable Foundations

Jenkins, R and Rogers, K, 2013, *For good and not for keeps: how long-term charity investors approach spending on their charitable aims*, London: Association for Charitable Foundations

Leat, D, 2007, *Just change: strategies for increasing philanthropic impact*, London: Association for Charitable Foundations

Lester, E, 2011, *Advancing upstream: philanthropy's aspirations for social justice*, MA Dissertation, Tucson, AZ: Arizona State University

Luxton, P, 2009, *Making law? Parliament v the Charity Commission*, London: Politeia

Mayer, S, 2008, *Saving the babies: looking upstream for solutions,* brief report, www.effectivecommunities.com/pdfs/ECP_SavingBabies.pdf

Morgan, G, 2012, Public benefit and charitable status: assessing a 20-year process of reforming the primary legal framework for voluntary activity in the UK, *Voluntary Sector Review*, 3, 1, 67–91

Nickel, P and Eikenberry, A, 2009, A critique of the discourse of marketized philanthropy, *American Behavioral Scientist*, 52, 7, 974–89

Pharoah, C and Bryant, L, 2012, *Global grant-making: a review of UK foundations' funding for international development*, London: Nuffield Foundation

Pratt, B, Hailey, J, Gallo, M, Shadwick, R and Hayman, R, 2012, *Understanding private donors in international development*, INTRAC Policy Briefing Paper no. 31, www.intrac.org/data/files/resources/747/ Briefing-Paper-31-Understanding-private-donors-in-international-development.pdf

Prewitt, K, Dogan, M, Heydemann, S and Toepler, S (eds) 2004, *The legitimacy of philanthropic foundations: United States and European perspectives*, New York: Russell Sage Foundation

Raddon, Mary-Beth, 2008, Neoliberal legacies: planned giving and the new philanthropy, *Studies in Political Economy*, 81, 27–48.

Rawls, J, 1999, *A theory of justice*, revised edition, Oxford: Oxford University Press

Rabinowitz, A, 1990, *Social change philanthropy in America*, Westport: Quorum Books

Rogers, R, 2012, Why philanthro-policymaking matters, *Society*, 48, 5, 376–81

Ruesga, A and Puntenney, D, 2010, *Social justice philanthropy*, www.p-sj.org/files/Social%20Justice%20Philanthropy%20Traditions_0.pdf

Sandberg, B, 2012, Constructing society's aide, *Administration* and *Society*, 44 , 8, 936–61

Sayer, A, 2012, Facing the challenge of the return of the rich, in Atkinson, W, Roberts, S and Savage, M, eds, *Class inequality in austerity Britain*, Basingstoke: Palgrave Macmillan, pp163–79

Sayer, A, 2015, *Why we can't afford the rich*, Bristol: Policy Press

Sealander, J, 2002, 'Curing evils at their source': the arrival of scientific giving, in Friedman, L and McGarvie, M (eds) *Charity, philanthropy and civility in American history*, Cambridge: Cambridge University Press, pp217–40

Sen, A, 2009, *The idea of justice*, Cambridge, MA: Belknap Press

Shaxson, N, 2011, *Treasure islands: tax havens and the men who stole the world*, London: Bodley Head

Singer, P, 1972, Famine, affluence and morality, *Philosophy and Public Affairs*, 1, 3, 229–43

Smith, A, 1976, *The theory of moral sentiments*, Indianapolis: Liberty Fund

Charity deserts and social justice: exploring variations in the distribution of charitable organisations and their resources in England

John Mohan[1]

Introduction

In December 2013 the Conservative think tank, the Centre for Social Justice (CSJ), reprised its arguments that 'charity deserts' existed in the UK, and that this constituted evidence of a dearth in social action in communities. Their argument rested on comparisons of variations in the ratio of charitable organisations to population between local authorities in England. The CSJ was relatively silent on what might be done about this situation, apart from expressing the hope that 'something's got to give': in other words, an increase in philanthropic activity was desirable. Whether this will have much effect on the manifest variations in the distribution of charitable resources is the subject of this paper.

The CSJ were by no means the first commentators to consider whether charitable giving promotes a socially just distribution of resources. John Stuart Mill argued that 'charity almost always does too much or too little. It lavishes its bounty in one place, and leaves people to starve in another' (1907, V.11.47). A more recent academic analysis argued that philanthropy has four distinct limitations: philanthropic

[1]   Financial support from ESRC, the Scottish Office and the Office for the Third Sector (OTS) through the Centre for Charitable Giving and Philanthropy (CGAP) (www.cgap.org.uk) is gratefully acknowledged. I am grateful to my colleagues in CGAP, particularly Beth Breeze, Rose Lindsey and Peter Backus, and also to David Clifford and Steve Barnard of the Third Sector Research Centre, University of Southampton.

amateurism, insufficiency, particularism and paternalism (Salamon, 1987, p40). The second of these, the inability of philanthropy to allocate resources to places and causes where they are most needed, is closely related to the concerns of the CSJ, and in this chapter I consider the challenges of mapping the distribution of charitable resources. There is a need for clarity in our assessments of this question. Considerable hopes are currently vested in voluntary initiatives and philanthropy, and there is optimism about the promise of the new philanthropy. Yet without a realistic appraisal of the current distribution of charitable resources, there is a risk that the new philanthropy might replicate the weaknesses of the old.

An assessment of the degree of social justice and redistribution achieved by charitable resources raises a number of questions. Donors may have a range of motivations for their generosity, and achieving social justice may not be one of them. Charitable activity has direct and indirect impacts on people and communities. The benefits might include the delivery of services, advice and support, and the provision of access to resources, whether in cash or in kind. The benefits of charitable activity may, however, be indirect, non-monetary and difficult to quantify. For example, Clotfelter (1992) points out that a foundation grant for a project designed to deter at-risk youth from crime might have a direct impact on the area in which the organisation running it is based, in terms of employment and volunteering opportunities. However, such a project might also have indirect benefit for the surrounding areas, in the form of greater peace of mind for residents. Some commentators also argue that voluntary activity can contribute indirect benefits to communities by contributing to the formation of social capital (Rupasingha et al, 2006; Saxton and Benson, 2006; Scheffler et al, 2008).

What sources are available for investigations into the distributional outcomes of charitable activity? There are no reliable sources of data on the extent to which individuals receive direct benefits from charitable organisations. Some surveys do ask people about whether they receive services from voluntary organisations, but their enquiries are confined to a limited range of activities such as social care. Given the complexities of such work, an alternative is to take Mill's comment as a point of departure for an investigation of the distribution of charitable resources across *communities*. This is consistent with a tradition of social policy investigation into territorial justice; given normative notions of need, do communities have more or less than their expected share of charitable resources (Davies, 1968)?

I pursue this line of enquiry by first reviewing historical studies of the distribution of charitable resources in the UK and also some contemporary studies of the US. I then outline sources of evidence for similar work in England and Wales. The substantive discussion presents illustrations of variations in communities in the availability of charitable resources, but also draws attention to the challenges of interpretation of those patterns. In conclusion, I reflect on the implications for new philanthropy.

Previous literature

We have ample historical evidence of variations in the availability of charitable resources. A late-19th-century enquiry into the distribution of endowed schools revealed a tenfold variation in the availability of places supported by charity between southern counties and parts of Lancashire (Owen, 1964). Writing in the 1940s, Jennings (1945, p29) observed that the 'haphazard and partial distribution of [voluntary social] services [was] a natural result of dependence on local initiatives and self-support'. In the Second Reading of the NHS Bill in 1946, Aneurin Bevan polemically argued that voluntary hospital services were distributed according to the 'caprice of charity' so that resources were supplied where they were least needed.[2] This assertion was given some empirical substantiation decades later through Mohan's (2003) reconstruction of the pattern of hospital utilisation and Gorsky et al's (1999, 2002) analyses of the distribution of hospital resources and finances. The authoritative Wolfenden Committee commented that the soil for voluntary action was 'much more fertile' (Wolfenden Committee, 1978, p58) in some areas than others, but these remarks were based largely on a study of the distribution of branches of some large national voluntary organisations, complemented by an investigation of the distribution of voluntary organisations in three contrasting local authority areas (Hatch, 1980).

More recently the Conservative Party's policy document, *Voluntary action in the 21st century*, used the term 'charity deserts' to denote areas in which there were relatively few charitable organisations (Conservative Party, 2007, p21). The context was the argument that unless opportunities for voluntary action were available in such areas, levels of social capital would remain low. Little has been heard subsequently from the Conservative Party or their coalition partners about how to irrigate charity deserts; instead, their policies have focused

[2]   H.C.Deb., 5th series, v 422, c 46–7

on creating a climate of general support for voluntary action rather than targeting resources or initiatives on particular communities. The Coalition Government's advocacy of the 'Big Society' is also relevant to discussion of variations in the distribution of voluntary organisations. There is a strong emphasis on local community action – for example, the Prime Minister's wish that every adult in the country should be part of a neighbourhood group – and a stress on localism in public policy (evident in encouragement of community groups to take over the running of public services, or in support for greater neighbourhood involvement in planning). Both of these imply a need to understand more about the distribution of charitable organisations and their resources. In Wolpert's (1996) evocative phrase, we need to know 'who is holding the safety net', and we also need to know something about the size of the mesh and the distribution of any holes in that net. What can be learned from previous exercises to map the distribution of charitable resources?

There is a considerable body of North American scholarship on the geographical distribution of nonprofit organisations, particularly those receiving tax reliefs for charitable purposes (for example, Wolch & Geiger, 1983; Wolpert, 1988,1993; Wolch, 1990). Research found significant variation in the distribution of nonprofits between and within states and metropolitan areas (Wolch & Geiger, 1983) and related these distributions to levels of regional and urban prosperity, local variations in charitable giving, and indicators of population composition and economic distress. Communities varied widely in terms of private generosity towards, and public sector support for, nonprofits (Wolch, 1990). These conclusions have been echoed by recent studies (Gronbjerg & Paarlberg, 2001; Joassart-Marcelli & Wolch, 2003; Bielefeld & Murdoch, 2004; Wolpert & Seley, 2004; Rupasingha et al, 2006; Scheffler et al, 2008).

To date, such studies have not been replicated in the UK. Some studies (Marshall, 1997; Fyfe & Milligan, 2004) relied on local listings of organisations, but these are known to offer a partial and unrepresentative picture; they are likely to overemphasise the larger charities in a local authority, particularly those engaged in delivering public services and those which have dual registration as charitable companies. Such organisations are most likely to be on the radar of infrastructure bodies, such as Councils for Voluntary Service (CVSs). Conversely, such listings are likely to contain very small numbers of small charities (Mohan et al, 2011; Mohan, 2012).

Nevertheless, in England and Wales considerable volumes of data on registered charities are gathered by the Charity Commission.

Registration is required for organisations above a certain size/ turnover and the relevant data are publicly available for the 190,000 registered main charities. The data includes: location; assets, income and expenditure; the nature of their activity by sector (for example, health, disability, overseas aid or arts/culture); function (how they carry out their charitable purposes: for example, through grantmaking or service provision), and beneficiaries (for example, children, youth, the elderly or those from a particular religious or ethnic background). Note that some of the more detailed regulatory data – particularly that which gives a breakdown of income sources – are only available for organisations with incomes greater than £500,000.

The focus of this chapter is on England and Wales. Comparisons with Scotland must be undertaken with care due to differences in regulatory requirements (Mohan & Barnard, 2013a), while the Charity Commission for Northern Ireland has only recently been established and is still compiling an authoritative register. The emphasis is on the difficulty of making appropriate comparisons of the level of charitable activity in different communities.

Mapping the distribution of charitable organisations and resources

Here, consideration is given to methods for mapping variations in the distribution and expenditure of charitable organisations, and to some of the challenges for such exercises. A first question to consider is whether *all* charities are of interest.

The National Council for Voluntary Organisations (NCVO) has worked with the Office for National Statistics on the definition of 'general charities'. They identified several types of charity which either provide benefits *only* to a limited class of individuals or are ultimately controlled by other, non-charitable, organisations (NCVO, 2014). The principal exclusions are: independent schools; non-departmental public bodies which receive nearly all their funding from government; NHS-controlled charities; and benevolent societies. In developing the classification, it was argued that such organisations would not be regarded by the public as being genuinely charitable. The great bulk of charities – some 90% – are described as 'general charities'. The other principal categories are religious bodies (approximately 6%), independent schools and colleges (approximately 1.5%) and benevolent institutions (approximately 1.5%). There are several other categories containing only a few hundred organisations each. While few in number, these organisations can account for considerable proportions of total spending, and because they are not distributed randomly across the country they can pose challenges when we seek to compare the distribution of resources between geographical areas. For instance, if we regard the aggregate level of expenditure by charitable organisations in communities as an index of variations in the distribution of voluntary resources, we should acknowledge that that measure will be influenced by the mix of organisations in any given area.

Thus the majority of independent schools which are registered as charities are located in south-east England. That is not surprising, since historically this has been the most prosperous part of the country. Such schools are the largest single charity in about 20% of local authorities, while in a small number of local authorities over 50% of expenditure by charitable organisations is disbursed by independent schools. Conversely, a small number of local authorities have no such organisations. Religious organisations account for over 50% of expenditure by charities in one local authority, although in 90% of cases the figure is below 20%. While general charities, as defined by the NCVO, account for the great bulk of charitable spending in most local authorities (the 50th percentile is 63% of total spending), there are a small number of local authorities (around thirty) in which general charities account for less than 30% of total expenditure by charitable organisations. These compositional differences caution against easy generalisations about the level of charitable activity in particular communities.

Similar arguments can be made about the distribution of expenditure by non-departmental public bodies, since these, while charitable, receive almost all of their income from government. Hence, some would argue, they should not be included in maps of the local and regional distribution of charitable activity. Finally, large grantmaking foundations have little effect on the pattern of organisations but would clearly give rise to a further problem of double-counting if financial statistics were being analysed. Such considerations may not have much impact on maps of ratios of organisations – but they certainly would have an effect on comparison of the level of expenditure between communities.

The distribution of organisations

In what follows, the focus is on general charities. What does the pattern of these organisations suggest about the notion of charity 'deserts'? The idea could be explored by looking at the characteristics of those areas that either have no registered charities in them or very few. It is really only at the local scale that this is the case, and some of these places are sparsely populated. There are no middle range *super output areas* (MSOAs),[3] the typical population of which is around 7,500, in England and Wales that do not have any charities in them at all, but 662 of them have five or fewer. The total population living in these areas is some 4.55 million, representing around 9% of the population; but these numbers represent 1.6% of the total number of charities in England and Wales. Ranking upwards by numbers of charities in each MSOA, 10% of charities are distributed across areas with a population of 15.4 million. Conversely, at the other end of the spectrum, there are 100 MSOAs containing 10% of the registered general charities in England; but fewer than one million people, or around 2% of the population, live in these areas. If we interpret 'desert' as the total absence of charitable activity and organisations, it suggests that there are few *genuine* charity deserts, although there are certainly areas where the presence of charities is less visible than others.

But with regard to unitary or upper-tier local authorities there are substantial variations. There are approximately 126,000 general charities in England, giving an average ratio of 2.56 organisations per 1,000 population. For the 149 upper-tier local authorities in England, there are 14 local authorities with a ratio less than half that. These authorities are: Blackpool; Knowsley; Stoke; Sandwell; Barking and Dagenham; Walsall; Oldham; Tameside; Middlesbrough; Hull; Rochdale; Wolverhampton, Hartlepool and Bolton. Conversely, in seven areas – mostly prosperous rural communities (Gloucestershire; Suffolk; Shropshire; North Yorkshire; Wiltshire, Oxfordshire and Rutland) – the figure is more than 50% above the national ratio. The City of London is left out of this calculation; with a population of just over 7,000 and 900 registered charities, its ratio of 127 organisations per 1,000 population is 30 times that of any other local authority. This

---

[3]   The 2001 census data is provided at various levels of aggregation; census output areas are the smallest units for which data are available, but with a typical population of 150 households the majority of them actually have no charities at all. For the calculation of reasonably stable ratios of organisations to population, MSOAs are the smallest appropriate scale.

reflects the presence there of many legal firms and companies which provide the correspondence addresses for large numbers of charities.[4]

However, we cannot be sure that the presence of an organisation registered in an area means that it actually operates there. We need more precise information on the areas in which charities carry out their work. They may, but are not required to, identify an 'area of benefit' (AOB), and if they do they must confine their activities within it. The complexity and coverage of the AOB information does not lend itself to the precise identification of which charities operate in which local authorities; AOB descriptions are often very vague, specified in relation to obsolete administrative units, or not specified at all (Mohan and Barnard, 2013b). An alternative is to use information reported by charities about their area of operation (AOO); they are asked to indicate which local authorities they operate in, and to name them if there are ten or fewer. Such data can be used to apportion expenditures between communities, albeit with accuracy only for those that operate within a single local authority.

Even allowing for such challenges, there are at least three respects in which a map of registered charitable organisations will not capture the full detail of charitable flows. First, certain categories of charitable organisation are exempt from registration with the Charity Commission – notably certain educational institutions and religious establishments – and limited public information is available about their income and expenditure. However, these bodies may be in receipt of substantial charitable income. For instance, flows of charitable support for academic (notably medical) research are comparable with levels of expenditure by the largest charities in certain regions of the country. As an example, statistics from the Higher Education Funding Council for England (HEFCE) suggest that medical research at Newcastle University receives around £15 million per annum from charities, a figure rarely exceeded by the largest charitable entities in its region apart from housing associations. Second, funding will flow to places outside the UK through the thousands of general charities operating in the sphere of international development. At present, detailed information on the flows of such expenditure by country is limited, but the Charity

[4]   For reasons of brevity, discussion has been omitted of other adjustments that may be made before estimates of ratios of charities to population are calculated. One is that many charities may share a postcode because they combine to achieve administrative efficiencies. Although the charities that share postcodes are overrepresented in London, that by no means accounts for the differentials between London and other parts of the country in terms of the ratio of charities to population.

Commission is now collecting data on it. Third, we should note the presence, particularly in London, of charities that are the headquarters of large national organisations that have branch or federal structures elsewhere. In practice, most of their activity takes place in areas other than the local authority in which they are based. Charity Commission data is not informative here but the 2008 National Survey of Third Sector Organisations (NSTSO: Ipsos MORI, 2009) showed that at least 60% of charities with incomes greater than £1 million characterised themselves as being the head office of an organisation with branches in other regions; 35% of such charities were in London (nearly twice London's share of charities, which was 18%). Other research focused on North East England showed that numerous large national voluntary organisations whose head offices were outside the region (mainly in London) were operating projects within the North East (Mohan et al, 2011). Information from the area of operation supplied by charities to the Commission suggests that the number of charities actually operating in specific local authorities is rather larger than would be inferred from the number of organisations registered there: sometimes two or three times as great.

One way to focus our analytical lens is, therefore, to consider only those charities which state that they operate within a single local authority. There are 73,000 such organisations, with a combined expenditure of £5.4 billion. They represent 63% of all general charities and around 20% of total expenditure by those organisations. The distribution is illuminating. There are 1.6 such charities per 1,000 population, but in 48 local authorities the ratio is less than half of that; those local authorities have a total population of 11.8 million. At the bottom of the rankings are Barking and Dagenham; Brent; Luton; Bedfordshire; Stoke-on-Trent; Blackpool; Bexley; Wigan; South Tyneside; Bournemouth, Slough and Knowsley. All have fewer than 0.6 'within local authority' charities per 1,000 population; five of them are in the lowest quartile of local authorities by index of material deprivation: that is, they are among the most disadvantaged areas in England. Conversely, in seven local authorities, mostly prosperous and rural, the ratio of 'local' charities to population is more than double the national average. These areas are Wiltshire; Somerset; Rutland; Devon; Cumbria, North Yorkshire and Herefordshire: with a combined population of 2.9 million. Once again, the City of London is an outlier.

Expenditure by charitable organisations

The contribution that charities make to the community cannot be measured just in terms of the numbers of organisations registered in a particular area; we also need to consider the resources which they have available to them. A lower ratio of charities to population might simply mean that charitable activity is organised through a smaller number of large entities; this was recognised by the Wolfenden Committee (Wolfenden Committee, 1978; see also Hatch, 1980). But measures of the scale of activity in a given community, such as average or aggregate expenditures, can be significantly affected by the presence of very large single organisations. As an example, calculation of the mean expenditure for charities in Swindon would be substantially inflated because of the presence of the National Trust (expenditure typically above £300 million), the largest charity in South West England and in the top 20 nationally and a charity which has activities throughout the country. More generally, we know that the size distribution of organisations varies greatly between regions. For example, Table 11.1 shows that while London only has 19% of the general charity population, it contains three-fifths of those with budgets in excess of £10 million and two-fifths of those with budgets over £1 million. By definition most other regions of the country, therefore, have lower shares of these organisations. As indicated previously, numerous charities in London are HQs of national organisations. Thus, much as there is a concentration of control functions in the wider economy in London and the South East, that also seems to be the case in respect of charitable organisations.

To minimise the influence of very large organisations, comparisons between local areas are better done using *median* expenditures. We see variations between local authorities along socioeconomic lines, as we found with the ratio of organisations to population, but a strong urban–rural contrast is also evident (Figure 11.1). Nationally, the median expenditure for general charities is just under £7,300, but there are 36 local authorities in which the figure is lower and, in contrast, 29 in which median expenditure is more than twice the national figure. It appears to be predominantly rural areas in which median expenditure is relatively low, while conversely it is particularly high in London. Of the 15 local authorities recording the largest median expenditure, 14 are in London (the other one is South Tyneside, a local authority with a low ratio of charities to population).

If we take these ratios and medians as a measure of organisational capacity, we might conclude that there are significant variations between places. Another graphical way to consider this is to divide

Table 11.1: Regional distribution of general charities by size band

Region		<10,000	£10-100k	£100k-1mn	£1mn-10mn	>£10mn	Total
							Expenditure band
North East	Number	2,130	1,589	756	110	7	4,592
	Col. %	4.02	3.84	4.65	3.7	2.3	4.03
North West	Number	6,361	4,565	1,831	325	22	13,104
	Col. %	12.01	11.02	11.27	11	7.21	11.5
Yorkshire and the Humber	Number	5,107	3,615	1,418	204	12	10,356
	Col. %	9.64	8.73	8.73	6.9	3.93	9.09
East Midlands	Number	6,038	3,656	1,120	134	10	10,958
	Col. %	11.4	8.83	6.89	4.5	3.28	9.62
West Midlands	Number	6,161	3,878	1,420	261	16	11,736
	Col. %	11.63	9.36	8.74	8.8	5.25	10.3
East of England	Number	8,811	6,008	1,598	253	12	16,682
	Col. %	16.63	14.51	9.84	8.5	3.93	14.65
London	Number	7,009	8,080	5,253	1,193	188	21,723
	Col. %	13.23	19.51	32.33	40.3	61.64	19.07
South East	Number	11,362	10,025	2,850	478	38	24,753
	Col. %	21.45	24.21	17.54	16.2	12.46	21.73
South West	Number	9,337	6,343	1,736	251	21	17,688
	Col. %	13.84	12.42	9	7.45	6.1	15.52
Total	Number	52,979	41,416	16,246	2,958	305	113,904
	% of total	46.51	36.36	14.26	2.6	0.27	100

median expenditure and charity/population ratios into quartiles and cross-reference them. This gives a 16-fold classification of local authorities, which is informative (Figure 11.2). All ten local authorities that featured in the top quartile on both indicators are in London and a further 12 local authorities, again largely in London, reached the top quartile on median expenditure per charity and were in the second quartile on the charity/population ratio. At the other end of the spectrum, six local authorities (Bolton; Wakefield; Barnsley; Redcar and Cleveland, Oldham and Tameside) fall into the bottom quartile on both indicators. Dudley and Darlington are in the lowest quartile on median expenditure, and the second lowest quartile on charity/

Figure 11.1: Median expenditure for general charities, 2005-9, for upper-tier local authorities, England

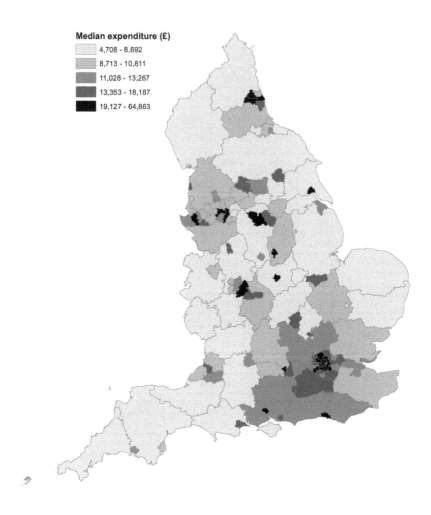

population ratio. In terms of levels of deprivation, three members of this group are in the most deprived quartile of local authorities, and the rest have above–average levels of deprivation. There does seem a strong prima facie case, therefore, that considering only those organisations which operate within a single local authority, charity does not do a particularly good job of matching resources with needs.

Figure 11.2: Charity–population ratios and median charity expenditures, upper-tier local authorities, England

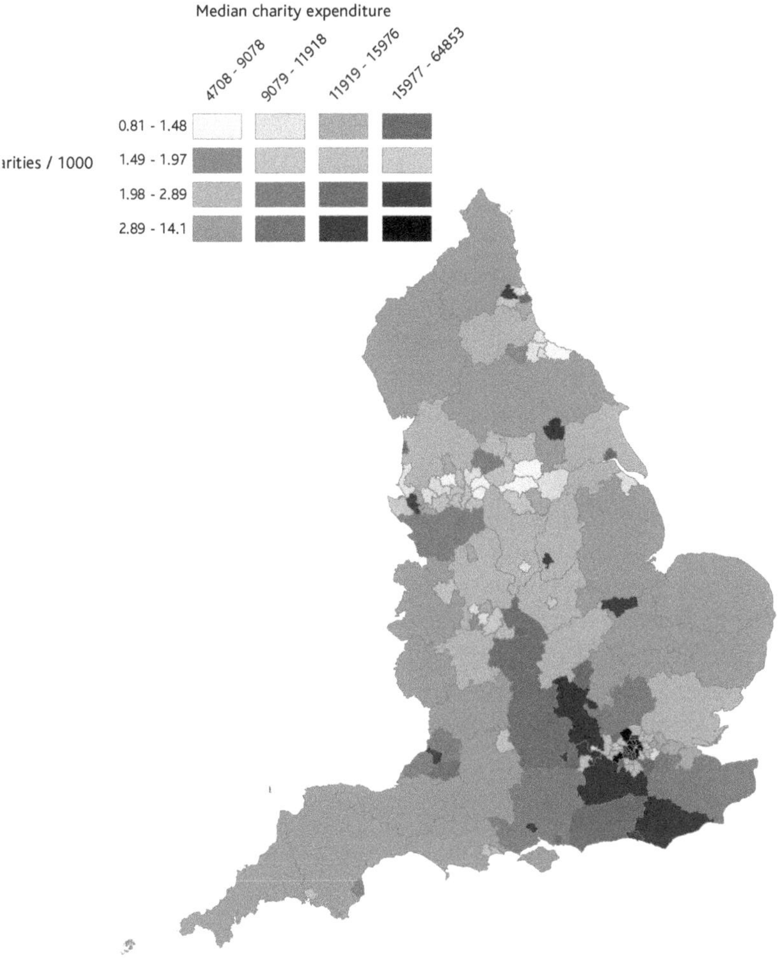

Comparing organisations across communities

A potential criticism of the discussion so far is that comparisons are not being made of like with like. Inevitably, the needs that voluntary organisations are established to meet will vary from place to place. Boroughs in inner London are far more likely, for example, to have organisations responding to the needs of migrant communities, some of which are quite long-standing (for example, charities associated with waves of immigration), whereas rural areas will exhibit a quite different mix (e.g. village halls; farmers' clubs) a range of environmental charities and so on. And aggregation to the scale of local authorities ignores the fact that, as survey data has shown (Clifford, 2012), many charitable organisations operate only at the neighbourhood scale. It is therefore useful to focus on types of organisations that are comparable between different communities.

Parent–Teacher Associations (PTAs)

A good example is that of PTAs (Parent–Teacher Associations), which exist to support individual schools; several thousand are registered as charities. The research of Reich (2006) in the USA is relevant here, although the organisations he investigates raise funds for *all* schools within a particular local area, rather than for a particular school as in England and Wales. He identified very considerable variations between school boards in the resources available to them, and suggested that this conferred additional advantage on those who are already well off, since the resources generated in this way could equate to some thousands of dollars per pupil. In England and Wales, thousands of schools raise charitable funds through vehicles such as PTAs; some 12,000 such organisations are registered charities. We can compare the resources that they generate, both by region and within region, with the level of deprivation of the area in which they are based; in Figure 11.3, the most disadvantaged areas are on the left. The great majority of organisations registered are located in the most prosperous localities, and the median level of income is also greatest there (Figure 11.3). Median incomes

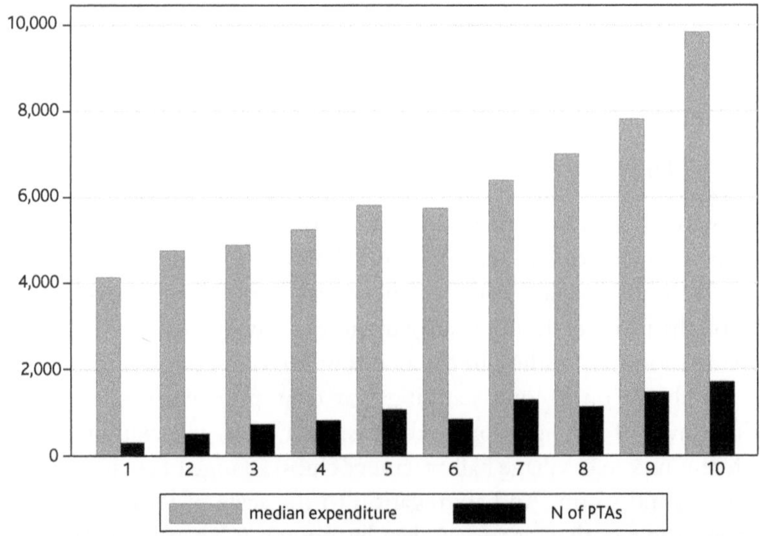

Figure 11.3: Median PTA expenditure and number of PTAs by decile of deprivation

range from around £4,000 in the areas where deprivation is highest to around £10,000 in the most prosperous communities. There are clearly more organisations in the most prosperous communities, but note that these figures are not standardised by population.

The overall sums of money involved are not large, and should really be compared to the numbers of pupils in the schools rather than to the population of the surrounding area, but it is clear that the position of individual schools varies greatly. There are around 900 PTAs that raise £25,000 or more in a given year. Indeed, in London and the south east there are several organisations in which annual expenditures are in the £100,000-plus bracket.

Although the pattern revealed in this graph appears a fairly clear one, one can think of potential objections to it. Not all charitable organisations choose to, or are required to, register with the Charity Commission so the numbers of PTAs could be underestimated, but since the financial threshold for charity registration is annual income or expenditure of £5,000 or more, one would expect the number of non-registrants to be small. Schools without PTAs may develop other fundraising vehicles; some establish general school funds, which may not be accounted for separately. Some charitable organisations are also exempt from registering with the Charity Commission, such as churches, and if they run schools it is possible they would not be required to disclose funds raised through charitable sources. Nevertheless, we can observe the pattern of charitable giving for several thousand PTAs and it seems reasonably clear that the funds raised in this way operate to the benefit of the more prosperous communities.

Hospices

The hospice movement is justly celebrated as an example of voluntary initiative. There are over 200 hospices in England registered as charities, with a combined total expenditure of around £500 million. Over 50 hospices featured in the largest 1,000 charities, and over 60 hospices would rank in the largest 100 charities in their region. However, is the pattern of expenditure by hospices distributed systematically with reference to need? A very simple answer to this question is presented in Figure 11.4, which compares each region's share of total hospice expenditure with its share of the population. Briefly, a score of 'one' would indicate that the region was receiving a share of expenditure that was broadly comparable with its share of the population; anything above that indicates an above-average share. These are not adjusted for need in any way, but one might argue that even without adjustment the pattern

Figure 11.4: Regional shares of hospice expenditures compared to regional populations

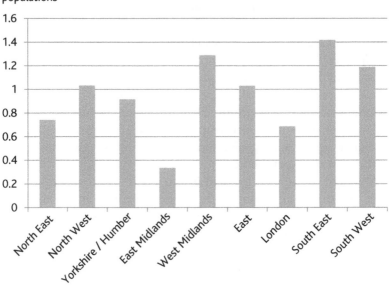

revealed does not represent a very good match of resources with the need for hospice care. The south east, the most prosperous region, has a share of resources some 40% greater than its population would indicate, while the East Midlands has about one-third and the North East and London have some 70% of their notional share. A better comparator might be the total number of deaths from causes requiring hospice care, but it does seem unlikely that the pattern would reflect this. And a word of caution is in order: not all of the variation is explicable in terms of Salamon's 'philanthropic insufficiency' (Salamon, 1987, p40); in addition to charitable support, many hospices receive funds from the NHS for end-of-life care, and variations between Primary Care Trusts in expenditure might account for some of the pattern.

Some further complications: charitable expenditure or expenditure by charitable organisations?

A further complication, which is not addressed in this paper, is that we don't know very much about *types* of income sources. Of course, charities are at liberty to obtain income from any source as long as it is applied in a manner consistent with their charitable objectives; but the reliance of many charitable organisations on public funding can complicate attempts to trace the destination of charitable funds. If we take this to its logical conclusion and focus only on charities that do *not* receive public money in any form, we would find that the charitable landscape looks somewhat different. For example, Clifford et al (2013) used detailed survey data providing reliable responses on income sources for 40,000 charities. While 63% of English charities received no public funding, the proportion was as high as five-sixths for unincorporated (generally quite small) charities in the most prosperous parts of London (and in areas with similar levels of prosperity) was three-quarters or higher. Clearly, therefore, the map of charitable organisations would look rather different to the national pattern if we focused only on those organisations that relied solely upon income from fundraising and charitable donations.

Conclusion

In this paper, I have considered the challenges that confront us when we analyse variations in the distribution of charitable resources. Care needs to be taken in ensuring that *appropriate* comparisons are being made. While there are important variations between places in terms of the distribution of organisations, on its own this is not evidence of the existence of 'charity deserts' and it does not mean that we can be confident of a straightforward correspondence between local economic conditions and patterns of prosperity, on one hand, and the distribution of charitable activity, on the other. Nevertheless, there does seem to be *some* evidence that broadly supports the contention advanced over 150 years ago by John Stuart Mill.

I have not engaged with the challenge of explaining why these variations come about. Some of these patterns will reflect long-term trends in the charitable landscape. For instance, many will reflect socioeconomic conditions pertaining in previous periods of economic distress, while others appear to be related quite strongly to various urban regeneration initiatives from the 1960s onwards. Other variations will undoubtedly reflect the availability of financial and human resources. Communities possessed of prosperous, well-educated populations are more likely to be able to establish and sustain local voluntary organisations (Mohan & Bulloch, 2012).

Do the variations discussed in this chapter constitute a matter of injustice? From one perspective, no. It could be argued that the extent of voluntary effort and charitable support is a matter of individual choice, and that communities themselves choose the 'package' of voluntary resources that best meets their needs and preferences (Wolpert, 1988). On the other hand, these variations do matter if public policy is going to place greater reliance upon the voluntary sector. This chapter urges realism in assessing what can and cannot be achieved through philanthropic effort alone. Clearly the charitable capacities and resources available to communities in England vary considerably, and the substantial reductions in public spending that are currently taking place are most likely to affect communities with the lowest level of charitable resources. There are strong negative associations between levels of deprivation and the distribution and median expenditure of voluntary organisations. Moreover, when we consider the expectations implicit in the government's idea of the 'Big Society' the evidence suggests that such policies may result in widening gaps between communities. The organisational base for voluntary action is clearly much better developed in some communities than in others.

There are some limitations to this kind of work. Without administrative data from individual charities about their projects and clients it is difficult to form a judgement about how far they are reaching the most needy groups in society, and it should be reiterated that the conclusions of this paper relate to geographical areas. We also need a better understanding of how the pattern of charitable activity relates to the pattern of activity by the state and the market: is charitable activity a complement to, or a substitute for, public provision? Work on the dynamics of the formation and dissolution of charities, and the connection with long-term changes in the pattern of regional development, is also essential. However, it is hoped that this paper provides a cautionary tale about mapping the distribution of resources and that it highlights the need for scepticism about how well voluntary effort will match resources to social needs. Finally, it is worth recalling that deserts result from *long-term* climatic change, so we should not expect the irrigation of 'charity deserts' any time soon, and the historical evidence points to considerable stability in the patterns.

As to new philanthropy, the evidence from this paper suggests that the challenge of philanthropic insufficiency, hinted at by John Stuart Mill and elaborated and developed by Lester Salamon, remains important. If we can legitimately identify an 'old' philanthropy then its inability to match resources and need would represent a valid criticism. Critics have pointed out (Odendahl, 1989) that the result has been the allocation of money to causes and projects that reflect the concerns of a social elite. The new philanthropy, with its strong connections to business leadership and its strong emphases on corporate support, seems likely to develop most rapidly in communities with a strong private sector. There is much evidence to suggest that philanthropy is least developed in the parts of England that arguably need it most. Whether the new philanthropy will do much to change that remains to be seen.

References

Bielefeld, W and Murdoch, J, 2004, The locations of non-profit organisations and their for-profit counterparts: an exploratory analysis, *Non-Profit and Voluntary Sector Quarterly*, 33, 221–46

Clifford, D, 2012, Voluntary sector organisations working at the neighbourhood level in England: patterns by local area deprivation, *Environment and Planning A*, 44, 5, 1148–1164

Clifford, D, Geyne Rajme, F and Mohan, J, 2013, Variations between organisations and localities in government funding of third sector activity: evidence from the National Survey of Third Sector Organisations in England, *Urban Studies*, 50, 959–76

Clotfelter, C T, ed, 1992, *Who benefits from the nonprofit sector?*, Chicago: Chicago University Press

Conservative Party, 2007, *A stronger society: voluntary action in the 21st century*, www.conservatives.com/~/media/files/green%20papers/voluntary_green_paper.ashx?dl=true

Davies, B, 1968, *Social needs and resources in local services*, London: Michael Joseph

Fyfe, N and Milligan, C, 2004, Putting the voluntary sector in its place: geographical perspectives on voluntary activity and social welfare in Glasgow, *Journal of Social Policy*, 33, 1, 73–93

Gorsky, M, Mohan, J and Powell, M, 1999, British voluntary hospitals 1871–1938: the geography of provision and utilisation, *Journal of Historical Geography*, 25, 4, 463–82

Gorsky, M, Mohan, J and Powell, M, 2002, The financial health of voluntary hospitals in inter-war Britain, *Economic History Review*, 55, 3, 533–7

Gronbjerg, K and Paarlberg, L, 2001, Community variations in the size and scope of the non-profit sector: theory and preliminary findings, *Non-Profit and Voluntary Sector Quarterly*, 30, 4, 684–706

Hatch, S, 1980, *Outside the state: voluntary organisations in three English towns*, London: Croom Helm

Ipsos MORI, 2008, National Survey of Third Sector Organisations: Analytical Report, London: Cabinet Office

Jennings, H, 1945, Voluntary social services in urban areas, in Mess, H (ed) *Voluntary social services since 1918*, London: Kegan Paul, pp28–39

Joassart-Marcelli, P and Wolch, J, 2003, The intrametropolitan geography of poverty and the non-profit sector in Southern California, *Non-Profit and Voluntary Sector Quarterly*, 32, 1, 70–96

Marshall, T, 1997, *Local voluntary activity surveys: research manual*, London: Home Office Research and Statistics Directorate

Mill, J S, 1907, *Principles of political economy*, 7th edn, London: Longman's, Green and Co, www.econlib.org/library/Mill/mlP73. html#Bk.V,Ch.XI

Mohan, J, 2003, Voluntarism, municipalism and welfare: the geography of hospital utilization in England in the 1930s, *Transactions, Institute of British Geographers*, 28, 1, 55–74

Mohan, J, 2012, Entering the lists: what can we learn from the voluntary sector in England from listings produced by local infrastructure bodies?, *Voluntary Sector Review*, 3 2, 197–215

Mohan, J and Barnard, S, 2013a, *Comparisons between the characteristics of charities in Scotland with those in England and Wales*, CGAP Working Paper, www.cgap.org.uk/research/research-outputs.html

Mohan, J and Barnard, S, 2013b, *AOO, AOB or NSTSO? Using geographical information to estimate the local distribution of charitable resources*, CGAP forthcoming Working Paper.

Mohan, J and Bulloch, S, 2012, *The idea of a 'civic core': What are the overlaps between charitable giving, volunteering and civic participation in England and Wales*, TSRC Working Paper no. 73, www.birmingham. ac.uk/generic/tsrc/publications/index.aspx

Mohan, J, Clark, J, Kane, D and Wilding, K, 2011, *Trends in the North: what we have learned from the quantitative programme of the third sector trends study*, www.nr-foundation.org.uk/wp-content/uploads/2011/08/ trends-in-the-north.pdf

NCVO, 2014, Why are our estimates lower than the Charity Commission's figures? http://data.ncvo.org.uk/a/almanac14/why- are-our-estimates-lower-than-the-charity-commissions-figures-2/

Odendahl, T J, 1989, Charitable giving patterns by elites in the United States, in Hodgkinson, V and Lyman, R W (eds) *The future of the nonprofit sector: challenges, changes and policy considerations*, San Francisco: Jossey-Bass

Owen, D, 1964, *English philanthropy, 1660–1960*, Boston: Harvard University Press

Reich, R, 2006, 'Philanthropy and its uneasy relation to inequality', in Damon, W and Verducci, S (eds) *Taking philanthropy seriously*, Bloomington, IN: Indiana University Press, pp27-49

Rupasingha, A, Goetz, S J and Freshwater, D, 2006, The production of social capital in US counties, *The Journal of SocioEconomics*, 35, 1, 83–101

Salamon, L, 1987, Partners in public service: the scope and theory of government-non-profit relations, in Powell, W W (ed) *The non-profit sector: a research handbook*, Newhaven: Yale University Press

Saxton, GD and Benson, MA, 2006, Social capital and the growth of the nonprofit sector, *Social Science Quarterly,* 86, 1, 16–35

Scheffler, RM, Brown, TT, Syme, I, Kawachi, I, Tostykh, I and Iribarren, C, 2008, Community-level social capital and recurrence of acute coronary syndrome, *Social Science & Medicine,* 67, 7, 1603–13

Wolch, J, 1990, *The shadow state: government and voluntary sector in transition,* New York: The Foundation Centre

Wolch, J and Geiger, R, 1983, The distribution of voluntary resources: an exploratory analysis, *Environment and Planning A,* 15, 8, 1067–82

Wolfenden Committee, 1978, *The future of voluntary organisations: report of the Wolfenden Committee,* London: Croom Helm

Wolpert, J, 1988, The geography of generosity: metropolitan disparities in donations and support for amenities, *Annals of the Association of American Geographers,* 78, 4, 665–79

Wolpert, J, 1993, *Patterns of generosity in America: who's holding the safety net?,* New York: The Twentieth Century Fund Press

Wolpert, J, 1996, *What charity can and cannot do,* New York: The Twentieth Century Fund Press

Wolpert, J and Seley, J, 2004, *New York City's nonprofit sector,* Toronto: University of Toronto Press

Conclusion

Behrooz Morvaridi

There is a broad consensus among the scholars contributing to this book that traditional philanthropy, which is driven by the 'love of humankind' and the wellbeing of others, has the potential to be transformative and address inequalities and injustices as well as to provide relief to the poor. Some of the activities of contemporary charity organisations, such as War on Want, Action Aid, Open Society and Oxfam, to name a few, also support advocacy work that is motivated by a social justice agenda. However, *New Philanthropy* is more contentious as it reflects a relationship between giving and business interest, and the associated agency puts new philanthropists into a position of power and influence over the political and economic control of outcomes. The generosity of super-rich philanthropists is undoubted and we have seen plenty of that in recent years. The question of concern is not whether new philanthropy is good or bad, but what motivates this form of giving and whether the sources of new philanthropy funding are legitimate (Sayer, 2014).

The often-stated rationale for new philanthropists' involvement with charity is to help others benefit from their 'wealth creation'. Some philanthropists establish their own foundations through which they channel significant donations, but they also serve to apply technocratic, market-based approaches and business principles to identify 'solutions' to complex problems, such as global poverty, social protection and food security. While traditional philanthropists were motivated, in part, by their belief that giving would help protect the poor and reduce inequality, the focus of new capitalist philanthropists is addressing the growing gap between the rich and the poor within the global marketplace (upon which many have in fact built their wealth). There are many high-profile examples of philanthropist activity that have assisted poor people, but the 'innovative' solutions to poverty are typically targeted at dealing with the symptoms of poverty and not the underlying inequality. As Edwards (2010, p12) points out, there aren't many new philanthropists who 'are prepared to invest in the challenges of long-term institution building, the deepening of democracy, or the development of a different form of market economy in which inequality is systematically attacked'. Super-rich philanthropists support poverty reduction, so long as it does not threaten the hegemonic structure through which they augment their asset base or even draw attention to its origins.

Any serious approach to tackling inequality requires redistribution. But this is not in the interests of the rich philanthropist. New philanthropy in fact depoliticises poverty in making no attempt to tackle the underlying structures and processes of inequality, whereas poverty and inequality are quintessentially issues of social justice. Under neoliberalism, inequality has been consistently rising more or less in parallel in all countries where government strategy and economic policy see economic growth as the solution to all social problems. New philanthropy is essentially a product of neoliberal economic globalisation that encourages wealth concentration in the hands of the 'super-rich' from both the Global South and North.

In describing the accelerated concentration of wealth in the hands of the super-rich in his book *Capital in the twenty-first century*, Piketty provides cross-country and historical evidence to support the assertion that 'capitalism, in short, automatically creates levels of inequality that are unsustainable. The rising wealth of the 1% is neither a blip, nor rhetoric' (Piketty, 2014a, p15). According to Piketty the rate of return on capital is always higher than economic growth rates; even when the economic growth rate is zero there is a return on assets. In concluding that 'wealth concentration is incompatible with democratic values' (Piketty, 2014b, p107), Piketty is of the view that market institutions neither produce social justice nor reinforce democratic values. As the concept of price knows neither limits nor morality, Piketty proposes effective regulation of capitalism to achieve more effective distribution.

This is relevant to our discussion of new philanthropy. More than 120 billionaires have signed up to the 'Giving Pledge' initiated by Bill Gates, through which they have agreed to donate half of their wealth to philanthropic foundations either during their lifetime or posthumously (and in doing so benefit from tax exemptions). Some of the initiatives supported, for example Gates's philanthropic activities in health, immunisation programmes and anti-malaria initiatives, attract global attention that recognises the good philanthropists do for the wellbeing of humanity; but they also reinforce their power and status and that of their corporate organisations. Why should rich philanthropists decide how the health of the poor is managed or the kind of education system reforms that are needed and where investment is a priority? This state of affairs has the potential to create an extremely brittle and potentially pernicious livelihood support structure where social protection instruments are contingent on disparate charity obligations, rather than claimable entitlements based on equal rights and social justice.

Bill Gates has criticised Piketty's position, arguing that in focusing on wealth and income, Piketty ignores inequality in consumption: 'rather than move to a progressive tax on *capital*, as Piketty would like, I think we'd be best off with a progressive tax on *consumption*' (Gates, 2014). In the same review Gates also suggests that, as well as helping society, philanthropy has the wider benefit of reducing dynastic wealth. Evidence does not suggest that this is the case.

New philanthropists are an intrinsic part of a neoliberal market approach to social justice, which assumes that charity and philanthropy organisations can effectively operate as delegated agents of the state. They are, however, neither elected nor representative of civil society. It is unclear how new philanthropy can fulfil the state's responsibility for social justice as enshrined in human rights treaties given that it does not operate within an accountability framework. Imposing an accountability mechanism on new philanthropy actors would be complex given the increasing diversity of the partnerships now involved in delivering elements of social policy. It also brings into question some of the more fundamental political motivations and structures that underpin these partnerships.

New philanthropic activities tend to be carefully targeted, focusing on measurable market-based outcomes. There is no guarantee that new philanthropists have the capacity or the will to provide support more widely or over the long term. New philanthropy could never constitute a system-wide social protection and inequality reduction strategy, delivering measures that provide income support, consumption transfer and employment opportunities for the poor. Recent activity suggests that the generosity of new philanthropists intensifies in times of growing inequality. While the reasons are not clear, it certainly serves to ease the conscience of the rich who, to some degree, have built their wealth by trading on the gap between rich and poor. Bill Easterly (2014) considers new philanthropists' obsession with international aid to be a 'condescending fantasy' built on an exaggeration of the value of western elites and lack of recognition of the hard work and commitment that ordinary people make to improve their lives.

So what is the alternative? Piketty provides a possible way forward in arguing for government and global institutions to play a role in delivering market corrections and redistributing wealth through accountable channels. As it stands, most of these institutions allow wealth concentration and as a result perpetuate inequality. Even billionaires who pledge to give away half of their money will continue to accumulate capital on a large scale. According to a recent Oxfam report, Bill Gates's wealth increased by 13% in the financial year

2013/14 (from US$67 billion to US$76 billion); his wealth increased by US$24m a day, or US$1m an hour (Oxfam, 2013, p8). New philanthropists, who are mostly billionaires, are wealth extractors: they tend to control assets such as property, land and investments that extract wealth through rents or interest, which is effectively unearned income. Unless there is some form of government policy intervention, extreme inequality will continue.

It is hard to argue against Piketty's call for a progressive global tax on capital wealth, as the current system of income tax does not prevent the accumulation of wealth and assets in the hands of a few nor deliver the social protection that is needed to address social injustice. In the US, for example, the top 1% of the rich get 38% tax relief for charitable giving, leading to annual losses to the US treasury of approximately US$45 billion. There are now 1,645 billionaires in the world. According to an Oxfam report on inequality, a 1.5% tax on the world's billionaires would raise US$74 billion and would be sufficient to meet the funding gap to ensure every child went to school and to provide health services in the poorest 49 countries (Oxfam, 2013, p9). The intention of such a tax on the 'patrimonial capitalism' of the 21st century, in which wealth and power are concentrated in the mega-rich, would help to combat rising inequalities (and poverty), with each taxed according to their wealth.

A steeply progressive capital tax would help to keep the dynamics of global wealth concentration under control. We have all seen the interaction between outlandishly extreme salaries paid to top business executives and wealth inequality. The enormity of this challenge cannot be underestimated, because 'if we are to regain control of capitalism, we must bet everything on democracy' (Piketty, 2014b, p115). The income generated from a tax on wealth could be redistributed to strengthen social protection and investment in health, education and food security through accountable agencies. The alternative is that new philanthropy stays with us as a sticking plaster that does not deliver long-term results because it does not tackle social injustice or the structural reasons for inequality.

References

Easterly, W, 2014, *The tyranny of experts: economists, dictators, and the forgotten rights of the poor,* London: Basic Books

Edwards, M, 2010, *Small change: why business won't save the world,* San Francisco, CA: Berrett-Koehler Publishers

Gates, B, 2014, Wealth and capital: why inequality matters, www.gatesnotes.com/Books/Why-Inequality-Matters-Capital-in-21st-Century-Review

Piketty, T, 2014a, *Capital in the twenty–first century*, Harvard: Harvard University Press

Piketty, T, 2014b, Dynamic of inequality: interview, *New Left Review*, 85, 85–114

Oxfam, 2013, Time to end extreme poverty, www.policy-practice. oxfam.org.uk/publications/even-it-up-time-to-end-extreme-inequality-333012

Sayer, A, 2014, *Why we can't afford the rich*, Bristol: Policy Press

Index

'helping others to help themselves' ethos 122, 145, 164
high net worth individuals (HNWIs) 163, 166
high signalling density 53–4
Himmelfarb, G 119, 121–2, 151
Hindmarsh, R 106, 110
Hindmarsh, S 106, 110
Hinduism 138–9, 143
history of philanthropy 17–30, 118–23, 149–50, 151, 193–5, 208
Hobhouse, Lord 24
holiday homes 92, 94
holistic approaches to development 12, 164
Holmes, G 82, 83, 84, 86, 96
horizontal philanthropy 163, 169
hospices 205–6
housing 28, 88, 91
Howard, J 20
HSBC 147
Huilo Huilo Biological Reserve 91
Hultman, T 5
'humanitarian licenses' 104, 106
Hume, D 19
hybrid institutions/ finance models 42, 152
hyper-agents, philanthrocapitalists as 83

I

idle, poor seen as 18–19, 121, 129
Igoe, J 86
Illingworth, P 66
impact investing 34, 37
impossible causes 25–6
independent schools 195–6
India
  corporate social responsibility (CSR) 161
  Dalit Fund (India) 43
  Indian philanthropists 1
  philanthropic foundations 163
'indigenous charity' 11–12, 137, 163, 167
indigenous communities 95
indirect benefits of giving 27, 70n, 103, 142, 192
indiscriminate giving 21, 22
individual philanthropists
  and the changing nature of global philanthropy 1, 160
  vs corporate philanthropy 55
  and NGOs 158–9
  and philanthrocapitalism 82–3, 87, 88, 92
individualisation
  vs collective action 38
  particularistic vs universalistic approaches 144
inequality
  and 'charity deserts' 207–8
  and giving forward vs giving back 43
  global inequality and social justice approaches 185
  and hybrid finance models of philanthropy 42
  and inter-institutional relationships 120

lingering inequality in voluntary sector provision 123
money at the heart of 40
and the need for a capital tax 216
as part of the cycle of capitalism 35, 177
reinforced by philanthropy 74
and religion 121, 128
and super-rich elites 185–6, 215
influence, philanthropy has undue 12, 38, 42, 74, 83, 165, 214
informal charity vs organised charity 142, 152
information goods 53
inheritance 24
in-kind assistance 131, 140, 159, 192
innovation
  as means to solve the poor's problems 5, 213
  and philanthrocapitalism 89
  philanthropic foundations supporting 179
  some philanthropy less innovative than claimed 35
  and transformation 37
Innovation Funds 43
institutions
  agribusiness and institutional experiments 101–10
  globally shared institutions and the global poor 69
  'humanitarian licenses' 106
  in a philanthropic ecosystem 43
  as poor relief 27
  welfare state- philanthropy relationships 119–20
instruments of redistribution (of resources) 7
intellectual property 104, 106, 107, 109
international aid 137–8, 157, 184–5
International Aid Transparency Initiative 168
International Communities programme 180
international development
  and civil society 157–71
  development aid vs private investment 110
  and philanthropy 137–52
International Development Committee (UK) 159, 164
International Maize and Wheat Improvement Centre (CIMMYT) 102, 107
International NGO Training and Research Centre (INTRAC) 157, 165, 168
International Program on Rice Biotechnology (IPRB) 103–4
International Rice Research Institute (IRRI) 102, 104, 105, 110
INTRAC (International NGO Training and Research Centre) 157, 165, 168
investment
  5% philanthropy (social housing) 28
  collective ownership arrangements reinvest profits 42
  ethical/ unethical investment by foundations 184–5
  impact investing 34, 37
  mission-related/ social investments 184

Contemporary Issues in Social Policy

Series editor: Charles Husband

This exciting new series brings together academics, professionals and activists to link cutting-edge social theory and research to contentious issues in social policy, challenge consensus and invite debate. Each text provides a critical appraisal of key aspects of contemporary theory and research to offer fresh perspectives.

Research and policy in ethnic relations: Compromised dynamics in a neoliberal era
Charles Husband (editor)

New philanthropy and social justice and social policy: Debating the conceptual and policy discourse
Behrooz Morvaridi (editor)

Political disengagement: The changing nature of the 'political'
Nathan Manning (editor)

See more at http://bit.ly/1AWjClV